Crossing

Crossing

How We Label and React to People on the Move

Rebecca Hamlin

Stanford University Press

Stanford, California

STANFORD UNIVERSITY PRESS
Stanford, California

Printed in the United States of America on acid-free, archival-quality paper

Library of Congress Cataloging-in-Publication Data

Names: Hamlin, Rebecca, author.
Title: Crossing : how we label and react to people on the move / Rebecca
    Hamlin.
Description: Stanford, California : Stanford University Press, 2021. | Includes
    bibliographical references and index.
Identifiers: LCCN 2020037819 | ISBN 9781503610606 (cloth) | ISBN 9781503627871
    (paperback) | ISBN 9781503627888 (epub)
Subjects: LCSH: Emigration and immigration law. | Emigration and
    immigration—Government policy. | Refugees—Legal status, laws, etc. |
    Refugees—Government policy. | Office of the United Nations High
    Commissioner for Refugees.
Classification: LCC K3275 .H36 2021 | DDC 342.08/2—dc23
LC record available at https://lccn.loc.gov/2020037819

Cover design: Rob Ehle
Cover art: Enrique Chagoya, *Thesis/Antithesis*, 1989
Typeset by Motto Publishing Services in 11/13.5 Adobe Garamond Pro

To Tom

"Nothing to declare"
As if in a sea of red tape
The faulty life-jackets tossed:
There is no custom house, no guards,
At the border these have crossed.

—A. E. Stallings, 2018

Contents

Acknowledgments

As I sit reflecting on my gratitude in my home office, where I have worked alone for many months due to the global pandemic of COVID-19, it strikes me how widely this book has traveled. I thank first and foremost the staff at UNHCR headquarters in Geneva, who were so generous with their time when I visited them in 2019, and who work so hard to protect vulnerable people.

I also thank the organizers and participants in three separate workshops where this book was incubated: first, the UMass Interdisciplinary Studies Institute's yearlong seminar on "trespassing" in 2016–17; second, the Smith College Kahn Institute's yearlong seminar on "refugees" in 2018–19; and third, the UMass Social and Behavioral Sciences Migration Working Group, an ongoing collective of faculty and graduate students that has proved to be a dearly beloved intellectual home for me.

Portions of this project have also been presented at Brandeis University, Concordia University, Middlebury College, Nichols College, Smith College, University of California Los Angeles, University of Pennsylvania, and the Law & Society Association's Annual Meetings, 2018 and 2019. I thank all of the audience members at these presentations for their engagement and useful commentary.

I would also like to thank the following individuals, who have provided thought-provoking feedback on this project along the way: Lamis Abdelaaty, Tendayi Achiume, Alex Aleinikoff, Tally Amir, Rawan Arar, Amada Armenta, Anna Boucher, Darcy Buerkle, Heath Cabot, Charli

Carpenter, Ming Hsu Chen, Cathryn Costello, Catherine Dauvergne, Rodrigo Dominguez-Villegas, Shannon Gleeson, Jill Greenlee, Peter Haas, David Hernandez, Salman Hussain, Betsy Krause, Meredith Loken, Audrey Macklin, David Mednicoff, Hillary Mellinger, Joya Misra, Hiroshi Motomura, Jaya Ramji-Nogales, Mirelle Paquet, Margaret Peters, Nikolas Feith Tan, Greg White, Phil Wolgin, Kevin Young, and Basileus Zeno. I would like to particularly thank my amazing colleagues Scott Blinder and Adam Dahl, who each read several parts of the manuscript very closely and gave critical yet supportive feedback at just the right moments.

I was also extremely fortunate to have the assistance of nine excellent UMass students through the Undergraduate Research Experience Program. I thank Ahmad Bakrin, Caroline Collis, Sarah Coomey, Julia Engel, Nicholas Groblewski, Kelsey Kenney, Abigail McDonough, Sara Nasah, and Willow Ross for their work on this project.

Thank you to other wonderful UMass colleagues and friends who have provided crucial moral support through some difficult times: Paul Collins, Jane Fountain, Alan Gaitenby, Justin Gross (Adirondack lyfe 4 eva!), Kirsten Leng, Jennifer Lundquist, Lauren McCarthy, Tatishe Nteta, MJ Peterson, Jesse Rhodes, Doug Rice, Meredith Rolfe, Jamie Rowen, Libby Sharrow, and Leah Wing.

I am eternally grateful to some other friends who may as well be family at this point: Kerri Berkowitz, Emma Berndt, Rachel Deutsch, Chloe Drew, Emily Gregory, Jenny Lancaster, Elise Lawson, Ali McKleroy, Jesse Sage Noonan, Lenore Palladino, and Alison Watkins. Special thanks to my title consultant, Ben Hurwitz, and to Albert Lacson, who was my writing retreat buddy in the summer of 2019, and a sunny presence in my life all the time.

I am indebted to both of my editors at Stanford University Press: Michelle Lipinski, who encouraged the project enthusiastically from the beginning, and Marcela Maxfield, who took over midstream with aplomb.

I cannot adequately express my gratitude to my family, who have been tremendously and endlessly supportive of my obsession with this book that sometimes took me away from them, literally and figuratively. My parents, Bryan and Anne Hamlin, are the best cheerleaders. My in-laws, Tom and Drewcilla Annese, have been so kind and generous. My brother and his family, John, Christina, and Elijah Hamlin, are a source of joy and support. My dog, Charlie, has been by my side for almost every word. My children, Althea and Lorenzo, are delightful people who are already full of ideas of their own. And finally, my husband, Tom Annese, who brings me coffee and asks for updates and who has more faith in me than I do in myself: I dedicate this book to you.

Florence, Massachusetts, June 2020

Crossing

1

The Migrant/Refugee Binary

EVERY DAY, PEOPLE CROSS. Hundreds of thousands of people cross borders in airplanes and go through customs at an airport. Millions cross borders at land checkpoints, show paperwork, and keep moving. Other crossings are more difficult, more dangerous. They involve deserts, or oceans, or barbed-wire fences. In these scenarios, many people do not survive the crossing.[1] Some plan their crossing carefully, packing treasured belongings with a clear vision of their destination. Others leave more hastily, carrying little, the future uncertain. Some border crossers are welcomed, others are treated as invaders and threats. Some people are recognized as vulnerable and viewed as deserving of protection and assistance, others must fend for themselves.

In/out, safe/dangerous, planned/spontaneous, desirable/threatening, legal/illegal, deserving/undeserving, genuine/fraudulent, citizen/alien. There are many labels and contrasts associated with crossing borders. This book is about the persistence and pervasiveness of one specific way we label and react to people who cross: what I call the migrant/refugee binary. Today, the concept of "the refugee" as a figure who is distinct from other migrants looms large. International law and the immigration laws of most receiving states have developed to mimic and reinforce a conceptual dichotomy between those viewed as voluntary (often economically motivated) migrants who can be legitimately excluded by potential host states and those viewed as forced (often politically motivated) refugees who should be let in. According to this binary logic, refugees "pose a problem for the international community quite different from that of other foreigners" whose "transnational movement has been one of choice" (Haddad 2003, 297–98). In other words, "the refugee" has come to be viewed as an exception to the rule that states have a sovereign right to control their borders. In this sense, border crossers who are categorized and recognized as refugees have a privileged legal position compared to other crossers who also might need help but cannot access it.

This book is about the relationship between legal categories and the social and political world. It is based on the idea that how we think and talk about border crossers shapes how border crossers are treated. Especially since the mid-twentieth century, people whose stories have been viewed as fitting within the conception of a refugee as set forth in the 1951 Convention Relating to the Status of Refugees have consistently had more success in accessing rights than other categories of migrants. The internationally recognized definition of a refugee, which is heavily focused on protecting people from political and identity-based persecution, has achieved widespread global acceptance. It has now been adopted by 148 signatory states.[2] In contrast, international legal instruments that enumerate the rights of migrants more generally have not been widely ratified, especially not by the states that actually host the vast majority of people on the move (Ruhs 2012).

The fact that refugees have more protections under international law than other types of border crossers is reflected in how publics in popular destination states think about deservingness. A recent public opinion survey from the Pew Research Center found that people around the world were significantly more likely to support admitting refugees, as opposed to migrants, to their countries.[3] To test this point further, I conducted a survey experiment embedded within an American public opinion poll, in which a randomly selected half of respondents were asked if they believed the United States has a moral obligation to admit vulnerable refugees (50.6% agreed), and the other half were asked if they believed the United States has a moral obligation to admit vulnerable immigrants (42.8% agreed). In other words, even when both groups are explicitly labeled as vulnerable, and the only difference in the question is the word refugee versus immigrant, I found a statistically significant difference in public support for people who are labeled as refugees.[4]

These data show that binary logic makes a very clear distinction between those to whom an obligation is owed and those who are less deserving of an international response. Such logic creates warped incentives.

It helps to prop up legal regimes that promise people refugee protection only if they can access it, incentivizing risky journeys while at the same time allowing powerful states to invest in preventative measures that make the journeys even more dangerous. Because refugees are recognized as deserving of protections that other border crossers cannot access, when faced with large numbers of spontaneous arrivals, states all over the world are quick to insist that the people arriving are "just migrants," not "genuine" or "real refugees." This insistence is used to justify the harsh deterrent measures that prevent people from accessing the ability to claim protective status. In this way, the migrant/refugee binary benefits those states that want to keep people out by emphasizing the ways in which refugees are the exception to the rule. The idea of the rare and special refugee is central to upholding the sovereignty of powerful destination states, the majority of which are in the Global North.[5] The concept highlights a type of selective inclusion that is only possible through mass exclusion. Ironically, even criticisms of the elaborate deterrent measures undertaken by Global North states often reify the binary by focusing their critique on the concern that the measures are also screening out refugees, not just the migrants they are designed to stop.

The problem is that the nuanced patterns of global migration and the lived experiences of border crossers push against the binary, revealing it to be a constructed "legal fiction" (Fuller 1967). Legal fictions are concepts that are not accurate depictions of reality, but which are treated as if they are true for purposes of bureaucratic expediency and convenience. If we look closely at migration, we see that people with multiple and various motivations use the same routes and defy categorization at every turn. To be sure, some border crossers are totally forced and some are purely voluntary, some are solely economically motivated and some are exclusively politically motivated, some may be morally deserving of assistance and some may not be. But these distinctions fall along continua and elude clear-cut binaries. Further, these continua do not logically overlay one another such that

refugees = forced = politically motivated = deserving
migrants = voluntary = economically motivated = undeserving

The reality is much more complex. Economic development, political corruption, and armed conflict are closely linked processes. Even on their own, economic factors are forces that can compel people to move.

Similarly, climate disasters can force people to move in a hurry, while other, more gradual climate changes can affect crops or water supplies and cause major economic strain, which can directly force people to migrate, or indirectly lead to political instability and corruption, which can cause migration. Ongoing conflict destroys businesses, kills breadwinners, cuts off food and medical supply chains, and forces many people who have not been directly targeted by war to flee in order to survive (Crawley and Skleparis 2018). But binary logic continues to insist that there is no such thing as an economically motivated refugee because "the liberal worldview considers market activity to be natural and nonpolitical" (Nyers 2006, 50). So, people who cross borders to save themselves from starvation, for example, are sometimes labeled "survival migrants" to whom very little is owed (Betts 2013).

Based on their research examining migration patterns in North Africa, Collyer and de Haas (2012) have advocated that scholars of human mobility shift their attention away from static categories because they inadequately conceptualize how people in motion, now more than ever, cross categories and statuses throughout their migration journeys. Instead, Collyer and de Haas suggest that contemporary migration patterns should be viewed as "dynamic" processes. Even leading legal experts on migration, who as a group tend to place a heavy emphasis on legal categories, have also recently observed that the migrant/refugee binary is a "gross oversimplification" (Ramji-Nogales 2017b, 11), and that refugee law is "ill-suited to migration realities" because the line between refugees and other border crossers is "exceedingly difficult to draw" (Motomura 2020, 32).

And yet, even though it is known to obscure nuance, the binary persists. The distinction continues to dominate political thought about borders, scholarly studies of migration, and public discourse by policymakers, advocates, and the media. Rather than being driven by conceptual clarity, institutional factors (including the structures that shape academic scholarship and advocacy) continue to reify the distinction and lead many scholars and advocates to explicitly defend its use. The migrant/refugee binary may be a fiction, but it is a powerful, enduring, and deeply consequential one.

The argument I present here is that, like all legal fictions, the migrant/refugee binary endures because it is an "expedient but false assumption" that has utility for powerful actors in the system (Fuller 1967, 9). This particular legal fiction serves the purpose of depoliticizing the most difficult ethical decisions that receiving states must make about whose protection should be prioritized. Subsequently, it makes harsh border control measures more ethically palatable to the general public. As Fuller has argued, a legal fiction "becomes wholly safe only when it is used with a complete consciousness of its falsity" (10). The migrant/refugee binary is thus a dangerous legal fiction. By making these categories seem natural, the migrant/refugee binary masks the ways in which such categories have been politically constructed to elevate the suffering of some people above the suffering of others. Thus, this book argues that the migrant/ refugee binary is a key "ordering principle of the current international system," one that contributes to the precarity of an ever-increasing number of border crossers (Gündoğdu 2015, 11). Its power stems from its portrayal as objective, neutral, and apolitical, and its endurance "poses a central challenge to efforts to reinvent global migration law" (Ramji-Nogales 2017b, 11).

The arguments in this book are very much in the tradition of the subfield of scholarship that is sometimes known as "critical refugee studies" (Espiritu 2014). Beginning in the late 1990s, works by Tuitt (1996), Chimni (1998), and Soguk (1999) forged the claims that the contemporary international refugee regime had been motivated by more than just humanitarianism, that refugees have been used as geopolitical strategic tools, and that the international legal definition of a refugee privileges some forms of violation and delegitimizes others. These early scholars worked in the Third World Approaches to International Law (TWAIL) tradition, which centered the perspectives of formerly colonized people in the Global South, and which understood international law to be a tool of subordination. More recently, critical refugee scholars have described the ways in which the international refugee regime is based on a "grand compromise" (Cuellar 2006) through which Global North donor states contribute to humanitarian causes with the expectation that displaced people will be contained in the Global South (Arar 2017). These dynamics perpetuate the global wealth and power imbalances that stem from colonial legacies and neocolonialism (Achiume 2019). In the spirit of critical refugee studies scholarship, this book argues that the logic of the migrant/ refugee binary helps to obscure these power imbalances by guiding us to focus on internal explanations for why people are leaving countries in the Global South (corruption, war, poverty) rather than externalist forces such as globalization, postcolonialism, and the failures of neoliberalism (Chimni 1998).

The reorientation that a nonbinary approach would require is hardly a straightforward endeavor. It would involve a total reevaluation of the notion of responsibility and obligation toward the world's vulnerable people. It would call upon powerful and privileged actors to confront long-standing practices of oppression and domination. It would demand an openness to the notion that international human rights law and international humanitarian organizations do not always serve to protect the weak. Nevertheless, my argument is that we should not postpone this difficult work by using the migrant/refugee binary to stymie creative conversation. The binary limits the ability of scholars, advocates, and policy-makers to be imaginative and visionary about the future. In short, vulnerable border crossers do not benefit from its persistence as a dominant framework for public debate about border crossing.

Binaries, Categorizations, and Definitions

In describing binary opposition, which is the tendency of language to group concepts into pairs (good and evil, light and dark), philosopher Jacques Derrida ([1972] 1981) observed that for each binary, "one of the two terms governs the other . . . or has the upper hand." Thus, he says, binary opposition has a "subordinating structure" (41). This phenomenon of subordination is abundantly clear in many of the binaries that abound in the world of border crossing. Border crossers are routinely placed into binary categories that serve as moral distinctions between those who deserve compassion and those who do not (Ticktin 2016). Labels offer the "pretense of value-neutral categorization" (Sajjad 2018, 42). But categorization is never neutral.

One dominant binary in the realm of migration is legal/illegal. On the one hand, whether a person's crossing is authorized is a simple matter of fact. On the other, we need not dig very deep to see the ways in which this binary is constructed in public discourse, media, and culture to privilege certain types of border crossers and demonize others. In the United States, the illegal immigrant is a heavily constructed figure who lives in the public imagination as a poor Mexican person, conjuring up both racial and economic anxiety (De Genova 2004). Rarely does public discourse about migration acknowledge that unauthorized immigration comes in many forms, nationalities, ages, and classes, or that many undocumented people did not sneak across a desert. Instead, many of them arrived with a visa and overstayed. In Europe, the illegal migrant of the public imagination is an African and/or Muslim person, linked to fears about cultural assimilation, criminality, and security threats (Sajjad 2018). The legacies of European colonialism in Africa and the Middle East, or the US conquest of territory formally belonging to Mexico and its many interventions in Latin America, are rarely acknowledged in these discussions.

While it is clear in the binary opposition of legal and illegal that legality governs, which side is subordinated in the migrant/refugee binary? The answer is somewhat more complicated. There is certainly a stigma associated with the vulnerability of refugee status. Headlines are filled with references to refugee crises, and refugees are often depicted as abject figures in desperate need. Meanwhile, some world leaders openly express disdain for refugees, even suggesting that they are national security threats.[6] For these reasons, Pulitzer Prize–winning author and self-identified refugee Viet Thanh Nguyen (2016) lamented that "refugees are the zombies of the world" because they are so vulnerable and yet so threatening. Similarly, political philosopher Hannah Arendt, who was forced to flee Nazi Germany because she was Jewish, began her 1943 essay "We Refugees" with the words: "In the first place, we don't like to be called refugees."

And yet, because in today's world being a refugee is associated with legal status, for those who actually gain that legal status and the rights that come with it, it can be a privileged category. In the realm of migration, categorization is a way for states to control people's movement and simultaneously reaffirm their territorial boundaries (Thomaz 2018). By designating people as in or out, legal or illegal, deserving or undeserving, refugee or nonrefugee, the state exercises significant authority. So, accessing legal status is hugely significant in the lives of border crossers. It "highlights the central role the state still plays in shaping and regulating immigrants' lives" (Menjívar 2006, 1001). Migrant categorization is not just about ascribing legality; it is also "status-making" because the act of classification confers status on people (Robertson 2018). People who are in-between statuses, unclassified, or unlikely to be granted refugee status live in a world of "liminal legality," which can be a source of enormous anxiety with dire material consequences (Menjívar 2006). For this reason, many people who seek it view refugee status as a privilege because of the coveted access that it allows, and because it is unobtainable for people on the wrong side of political controversies and definitional divides (Menjivar 1993; Hamlin 2014).

In contrast to the legal status promised by the term refugee, "migrant" is not a technical legal term because it has no definition in international or domestic law. According to the International Organization for Migration (IOM), it is an "umbrella term" that reflects

the common lay understanding of a person who moves away from his or her place of usual residence, whether within a country or across an international border, temporarily or permanently, and for a variety of reasons. The term includes a number of well-defined legal categories of people, such as migrant workers; persons whose particular types of movements are legally-defined, such as smuggled migrants; as well as those whose status or means of movement are not specifically defined under international law, such as international students.[7]

This definition reveals a tension in the way that the major global governance organizations tasked with working on issues of border crossing describe the populations with whom they are concerned. While IOM insists that the word migrant encompasses all border crossers, the United Nations High Commissioner for Refugees (UNHCR) insists that "refugees are not migrants," but a category unto themselves (Feller 2005). Notably, refugees are not explicitly listed in the IOM discussion of the term migrant. Instead, it is implied that refugees are covered as "persons whose particular types of movements are legally-defined."

As this book will show, policy-makers, advocates, and scholars use a lot of terms to describe people who cross borders, some of which have official legal meanings and many of which do not. Further, terms with legal meanings also have other social and rhetorical meanings, and these "legal, discursive, and social definitions of a migrant's status may variously align with, inform or contest each other" (Robertson 2018, 226). Policy-makers, advocates, and scholars frequently use terms discursively in ways that do not match their official legal meaning. For instance, while the IOM insists it is merely an umbrella category, when the word migrant is used in direct contrast to refugee, it takes on the implication of an economic, or undeserving, border crosser, and thus is relegated to a subordinated status in the binary opposition of migrant and refugee. At the same time, people are sometimes referred to as refugees when they have not officially been categorized as such, so it would perhaps be more accurate to call them asylum seekers—people hoping to be granted refugee status. But public pronouncements that certain people "are refugees" can carry tremendous symbolic meaning, even when the people are, in a technical legal sense, still unclassified. If the public imagines a group to be refugees as opposed to migrants, their willingness to accommodate arrivals shifts. Conversely, people who are coming with the obvious intent of seeking asylum are often referred to by government officials as migrants, implying different and less sympathetic motivations behind their crossing.

Thus, for the purposes of exploring the migrant/refugee binary, I must move beyond positivist frameworks that take definitions at face value and instead examine the ways in which various terms are deployed discursively, particularly by people who wield the authority of the state, or who seek to appeal to that authority. For clarity, I will use the phrase border crosser as much as possible, and avoid calling people refugees or migrants unless I am referring to the terminology used by others or to official legal designations. Before moving on to my exploration of the life of the migrant/refugee binary, I elaborate next on three core assumptions that form the tripod of binary logic.

Assumption 1: Refugees and migrants have distinct and distinguishable motivations for crossing borders

At its most basic level, the migrant/refugee binary relies on the assumption that there are two distinct and distinguishable motivations for border crossing: voluntary and forced. However, there is a wealth of research that challenges this assumption. From a theoretical standpoint, Ottonelli and Torresi (2013) question the very notion of voluntary migration. They argue that the concept does "significant normative work" in reducing the sense of obligation that people and states feel toward those border crossers who are labeled as, or are assumed to be, voluntary (784). They also note that conceptualizing migration as either forced or voluntary (a close variant of the migrant/refugee binary) perverts our understanding of what it means for people to have agency when making major life decisions. In reality, people migrate for a wide variety of reasons across a broad spectrum ranging from the completely voluntary to the absolutely forced. A vast, and perhaps increasing, number of border crossers land closer to the middle of the spectrum. Nor do people remain static on that spectrum at various stages of their journey—perhaps seeking immediate refuge in one state, then moving on to another state to lodge an asylum claim, then moving yet again in search of better economic prospects than were available in the country of first asylum. People also make major life decisions about whether to leave their home based on a combination of factors, some of which map neatly onto the definition of a refugee and many of which do not.

Recent ethnographic work exploring people's internal motivations for leaving home has consistently belied the assumption that border crossers can be easily sorted into two groups. For example, multiple recent studies draw on interviews with people arriving in Europe from across the Mediterranean to demonstrate the ways in which people's motivations for leaving their homes, and the many stops often taken along the way, make it very difficult to classify them as voluntary or forced, as migrants or refugees (Crawley and Skleparis 2018; McMahon and Sigona 2018; BenEzer and Zetter 2015). A University of Warwick study, relying on interviews with 217 people who had crossed the Mediterranean by boat into Europe, consistently found that they had decided to migrate based on various and intersecting factors, some of which may qualify them for refugee status and some of which may not (Squire et al. 2017, 62). Similarly, Erdal and Oeppen conclude, based on fieldwork with Afghani and Pakistani people living in Europe, that it is impossible to clearly distinguish for most border crossers whether their decision to migrate was "entirely voluntary or entirely forced" (2018, 982). They found that people from both national groups left their home countries because of domestic instability and perceived lack of alternatives, although Afghanis were far more likely to be categorized as deserving refugees by European states (982). In a similar vein, based on interviews with Nicaraguans in Costa Rica, Lee (2011) found that it was impossible to distinguish among their various motivations for leaving Nicaragua due to that country's long-standing economic and political instability, combined with climate change.

When faced with the prospect of assigning people with a complex set of motivations to specific, and often inflexible, categories, destination states have generally failed to achieve consistency and predictability. Instead, studies of refugee status determination procedures reveal that the placement of the policy line separating refugees from other migrants is highly contested and politically constructed in receiving states. Despite a common refugee definition outlined in international law, there is wide variation across receiving states in terms of where that policy line is drawn. Even similarly situated liberal democracies grant refugee status to applicants from the same sending states at strikingly variable rates. In previous work I have shown how asylum seekers with remarkably similar stories, coming from the same countries of origin, have wildly varying likelihoods of gaining refugee protection depending on the liberal democracy in which they lodge their claim (Hamlin 2014). For example, asylum seekers from the People's Republic of China were granted refugee status at rates from under 15% in Australia to about one-third in the United States and almost two-thirds in Canada (ibid.). My in-depth country case studies found that the reasons for this variation lie in the differing degrees to which states organize the institutional structures of refugee status determination so that they are insulated from the exclusionary politics of border control. Gill and Good (2019, 12) found similarly alarming variation within the European Union, such that Syrian asylum seekers experienced average acceptance rates ranging from under 60% to close to 100% across EU member states, and Afghani applicants had an even wider range, from 5% to 96%.

Some scholars have convincingly argued that the refugee status determination practices of receiving states are transparently political, and have pointed to the hypocrisy of how geopolitics, not law, ultimately determines who gets classified as a refugee (Chimni 1998; Kukathas 2016). While much of this critique has been focused on the Global North, there is evidence of variation in state responses to border crossers seeking protection in the Global South as well. In a comparative study of six African states, Betts (2013) found a great degree of variation in response to arrivals that had little to do with the needs of the people seeking help, and a great deal to do with the capacity and willingness of the host state governments. Building on this work with an impressive quantitative data set and in-depth case studies of Egypt, Turkey, and Kenya as receiving states, Abdelaaty (2021) found that state responses to asylum seekers can be predicted by a combination of the relations between the sending and receiving states, and whether the ethnic makeup of the people seeking refuge matches that of the government in power in the host state.

Taken on their own, these findings about state-level variation do not necessarily disprove assumption 1. It could theoretically be the case that some host states are simply better at discovering who are the refugees among the crowd of applicants claiming to be refugees. However, other research has demonstrated the ways in which even *within* receiving states, the refugee status determination grant rates vary tremendously among otherwise identical applicants, based solely on characteristics of the individual decision-maker (Ramji-Nogales, Schoenholtz, and Schrag 2009; Rehaag 2009; Gould, Sheppard, and Wheeldon 2010). Not all refugee status determination regimes have the same levels of internal inconsistency, but the fact that all systems have it to some degree is revealing (Hamlin 2014; Macklin 2009). The reality that the decision-maker's personal background is often of more significance to the outcome than the life experience of the person making the claim undermines the idea that there is a coherent process through which people who truly are refugees are being discovered by large-scale bureaucratic processes.

The binary, then, is not an innocuous shorthand that glosses over minor complexities. Rather, the more nuanced understanding—that migration motivations take the form of a continuum, are multiple, and are not static—is hugely significant. These truths undermine the entire project of confidently sorting people into the "correct" categories, because they question the notion that each individual border crosser either possesses the qualities of refugeehood or does not. Instead, the idea that it is the role of receiving states to properly sort and separate the refugee wheat from the migrant chaff is exposed as problematically essentialist.

In gender studies and feminist theory, essentialism is the belief that categories of people exist because of particular qualities or characteristics that people in each group uniquely possess (Witt 1995). For example, an essentialist view of gender would assume that all people are either men or women, that men and women have fundamental differences, and that these differences are central to the experience of being either male or female. Anti-essentialist feminist theorists have been concerned with examining why and how such categorial distinctions emerge, and who they benefit and oppress (Butler 1990). Drawing on these long-standing insights from gender and sexuality studies, I imagine that an essentialist view of migration assumes that all border crossers are either migrants or refugees, that migrants and refugees are fundamentally different from one another in terms of their motivations for leaving home, and that these differences are centrally important to understanding everything else about these people's lives and to assessing their deservingness for hospitality. Rather than falling into the essentialist trap, this book assumes that "labelling processes involve relationships of power" (Moncrieffe 2007, 2). When and how they are employed and invoked carries a significant degree of political meaning and can have unexpected and long-lasting consequences. As this book will illustrate, essentialist conceptions of "the refugee" are common, and in fact a foundational component of binary logic.

Assumption 2: Refugees are the neediest among the world's border crossers

In addition to the most basic assumption that refugees and migrants truly are distinct and distinguishable, people who use the migrant/refugee binary tend to justify it by falling back on the second-order assumption that people who receive refugee protection are the neediest among the world's border crossers. This assumption is perpetuated by the fact that refugees have consistently been constructed in popular and political discourse as vulnerable subjects of persecution, not as actors with individual agency (Espiritu 2006). Gatrell outlines the ways in which refugees "are habitually portrayed as if they are without agency, like corks bobbing along on the surface of an unstoppable wave of displacement" (2013, 9). Even the famous quotation on the Statue of Liberty, referring to the "huddled masses, yearning to breathe free," invokes the image of anonymous hordes of pathetic, weak figures.[8] Many books and news articles about refugees perpetuate these conceptualizations through images and rhetoric.

And yet, this portrayal stands in contrast to the highly individualized model of the dissident in exile outlined in the 1951 Refugee Convention definition of a refugee. In other words, the huddled masses may not actually officially qualify as refugees if they apply. Betts echoes this point, arguing, based on his work on mass migrations in Africa, that "many people whom one might believe to be refugees fall outside the dominant legal interpretation of a refugee" (2013, 27). Similarly, FitzGerald and Arar (2018) explain that the "sociological meaning" of the term refugee encompasses types of suffering that are not covered by the definition. In this way, the term refugee often works "not as a legal classification but as an idea" (Espiritu 2006, 411). This argument is supported by the existence of a wide variety of complementary protection categories that allow states to offer some form of legal status for people who are found not to qualify for refugee protection (Hamlin 2014). These categories also make clear that the binary is not sufficient, since the concept of a refugee does not even fit the needs of everyone that states *want* to protect. Of course, the existence of these intermediate categories only matters if the person accesses the territory and is able to make an argument, a hurdle many seekers of protection are not able to clear.

The concept of complementary protection helps to reveal that there is some tension between the definition of a refugee in Article 1 of the 1951 Convention and the other core feature of international refugee law outlined in Article 31, which is the pledge by receiving states not to return people to home countries where their life or freedom will be in danger. This pledge, known as *non-refoulement* (or nonreturn), theoretically allows for the protection of a larger swath of people than those who would qualify for refugee status under the Article 1 definition. It theoretically offers protection to the most vulnerable by recognizing that their lives are at risk. But the relationship between the concept of non-refoulement and the concept of a refugee can be confusing, and can shift in the way it is deployed depending on the circumstances. States often treat the right to seek asylum and the right to non-refoulement as equivalent. Or they meet their non-refoulement obligations by offering temporary legal status to people whom they cannot return but whom they do not want to recognize as refugees. In sum, to the extent that it is recognized, the institutionalization of norms such as non-refoulement is an important step in developing the legal personhood of noncitizens and moving beyond the binary. And yet, like the concept of a refugee, states still get to decide who qualifies. In this way, the norm reaffirms state sovereignty by focusing on the exceptions to it (Gündoğdu 2015, 108).

Other examples abound that further complicate our idea of the refugee as the neediest category of people on the move. First, internally displaced people (IDPs) can be very vulnerable and are consistently about double in number worldwide compared to people classified as refugees (UNHCR 2019b). "In ethnically and politically fragmented post-colonial states, domestic moves may be just as significant if not more so than relocating beyond borders" (Landau and Achiume 2017, 1184). However, IDPs do not receive anywhere near as much attention in a state-centric world. Second, when terrified people flee their homes with nothing and arrive at the borders of a neighboring state, there is no guarantee that they will be recognized as refugees. Some of those people will gain refugee status and many will not; and gaining or failing to gain refugee status is not necessarily a reliable indicator of whether they will receive assistance and protection. In a study of displaced people across multiple sites in Africa, the authors found that "legal status is far less important than local social relations that enable people to access information, emergency shelter or the occasional form of material assistance" (Landau and Amit 2014, 537). Third, receiving states often decline to categorize people who might genuinely qualify for refugee status as refugees. For example, Brazil deliberately chose not to label Haitians arriving in the 2010s as refugees; rather, it called them "humanitarian immigrants," an "authorized but temporary category that provides the state with more control but also less responsibility over these migrants" (Thomaz 2018, 212). These examples illustrate some of the ways in which many people who desperately need protection are never classified as refugees.

There are also many examples of the ways in which those who *are* officially classified as refugees in liberal receiving states can ironically be some of the most privileged of the world's vulnerable people on the move. States with the most generous refugee policies tend to be the most difficult and expensive to access. This system does "not prioritize the substantive needs of the individual, but instead privileges ability to get close to the state or its agents—proximity that is determined by capacity (or special circumstances: luck, resources, gender, or physical traits such as youth, strength, and stamina)" (Paz 2016, 9). For example, Van Hear's (2014) study of people fleeing Sri Lanka found that class, not degree of persecution, was the determining factor in whether or not people who left their country ultimately gained refugee protection somewhere. Wealthier Sri Lankans accessed social networks in order to cross into the territories of liberal receiving states where they were able to lodge applications for refugee protection. Poor Sri Lankans often could only get as far as the Persian Gulf, where they avoided persecution in their home countries by becoming migrant laborers working in dangerous conditions with few, if any, rights. Further, we know that when choosing among the many people waiting in camps who have already been designated as eligible for refugee resettlement in the Global North, these wealthy states use all kinds of criteria, including religious affinity and employment skills, to select the lucky few who will get resettled (Mourad and Norman 2019a). It is therefore not at all clear that people who are resettled as refugees in the Global North are always the most vulnerable among their peers.

A great many people who access the territory of liberal democratic states in order to escape harm never gain refugee status. These people use other migration channels but still have harrowing tales, and also feel that they cannot go back home. For example, Cabot (2012) describes interviews with people residing in Greece who had been asylum seekers, but ultimately shifted gears and obtained work visas because the asylum process had placed them in a protracted state of limbo and uncertainty. One interviewee described his frustration and disappointment with that outcome because he felt "he was a refugee and should have been recognized as such" (18). Conversely, in her study of Liberians in the United States, Ludwig (2013) found that people will "identify as refugees when this identification leads to international protection, resettlement in the US, and access to government benefits, but, on the other hand, reject the refugee label when it is not tied to resources and is a reminder of past suffering and a stigma" (6). Others choose to live with a less protective status rather than risk applying for refugee status and failing, because the stakes of deportation are too high. These examples demonstrate how the binary can be constructed both from the top down and from the bottom up, as people must make claims that comport with the Convention definition in order to receive protection.

Assumption 3: True refugees are rare

The erroneous assumption that refugees are by definition the neediest and most vulnerable border crossers is closely connected to the assumption that the vast majority of people on the move are voluntary migrants and not refugees. In other words, a major assumption of binary logic is that refugees are rare. This assumption is compatible with a fundamental reality of liberal thought—that the vulnerable subject is constructed in opposition to the central figure of the autonomous liberal subject (Fineman 2008). According to this logic, refugees are rare because they are an anomaly in a stable system in which state membership is the norm. They are the exception that proves the rule stating that each person must be rooted in a place, due to the "national order of things" (Malkki 1995).

This assumption is supported and perpetuated by official data. The United Nations estimates that there are 272 million people living outside of their country of origin worldwide, and only 28 million of them are classified as refugees.[9] In other words, refugees represent approximately 10 percent of the world's border crossers. The confidence with which UNHCR, governments, and advocates alike present these refugee statistics is surprising, given how many obstacles exist to collecting accurate and reliable information about exactly how many people in need of protection there are in the world. It is also surprising how few scholarly analyses there have been on the topic of data collection, when such data is centrally important to refugee protection and advocacy (Crisp 1999).

First, it is essential to remember that there is a politics behind how people are counted that is directly linked to categorization (Andreas 2010). The only available statistics rely heavily on UNHCR, which only counts people who have already been officially classified as refugees through either a state's refugee status determination process or a UNHCR-run process. Unless and until people are officially recognized as refugees, they will not show up in the data as such. Further, FitzGerald and Arar have made the important point that counting the world's refugees based on official UN statistics that use the UN definition "risks circular reasoning" because "it may be that people fleeing other kinds of violence outside the statutory definition are refugees in a sociological sense but not counted as such by the official sources" (2016, 7). By this logic, if we counted the people whose situations the public believes and perceives to qualify one for refugee status, the numbers might be significantly larger than the 10 percent that a more restricted accounting suggests.

There is also evidence that official statistics undercount the number of people who would actually fit within the UN definition if given a chance to have their case thoroughly assessed. We know that many people attempting to gain access to the asylum systems of the Global North are screened out by policies of border externalization and "remote control" before they are even able to lodge an application. These efforts to control borders by keeping asylum seekers at arm's length are proliferating rapidly with increasing degrees of ingenuity and cruelty (Casas-Cortes, Cobarrubias, and Pickles 2015; Frelick, Kysel, and Podkul 2016; FitzGerald 2019; Ghezelbash 2018). Ultimately, while we know that these efforts are widespread and increasingly effective, we have no way of knowing just how many people who might have received refugee status are being deterred and screened out by these policies.

Global North states are also able to perpetuate the idea that refugees are rare by resettling a very small fraction of the total number of displaced people in the world each year. For example, in 2018 Canada resettled 28,000 people who had been granted refugee status overseas and the United States resettled 23,000 people (Radford and Connor 2019). Each of these major resettlement states took in about one-tenth of 1 percent of the world's officially recognized refugee population, leaving the vast majority to languish elsewhere.

In the Global South, receiving states may not have the same capacities to keep potential refugees at arm's length. However, Betts (2010) has shown how host states with limited resources often engage in a trade-off when large-scale movements across their borders occur. Some states elect to protect everyone minimally without providing official refugee protection, while others offer full refugee protection to a small group while excluding the rest. In other words, many of those host states may be deliberately undercounting people who might otherwise qualify for refugee protection in order to reduce perceptions of their obligations to them.

In sum, it is extremely difficult to know exactly how many displaced people in desperate need of protection there are in the world. The powerful players of the international community have agreed on a figure that suggests about one in ten border crossers fits that description. However, there is good reason to believe that if people were more closely and consistently accounted for, the number would be much larger.

A Guide to What Follows

The remaining chapters of this book apply a critical lens to the story of the life and homes of the migrant/refugee binary, and the intellectual, ethical, and geopolitical commitments that undergird it. I show how the binary shapes and constrains the academic study of border crossing, the work of global governance institutions, and policy debates in active crossing situations. Because I am trying to be as exhaustive as possible in revealing the binary at work, the chapters cover a lot of ground both geographically and in terms of discipline, using a wide variety of sources and methods.

In chapter 2 I look historically at the development of the refugee concept alongside the concept of sovereignty. In part, this story serves to further undermine essentialist notions of "the refugee" as a timeless figure. Instead, I argue that the refugee concept is deeply linked to questions of sovereignty and territoriality, neither of which was an organizing principle of the world until the modern period. Further, the chapter traces how the legal construction of sovereignty developed alongside and intertwined with the colonial project. The resulting hierarchies of sovereignty led some forms of displacement to be cast as examples of refugees in exile and others as byproducts of legitimate colonial expansion. The chapter then tracks these global power dynamics into the twentieth century, when the refugee was codified into international law through processes that privileged the interests of powerful states and routinely discounted the sovereignty of states in the Global South. These tales of colonial exploitation are the foundation upon which the binary rests.

Chapter 3 traces the role of the migrant/refugee binary in shaping, constraining, and ultimately bifurcating the academic study of migration. Especially since the birth of the field of refugee studies in the 1980s, scholars have tended to consider refugee movements separately from other forms of migration. The logic behind drawing this boundary was based in the belief that there was a particular "refugee experience" that was conceptually distinct from voluntary migration (Stein 1981). The refugee studies literature has generally followed the UNHCR's insistence that "refugees are not migrants" (Feller 2005). This isolation is mutually reinforced; standard theories of migration tend to be heavily focused on economic push and pull factors, and on the migration policies of Global North states (Cornelius and Rosenblum 2005; Adamson and Tsourapas 2019). A direct result of the isolation of refugee studies (later called forced migration studies) from the rest of migration studies is that generalist migration scholars tend to be more thoroughly integrated into their specific academic discipline (usually sociology, political science, or history). This lack of connection between the study of refugees and the social sciences results in real intellectual losses for the fields in question. For example, I argue that because they are by definition uncategorized, asylum seekers have been one of the groups most likely to fall between the stools of forced and voluntary migration studies.

Chapter 4 analyzes the historical and current role that UNHCR plays in the perpetuation of the migrant/refugee binary, revealing the binary to be a central part of UNHCR's public relations and communications strategy. I discuss the essentialist and positivist conception of a refugee that the agency promotes, and how that view fits with the inherent incentive for self-preservation that goes along with maintaining a specific institutional mandate. Drawing on the international organizations (IOs) literature from the field of international relations, I argue that the migrant/refugee binary is a key aspect of how UNHCR "sees like an IO" (Broome and Seabrooke 2012, 4). The rest of the chapter supports this claim with a close study of UNHCR's public relations work over the past decade, including interviews with communications and social media staff at the

agency, and an analysis of press releases and social media efforts to promote and protect the migrant/refugee binary. I find that UNHCR is
deeply invested in the binary in part because it helps the agency to reassure Global North publics that sympathy toward refugees is not equivalent to open borders.

Chapter 5 examines the life of the migrant/refugee binary in the
Global South. First, the chapter provides an account of the initial reluctance and abiding resistance on the part of many Global South states to
accept the wording of the 1951 Convention definition, to adopt the Convention after its ratification, and to implement the 1967 Protocol that sup-
posedly made the definition global. The chapter also chronicles the creation of two regional refugee definitions that are more expansive than
the 1951 Convention definition (the Organization of African Unity Convention of 1969 and the Cartagena Declaration on Refugees of 1984) and
UNHCR responses to these conceptualizations of a refugee. Finally, the
chapter presents two brief case studies examining how the binary functions in government rhetoric and reaction to direct arrivals in the two
largest contemporary displacement crises: Jordan and Lebanon (receiving
Syrians) and Colombia and Peru (receiving Venezuelans). These accounts
of South–South border crossing help to illustrate the ways in which the
migrant/refugee binary is a construct driven by the interests of wealthy
Global North states.

Chapter 6 analyzes European reactions to Middle Eastern and African arrivals at Europe's southern and eastern borders since 2014. Recent
mass arrivals into Europe have triggered an unprecedented public interest in the terminology of migration, while simultaneously helping to reveal that the categories are irremediably blurred. During the summer of
2015, nearly every major media outlet ended up taking a stand on terminology, and heated debates ensued, sparking an ongoing conversation. Inspired by the public discourse about the categorization of border crossers,
this analysis is particularly focused on the choice to refer to people as refugees or migrants, and the moments in which speakers or media outlets
defended or explained such choices. I conclude with the suggestion that
debates about terminology are fundamentally linked to larger anxieties
about both the past and future of Europe.

Chapter 7 examines reactions in the United States to Central American arrivals at the US/Mexico border since 2014, placing these debates in
an historical context that shows the continuing US reluctance to acknowledge itself as a destination for people seeking asylum. As in chapter 6, this

chapter also focuses on the moments in which public figures or media outlets refer to people as refugees or migrants, and how they defend or explain such choices. This time frame is particularly interesting in the case of the United States because it allows for a comparison across two presidential administrations, Obama's and Trump's. By examining the endurance of the migrant/refugee binary across administrations that have vastly different reputations on immigration and humanitarianism, I conclude that binary logic does not prevent refugees from being cast as a tiny fraction of the people advocates want to protect. Advocates in the United States have seized the moment to suggest that Central American arrivals represent a refugee crisis. Such entreaties have been generally unsuccessful, particularly under the Trump administration. I argue that while President Trump may seem to some like a post-binary figure due to his blanket hostility to all border crossers, binary logic is still apparent in both his harsh anti-immigrant policies and advocates' responses to it.

The concluding chapter 8 asserts that the migrant/refugee binary is not a useful frame for thinking about border crossing in a world that seems to have abandoned the notion of protecting vulnerable border crossers. The binary is still the central way in which destination states maintain control over their borders while paying lip service to humanitarian concerns. But the hypocrisy of the so-called "global" refugee protection regime is more apparent than ever, as wealthy states spend money that could be used to help people to instead keep them as far away as possible.

It is not surprising that policy-makers promote a binary way of thinking, but scholars and advocates need not follow suit. Perhaps the widespread resistance among advocates and scholars to question the stability of migrant categories stems from a fear of exposing the dilemma and eroding support for protecting refugees. Advocates run into trouble, however, when the tropes used to focus on the special needs of refugees automatically make nonrefugees harder to defend. Thus, I conclude that assessment of humanitarian need combined with an honest accounting of Global North responsibility for displacement is a preferable alternative for advocates. Finally, I assert that scholarship on border crossing would be radically enriched if it moved beyond the binary paradigm.

On Objections and Critique

I recognize that the arguments in this book will not be universally accepted or well received. In the process of writing it, I have heard a few expected objections. First, some people say, *We already know this.* This re-action often comes from scholars of refugees and forced migration. They are so familiar with the shortcomings of the binary that they do not be-lieve it is necessary to rearticulate them. My response is that while many of us already understand much of what I am about to say, scholars con-tinue to use the binary to a surprising degree, sometimes with a brief side note about how it is an oversimplification. In other words, while many scholars of refugees and forced migration are aware of the problems with binary logic, the fundamental structure of our field of study has not rad-ically changed. Instead, it mimics the categories of international law, and inadvertently reifies them in the process. Further, many, many people *do not* already know this. The average person has thought very little about the distinction, and takes cues about how to understand the terms "ref-ugee" and "migrant" from public discourse, which is often informed by and includes scholars. Even though we may know that the landscape is far more complex than the binary implies, we as scholars and/or advo-cates have not done an adequate job of passing on that knowledge to the general public. In other words, I believe that the limitations and legacies of binary logic, while known to many, still need to be discussed explicitly and in some detail.

Second, some people have said, *Sure, but don't we have to work with what we have?* Many lawyers who represent asylum seekers view the bi-nary as perhaps an oversimplification, one that excludes many vulnera-ble migrants from protection, but one that allows at least a few to access it. Thus, they understand it as an inadequate but valuable tool. They also see the level of global consensus around the definition of a refugee as a remarkable achievement, one that could not be replicated if the process were begun anew today. Much like US constitutional scholars who ac-knowledge that the wording of that centuries-old document is not ideal, but fear what would result from a constitutional convention held today, these refugee advocates believe that they (and all of us who care about protecting vulnerable people) should focus on the potential of existing le-gal tools instead of highlighting their limitations. My response to these objectors is that attorneys and other advocates who are working within existing frameworks to assist people absolutely do need to accept the bi-nary for those purposes, even as they may be working internally to stretch the reach of the refugee definition. However, that reality does not explain why nonpractitioners, advocates, and policy-makers need to perpetuate legal categories and make them the defining features of other work in this arena. It is not the limited use of the binary when it is attached to legal categories that I am most concerned with here. It is the widespread use of the binary in all other areas that I believe can only serve to constrain our imaginations and our conversations.

The third objection is the most difficult to address: *This argument is woefully misguided and will put refugees at risk.* Some people, usually those who have dedicated their lives to advocacy for refugees as a category of people, or to representing individuals who are seeking refugee status, feel very strongly that what I am saying here is dangerous. Some of them believe that refugees have been particularly and egregiously wounded, even abandoned by the system of states, and deserve more concern and protection than other people who cross borders. They believe that the definition of a refugee highlights something very important, and to suggest otherwise is to demean and threaten people who "are refugees." They may acknowledge that there is some blurring at the boundaries of the category, but the core of who constitutes a refugee is sacred and should be kept separate. They believe that if we poke a hole in the dam that keeps refugees at least theoretically protected, a wave of other claims will come crashing down and wash that important distinction away. They believe that lives are literally at stake, and some of the people who believe this get angry at people they view as deliberately poking holes.

My response to these objectors is that we may just have to agree to disagree. I do not believe that there is an essential quality of "refugee-ness" that some people possess and others do not. I believe that people who have qualified for refugee protection include among them some of the most abject, the most vulnerable people in the world. However, I also believe that there are many, many people with equally valid claims on our compassion, our assistance, and our protection who have no hope of qualifying for refugee status. And I believe that insisting on the particularity of refugees leads to an abdication of other responsibilities. I ask that readers put aside the suspicion that I do not care if refugees die, and understand that I believe passionately in the responsibility to protect vulnerable fellow humans. I just do not think that a binary logic that assumes two innately different kinds of border crossing is an effective way to achieve that goal.

I hope this last point helps elaborate my position on the practice of doing critical work. To say proudly that this book is a work of critical refugee studies is not to say that I am engaged in critique for the sake of it. It is absolutely not my aim to be destructive, but to better understand the implications of our ways of thinking. As Güngdoğdu has pointed out, Arendt's approach to this question is instructive. When Arendt expressed cynicism about the concept of human rights, it was not her aim to deconstruct the concept into oblivion. Rather than a nihilistic view of critique, she wanted a radical rethinking and reimagining of the concepts with which she was concerned (Güngdoğdu 2015, 27). Skepticism about a concept is not just about questioning and deconstructing, it is also "midwifery," delivering oneself from prejudgments that limit one's thinking, and reorienting toward a constructive end (34).

I appreciate Latour's (2004) lament that the practice of critique has too often devolved into intellectual warfare. Instead, he suggests that we imagine that the objects of critique are "matters of concern." In his imagined form, "the critic is not the one who debunks, but the one who assembles. The critic is not the one who lifts the rugs from under the feet of the naïve believers, but the one who offers the participants arenas in which to gather," because "if something is constructed, then it means it is fragile and thus in great need of care and caution" (246). In this spirit, my objective is to bring together people who study and care about border crossers and to bridge scholarly divides. Because I believe that uncritical attachment to the binary has left scholars and advocates unprepared for this newest phase of anti-immigrant politics, I aim to encourage and create space for all of us to have much more difficult, much franker conversations about what and who we value.

In sum, we have these three objections: that the binary has already been dismantled, that the binary is problematic but we need it, and that the binary is not just instrumentally but intrinsically significant. Interestingly, these three objections are not compatible with one another, which means that there is something more to be said on the matter. I will elaborate further on each of these objections and my responses throughout the course of this book. I hope for now to have convinced you that I am not embarking on this project blindly, and that as you follow my argument through the subsequent chapters, you will, at the least, remain engaged if not always persuaded.

2

Uneven Sovereignties

IN *THE ORIGINS OF TOTALITARIANISM* (1951), Hannah Arendt spoke of "the perplexities of the rights of man," referring to the ways in which rights abuses are usually carried out by vociferous proponents of rights. Based on her experience of persecution in and exile from Nazi Germany, and her observations about how vulnerable people had been abandoned by the world in their moment of need, Arendt was highly skeptical that those who had been displaced could make successful rights claims that would require the receiving state to act beyond its own interests. To her mind, refugees, stateless people, and others were without rights precisely because states are the rights providers, and states had decided not to provide them. Despite all kinds of pretty language about rights being developed by so-called liberal states at that time, Arendt (1951) concluded that "the world found nothing sacred in the abstract nakedness of being human." In other words, a person simply saying that they needed protection did not appear to compel the powerful to provide it, especially not in the absence of some other incentive.

Decades later, those who care about the plight of vulnerable people remain perplexed by the disconnect between a widespread formal commitment to the 1951 Refugee Convention and the practical rightlessness of so many border crossers. The contemporary international refugee regime is held up as a powerful instrument of protection, and yet those who are most familiar with it would be the first to admit that it is woefully inadequate. Even in the course of attempting to seek protection, many people find themselves suffering in the most abject ways. Italian philosopher

Giorgio Agamben (1995) described this experience as one of "bare life," in which people are stripped of all rights and exist only in the most basic form of humanity. A key component of bare life is the paradoxical way in which those who are most in need of rights protection are least able to assert or access it. In these moments, the continuing reliance of the system of rights on the *noblesse oblige* of powerful sovereign states is exposed.

Why has it continued this way? To understand the current moment, we have to look unflinchingly at the sordid histories that have brought us to this point. It would be impossible to exhaustively catalogue all of the processes that have led to the current dynamics of border crossing and border control. Instead, the goal of this chapter is to encourage the reader to think critically about the ways in which binary logic has shaped existing understandings of border crossings. In particular, the chapter attempts to illuminate some of the global power dynamics of refugee concept construction and its relationship to state sovereignty. In doing so, the chapter reexamines some of the accepted wisdom about the contemporary state of borders and protection in the world.

Once we understand the modern refugee concept not only as part of the bundle of universal human rights that emerged out of the Second World War but also as a product of nationalism after the fall of empire, persistent "rightlessness in an age of rights" is less perplexing (Gündoğdu 2015). Instead of wondering why rights violations for vulnerable border crossers abound despite their prohibition in international law, it becomes clear that state sovereignty concerns drove the institutional arrangements of the pre- and postwar periods, and powerful state interests are baked into the concept of a refugee.

The Appeal of Essentialism

Binary logic often relies on an essentialist version of history that portrays "the refugee" as an ancient category that existed long before it was officially recognized by law. These accounts can be very appealing, but they are often anachronistic, portraying some historical displacements as producing refugees, while tellingly ignoring many other displacements altogether. The refugee concept cannot be timeless if it is linked to the notion that territorial sovereignty must be protected, because territorial sovereignty has not always been the organizing logic of the globe. To guard against essentialism, we must acknowledge that the migrant/refugee binary is a construction, and that the concept of a refugee as a distinct category of border crosser is not ancient and continuous. As with all constructed categories, it has required and continues to require a lot of constructing. And the construction is surprisingly recent.

The field of refugee studies has sometimes obscured this point by nodding to the fact that since ancient times, Western thought has included the idea of protection from a pursuer or tormenter. Indeed, the word "asylum" comes from the Greek and refers to the notion of someone who cannot or should not be seized (Grahl-Madsen 1972). And so, proponents of international refugee law invoke the ancient roots of asylum-seeking in order to foster the belief that the figure of "the refugee" is timeless and natural. In contrast, I want to make a distinction here between seeking asylum, which is something a person *does*, and being a refugee, which binary logic treats as something a person *is*. The act of seeking protection is ancient. The idea that an individual is "a refugee" is not.

Greek literature and philosophy are certainly filled with tales that emphasize the themes of foreignness, hospitality, and belonging (Kasimis 2018). But this is not unexpected in light of the fact that mobility was the norm rather than the exception for much of human history. Recent studies of ancient Greece and Rome have concluded with increasing certainty that human mobility was a key feature of those ancient worlds (Isayev 2017; Tacoma 2016). These findings raise questions about whether the notion of being tied to a place (and thus being capable of displacement) was anywhere near as central for humans during ancient times as it is today. Perhaps it adds moral weight to current political debates to remind people that the idea of hospitality for the stranger dates back to the earliest recorded history, and was a central concern for the Greeks and Ancient Persians, and was a theme in the New Testament of the Bible (Kukathas 2016). But there is also much evidence to suggest that the ancient Greeks were hostile to new arrivals just as often as they were welcoming (Rubinstein 2018; Gray 2011). And the fact that ancient societies had debates about how and whether to show hospitality to foreigners is quite different from having a distinct concept of a refugee, a figure who makes a claim to access a sovereign territory. Hospitality to foreigners in the ancient world stemmed from a kind of moral obligation that was not a function of state sovereignty.

Thus, a key aspect of undoing binary logic is to remind ourselves that throughout the premodern era, there was no concept or category of a refugee as a distinct form of border crosser. For most of early European history and through the Middle Ages, there were a wide variety of terms used for people who were travelers, strangers, and outsiders, and the terms did not seem to be associated with a particular definition or used with the goal of categorization in mind. Mobility continued to be a big theme, but it would be anachronistic to suggest that it had anything to do with crossing an international border or appealing to a state for protection. Instead, appeals for protection could be made to families, individuals, or religious leaders. Similarly, throughout the Middle Ages, asylum existed as a concept in relation to churches as a place of sanctuary. Referencing ideas such as protection and sanctuary can be deceiving if the intent is to suggest a throughline from ancient to modern times, when there simply was no concept of a refugee as a distinct category of border crosser before the modern period.

Many refugee scholars also invoke seventeenth-century examples of displacement in order to suggest, in an essentialist vein, that there is something coherent about the experience of refugees across time and place. For example, Zolberg et al. (1989) begin their study of contemporary displacement with a mention of the French Huguenots, calling them the "classic type of refugee" because they were fleeing religious persecution. Similarly, Orchard has argued that after the French state banned Protestantism, the flight of 200,000 Huguenots from France in 1685 helped to create the norm that states should provide asylum (2014, 46). Other scholars point out that the flight of the Huguenots actually inspired the word refugee, which seems to have come into French usage at that time, and then was adopted into the English language as the Huguenots arrived in England (Soguk 1999, 59). So, a common way to tell the story is that the Huguenots were the first modern refugees. They were persecuted for being Protestant by the French state, they were labeled as refugees, and they fled to other European states where they were welcomed according to an emerging norm of providing refuge to those whose states of origin had abandoned them.

This story is tidy, but not entirely accurate. When probed, the binary logic driving it starts to break down. As Orchard later concedes, the Huguenots were largely welcomed by other European states not because of their persecuted status, but because they were a highly skilled artisan class of people, giving these states an economic interest in admitting them (2014, 62). Further, while this event does mark the first English use of the word refugee, it did not come into widespread use at that time, as many different terms were used interchangeably to describe the Huguenots, including exiles, strangers, emigrants, and "the distressed Protestants" (Soguk 1999, 60–61). It is also somewhat anachronistic to portray the Huguenots as fleeing one sovereign territory for another, as state borders were still very much in the process of crystallization at that time (Haddad 2003, 304). While it is true that the Huguenots were moving to escape the rule of the French king and ended up subject to the rule of other kings, even as recently as the late nineteenth and early twentieth centuries "the typology of human displacement . . . was not at all conceptually precise" or institutionalized (Soguk 1999, 64). There was no official process of admitting people, and no expectation of host state support for new arrivals. Displaced people either survived and integrated economically, or they did not, often based on their class background and skill set. To look back and place a refugee/migrant binary onto crossings of the past does not accurately reflect the realities of those events.

Another frequently cited example of early refugees comes from the US nation-building project. The "settler society" myth highlights the ways in which the territory that was to become the United States provided refuge for those seeking religious freedom (Dauvergne 2016). This story often casts the "Puritans"—radical Protestant separatists who left England to settle in an area of the Americas that they called New England in the seventeenth century—as refugees, implying that they were forced to seek safety in a new place (Taparata 2019). This analogy to contemporary displacement is even more wildly inaccurate and misleading than the narrative attached to the Huguenots, and binary logic breaks down here as well. Puritans had certainly fled religious persecution, but they also openly sought material wealth in a new land. Further, the distinction between these two motivations did not exist in the same way during that period. Historians are clear that it is "anachronistic" to argue about whether these settlers were motivated by religious freedom or economic desire because these factors were "interdependent in the lives of people who saw piety and property as mutually reinforcing" (Taylor 2002, 166). The Puritans were seeking their fortunes as a form of religious practice. And, crucially, they did not view themselves as seeking refuge in the arms of a sovereign state.

Ironically and somewhat outrageously, stories that paint these settlers as refugees ignore the displacement of indigenous people that colonial settlement required (Dahl 2018; Taparata 2019). They also obscure the fact that "European colonial economic migrants benefitted from an international legal and imperial regime that facilitated, encouraged, and celebrated white economic migration" which unfolded alongside mass resource extraction for the benefit of European states (Achiume 2019, 10). The dominant frame was one of conquest and domination, of building something new.

In addition to exposing the problems with essentialism in refugee history, the example of the Puritans also helps put a spotlight on a key argument of this chapter: some forms of displacement have been linked to the concept of a refugee, while other displacements have not. In order to understand these patterns, we must look to the history of the concept of sovereignty. The refugee was constructed alongside a world of uneven sovereignties. The Westphalian system combined with colonial conquest led to the displacement of many people, only some of whom perceived themselves as crossing borders between sovereign states. Then, as today, some of these people were viewed as deserving of assistance and protection, and others were viewed as threats.

Uneven Sovereignties

Postcolonial scholars have argued that "it should be impossible to inquire into the modern state without attending to its creation in a global context of colonialism and racism" (Mongia 1999, 529). It should be impossible, and yet the colonial project is overlooked in the vast majority of academic discussions on the concept of a refugee.[1] Attempts to contend with the modern state while ignoring the colonial project and its commitment to white supremacy have misunderstood the modern state and its legitimizing logics. And because the refugee and the state are deeply linked, our understanding of the refugee concept has suffered as a result of this blind spot. The colonial project actively denied sovereignty to much of the world, and imposed borders that did not meaningfully map onto people's lives. People displaced by these events were not considered to be refugees.

Traditional framings of the refugee concept often imply that international law scholars of the seventeenth and eighteenth centuries were preoccupied with outlining the obligations of territorially bound states to protect persecuted people. Despite nods to ancient roots, most histories of the refugee concept converge on the birth of what they call "the modern state," after the 1648 Peace of Westphalia led to the regularization of territorial sovereign states in Europe. According to this history, the newly formed European system of nation-states expected all people to be rooted in a place in order to have an identity, and conversely, states were expected to protect and contain their citizens. So that they could wage wars and extract taxes, modern states needed to be able to identify the group of people contained within them, and control their movement (Torpey 2000). As states began to imagine themselves to be nations, state-sponsored homogenization efforts framed as nation-building led to the persecution of minorities, and caused people to flee across newly crystallizing international borders (Anderson 1983). Displaced people were then understood to be the products of either the state's failure to protect their citizens, or the citizen's failure to fit within the state (Soguk 1999; Haddad 2003).

As European nation-states began to be more territorially bound, legal scholars of the time such as Grotius, Pufendorf, and later Vattel developed treatises that came to form the law of nations, using a juridical framework linking sovereignty to territoriality through the right of states to protect their borders. In discussing early international law, the field of refugee studies has pointed out that the Peace of Westphalia included a right of emigration and outlined a concept of religious toleration (Orchard 2014, 53). Similarly, in his massive *The Status of Refugees in International Law* (1972), Grahl-Madsen devotes some attention to the work of Grotius, Pufendorf, and Vattel. He describes how, in thinking through the difficult questions of the extent of sovereignty, these men actively debated how to draw the line between extraditing criminals who deserved punishment and protecting people who were likely to be punished for political acts if they were returned to their state of origin (18). Grahl-Madsen also points out that Grotius wrote about the rights of "suppliants," people who had been driven out of their homes (13). He cites these examples as evidence of his argument that, from the birth of the modern state, scholars were concerned about how to balance state interests against the obligation to offer protection to those in need (14).

In contrast to such a reading of early international law, this chapter builds on the claims of Third World Approaches to International Law (TWAIL) scholars, who have argued that international law was developed alongside the European conquest of the globe, and thus historically has served to justify colonial oppression (Anghie and Chimni 2003). While refugee studies as a field has not explored the topic, the early international law scholars of the seventeenth and eighteenth centuries were very concerned with colonialism. In many respects, the sovereignty doctrine emerged out of an effort to make sense of colonial encounters and resolve the inherent tension between the increased focus on territorial sovereignty in Europe and the expansionist efforts of these same states around the world (Anghie 2004). By emphasizing the ways in which states were deeply invested in the concepts of territoriality and borders within the continent of Europe, traditional histories of the refugee concept obscure the fact that these same states were simultaneously not "territorially circumscribed" in their approach to the rest of the world during the period of imperial expansion (Mongia 1999, 544).

Not only has refugee studies largely ignored the relationship between early international law scholars and the colonial project, the field has often recast these scholars as creating prototypes of the argument that states have an obligation to protect persecuted people. To cast these legal thinkers as early champions of refugee protection mischaracterizes their thought and serves only to prop up binary logic. To the contrary, early international law scholars believed unequivocally that sovereign states had the right to control and protect their territories, and particularly Vattel's work on sovereignty and nonintervention were hugely influential across Europe and for the founders of the United States (Song 2019, 25–26). This work was primarily focused on defending closure, exclusion, and territorial control. It was not yet concerned with thinking through the exceptions to those rules.

To demonstrate the dominance of the sovereignty doctrine in the seventeenth and eighteenth centuries, one need only contrast it with the thinking of moral philosopher Emmanuel Kant, a contemporary critic of those international law scholars. In 1795 Kant wrote that people should not be denied entry to a territory if they are at risk of being destroyed. Today, immigration scholars often reference Kant's writings on hospitality, reflecting on his depiction of hospitality as a right that belongs to everyone, and that governs interactions between peoples at borders. For example, Benhabib argues that Kant's "formulations presciently anticipate the distinctions in international law between migrants on the one hand, and refugees and asylum seekers on the other" (2004, 1782). It is certainly true that Kant's cosmopolitanism was ahead of his time, so much so that it was considered a fringe perspective when it was written. In fact, Kant's writings on the subject of hospitality received "negligible diplomatic and political reception" until at least the 1880s (Hunter 2013, 501). The dominant legal and moral arguments of the time were those of Grotius, Pufendorf, and Vattel, who Kant famously called "sorry comforters" ([1795] 1996, 326), a phrase which has also been translated as "miserable comforters" (Hunter 2013, 478) for the ways in which they came down squarely in favor of defending states' interests. If those dominant thinkers had been actively carving out the legal concept of protection for persecuted border crossers, Kant would not have been such a marginal figure in his time.

Meanwhile, as theories of territorial sovereignty and self-determination were developing in sophistication within Europe, millions of European colonialists left Europe to help build empires, with no sense that they were crossing into sovereign foreign territories overseas. The colonial project was explicitly built on the notion that the standard of territorial sovereignty was not granted to all people. Early international law served to justify the belief that the non-European world was not sovereign, because those peoples had not earned the right to sovereignty.

This logic then legitimated the process of conquest as a means to bring civilization to the uncivilized. For example, Vattel explicitly argued in relation to colonial possession that people who had not densely settled the land with buildings and agriculture could not be said to have any legal claim to it (Banner 2005, 102). These logics lasted over centuries. The British used this argument to declare Australia to be *terra nullius* (empty land), a legal doctrine that was used to justify the total conquest of that territory and the indigenous peoples who lived on it. Early US Supreme Court decisions used a similar logic to determine that while Native Americans lived on the land, they did not have any legal claim to own it. That right was granted solely to Europeans under the legal principle that "discovery gave title" to whichever European state claimed the land first.[2] Notably, the people who were displaced by these logics have never been considered by the field of refugee studies to be forcibly displaced people. Rather, as described above, the settlers themselves, the displacers, are sometimes constructed as early refugees. Building on these legal fictions of "empty land" and "discovery," many contemporary immigrant destination states outside of Europe were developed and sustained through mass emigration of people from Europe.

These enduring legal fictions are not incidental to our contemporary understanding of state sovereignty. They clearly outline the ways in which the concept was always based on a hierarchy of sovereignties, and true sovereign authority was only ever granted to the conquerors, because the conquerors defined what sovereignty was, and granted it to themselves. As colonial settler states gained tighter control of the territories they claimed, doctrines of sovereignty were invoked to protect their borders from foreign threats. For example, Vattel's argument that states had the right to exclude foreigners from their territories if they so desired formed the basis for the plenary power doctrine in US immigration law. This doctrine was used to justify the Chinese Exclusion Acts passed by the US Congress in 1882, and continues to form the basis of constitutional interpretations of the extent of congressional and executive power over immigration policy (Song 2019, 27).

In sum, sovereignty doctrines were never about equal sovereignty, they were about domination. The concept of state obligation to persecuted people as an exception to the sovereign right of states to pursue their interests was simply not a prominent nor widely accepted concept during the colonial era, a period that lasted centuries. Histories of the refugee concept that ignore the role of colonialism perpetuate misunderstandings of early international law and make it seem more humanitarian and cosmopolitan than it was. Concepts linking the territorial sovereign state and the right to control its borders came well before the refugee concept emerged. Misunderstanding that timing allows us to incorrectly believe that the modern state created a byproduct (the refugee), and alongside it, a solution (the notion of an obligation to protect refugees).

The End of Empire and the Rise of the Border

Unlike the traditional explanation that portrays the refugee as a byproduct of the Westphalian system that emerged in the seventeenth and eighteenth centuries, my retelling claims that the concept of a refugee was constructed much later. The birth of the modern European state did not immediately coincide with tight border control. Rather, it was the end of empire, not its rise, that led to the peak of anxiety about borders and containment. The earliest version of the refugee concept emerged as the Westphalian system was altered by the decline of the colonial project, increased global mobility in the late nineteenth and early twentieth centuries, and the rise of ethno-nationalism that these two phenomena produced. Decolonization is thus a key moment in the construction of the refugee concept. Rather than a seventeenth-century byproduct, the refugee is deeply intertwined with the "trinity of state-people-territory" that only emerged out of the nationalisms of early twentieth-century Europe, but which remains unevenly regarded worldwide (Arendt 1951).

Immigration historians often talk about the turn of the twentieth century as a period characterized by laissez-faire immigration policies, but that was only true for European border crossers. For non-Europeans on the move, it was a period of rapid closure based on newly articulated anxiety about racial purity and invasion. Further, whether new arrivals were viewed as a threat to the state or a potential benefit continued to depend not on an assessment of their need for protection, but often on highly racialized understandings of people's capacity to become productive democratic citizens.

Colonialism was central to the development of ethno-nationalism in the late nineteenth and early twentieth centuries. As Levine argues, "A growing interest in colonial populations and mostly celebratory attitudes towards European imperial expansion set the stage for acceptance of eugenics in the 20th century" (2010, 43). Colonial encounters led Europeans in a post-Darwinian world to construct pseudo-scientific accounts of biologically based race and racial hierarchies and Christian stewardship to legitimize the ongoing subordination of colonial subjects (Mayblin 2017). By the end of the nineteenth century, rising nationalism rooted in racist logics began to change the way in which states viewed migration. States began to imagine an alignment between nation and territory that was closer than ever before (Anderson 1983). For example, throughout the 1800s, the British had shipped Indian colonial subjects to all corners of the empire as indentured laborers. But when, in the early years of the twentieth century, Indian-origin British subjects attempted to emigrate to Canada and Australia, the British government began to institute a passport program in order to protect the white settler colonies from the arrival of people from other parts of the empire (Mongia 1999). Similarly, after having banned Chinese migration in the 1880s, the United States expanded the ban to all people from Asia in 1917 and then moved to nearly eliminate southern and eastern European migration in 1924. By 1930 every independent state in the Western Hemisphere had passed legislation limiting migration on racial grounds (FitzGerald and Cook-Martin 2014, 39).

Even within Europe, the chaos of the early twentieth century illustrates the significance of the end of empire for fueling both displacement and anxiety about borders. As ethno-national identity became more centrally important in Europe, "migrants began to be conceptualized as continuing to have memberships in their ancestral homeland" (Wimmer and Glick Schiller 2003, 588). It was during this period that the state-people-territory trinity began to crystallize and create "impossible subjects," people who do not fit neatly within the confines of a nation-state (Ngai 2004). Exiles and outsiders had been constructed as the anomaly in an otherwise "normal" rooted experience (Haddad 2003, 299). People who lacked this rootedness, who moved across this otherwise stable system, were therefore constructed as errors in an otherwise coherent organizational framework. Nation-state formation in Europe and the Middle East at that time took the form of violent erasure of ethnic and national minorities, assimilationist policies, and forcible expulsion and exchange of humans between states. The sudden dissolution of the Austro-Hungarian empire in 1918 led to the creation of newly hardened state borders, causing ethnic minorities to flee. The dissolution of the Ottoman empire involved the mass extermination and displacement of Muslim, Armenian, Greek, and Assyrian ethnic minorities. A staggering 1.5 million people fled Russia after 1917, and then had their citizenship rescinded by Russia en masse in 1921 (Hathaway 1984, 352). Greece and Turkey engaged in a mass exchange of people in 1923 (Xenos 1993, 424). So, in the early twentieth century, the powerful idea emerged that roots to a homeland were the most valuable, essential thing a person could have (Xenos 1993), and simultaneously, the process of alignment between nation and territory required active efforts to expel and exchange people who were foreign to the project of nation-building (Soguk 1999, 115).

This is the global political context into which the modern concept of the refugee emerged. While the concepts of asylum, protection, and hospitality were long-standing, the term "refugee" was not widely used until the years immediately following the carnage of the First World War and the Russian Revolution. It was a product of that period. During the 1920s the word began to emerge with more frequency and competitor terms were "relegated to oblivion" (Soguk 1999, 119; see also Gatrell 2013). It was also at this time that the issue of displacement was formalized as a problem for states, calling for an intergovernmental institutional solution (Soguk 1999). Notably, as the next section outlines, these solutions were always envisioned as a way of protecting the needs and interests of powerful states.

The Development of the Refugee
Concept in International Law

The first international refugee organization was created in 1921 out of a collaboration between the International Red Cross and the newly founded League of Nations. The League of Nations appointed Norwegian explorer Fridtjof Nansen as the High Commissioner for Refugees (LNHCR) in August 1921, and he went straight to work convincing European leaders to support coordinated efforts to help stateless former Russians. In 1922 the LNHCR created identity documents, known as "Nansen passports." With the advent of the passport age, everyone suddenly needed one in order to move, and so these documents significantly facilitated the freedom of stateless people to travel around Europe looking for work, although it was still left to the discretion of individual states whether to recognize Nansen passport holders (Torpey 2000).

In the 1920s and 1930s, the League of Nations also became very involved in managing displacement in the Middle East. But, unlike in Europe, where states could assert their sovereignty and decide the degree to which they wanted to admit displaced people, much of the Middle East was under European mandate, a supposed transitional phase out of colonialism that still greatly limited the sovereignty of mandate states. In particular, the League of Nations was very active in managing the resettlement of displaced Armenians and Assyrians in the French mandates of Syria and Lebanon. All of the interventions were designed to buttress continuing European intervention in the region.

Refugee resettlement policies could be enacted without permission from local populations and designed specifically to support a new form of European political authority. Refugee policy thus served both as a tool of colonial administrations and as a mode of differentiating sovereign from less sovereign political spaces. (Robson 2017, 628)

In this sense, unequal sovereignties were central to the international refugee regime from the very first moments of its existence, especially as it expanded beyond the borders of Europe.

Nevertheless, the earliest iterations of the international refugee regime were far less essentialist in their conception of a refugee than the binary logic of the contemporary regime. First, early conceptions were more focused on the consequences, not the cause, of displacement (Hathaway

1984). They focused on the ways in which statelessness would impede people's ability to find work. Nansen passports were designed to facilitate refugees' mobility so that they could economically integrate into new places.
Thus, Long (2013) argues that once they had been recognized as such,
"refugees were to be helped to become migrants" by meeting their most
basic survival needs and then allowing them to transition into economic
actors and away from being regarded as little more than objects of charity
(9). For this reason, Long concludes that there was "no clear distinction
made by the international community in the 1920s between political refugee and impoverished migrant" (10).

Whereas the concept of a refugee was now defined by law for the first
time, these early definitions were entirely group based, without a requirement of individualized assessment. They relied on the assumption that
each person had an ethnic or territorial origin that corresponded to their
national identity. If protection from that national home was revoked, the
international community stepped in. As Simpson argued at the outset of
his major 1938 report summarizing a survey of the various major refugee situations that were likely to affect Europe, the refugee's "defenseless-
ness lies in his inability to demand the protection of any state" (Simpson
1938, 3). In this moment, displaced people were not seen as people in exile as much as people who had no home to return to (Xenos 1993, 423).
This conflation between statelessness and displacement is revealing because it demonstrates just how much the linkage between territory and
nation had been cemented in this period. By the late 1930s, conceptions of
a refugee expanded to include people who had experienced de facto loss
of protection even if not officially made stateless by law—many displaced
people in that moment were technically German citizens even though
they had fled Germany and could not return (Hathaway 1984). However,
these conceptions were still entirely group based, granting protective status to entire ethno-national groups at once, without any attempt at individualized assessment. The individualized, personal aspect of the refugee
concept developed and was constructed over the course of later decades.

Once the global Great Depression took hold, the group-based approach to refugee protection ran into problems. There was a lack of will
among potential host states to protect people who were seen as economic
drains. Both Britain and the United States implemented highly restrictive immigration laws in the 1920s that did not distinguish between
refugees and immigrants (Orchard 2014, 118). The US was particularly

"isolationist" in its attitude, fueled by the Great Depression and anti-semitism (119). Due to the US's strict interpretation of its legal bar against admitting people who would become a public charge, the numerical migration quotas set aside for Germany went unfilled in the 1930s: "many of the persecuted who applied for entry to the USA were refused entry because they were also poor" (Long 2013, 12). Thus, they were excluded through the closure of migration channels that had previously been left open. Ultimately, as Orchard puts it, "over the interwar period, formal multilateralism had become an entrenched norm" that paid lip service to displaced people (2014, 139). Crucially, however, "no states sought to alter their own domestic restrictionist legislation" to admit large numbers of people that they viewed as an economic burden (139).

International organizations were stymied in their capacity to protect people fleeing Nazi Germany because they lacked the authority to influence or control powerful state interests. US president Franklin Delano Roosevelt (FDR) took on a leadership role by convening a conference in Evian, France, in 1938. The ostensible purpose of the Evian Conference was to set up an international organization to help with Jewish refugees. At Evian, FDR did not ask states to increase their immigration quotas. The purpose of the newly created Intergovernmental Committee on Refugees (ICR) was to help facilitate safe and orderly emigration of Jews from Germany and Eastern Europe, but reactions to these plans among European Jews were mixed (Zahra 2016). Some wanted to leave, others did not. European governments strongly encouraged emigration during the 1930s despite this reluctance, but this push coupled with immigration restrictionism in the Western Hemisphere led to disaster. The ICR devoted substantial effort to a global search for a potential Jewish homeland, considering both Madagascar and British Guiana quite seriously. These possibilities are sometimes referenced as amusing anecdotes, conjuring up imaginary parallel roads not traveled. But they are also an extremely revealing window into the hierarchies of sovereignty that existed at the time. The fact that, even in the mid-twentieth century, some powerful states believed they could dump a group of people into the territory of another state without the consent of either reveals the degree to which some states had sovereignty's autonomy, territorial control, and independence, and some did not.

Evian was a key moment in what Hathaway (1984) has called "the individualization of refugee law," because when the ICR was founded, it set forth a definition that focused for the first time on *why* people were being displaced (377). The seeds of the definition that would be codified in the 1951 Convention can be seen in the wording of this earlier ICR definition, which stated that a refugee was someone who had been displaced "on account of their political opinions, religious beliefs and racial origin" (371). This shift represented a significant change from the group-based models of previous decades, since it meant that refugee status determination would, at least theoretically, focus on the individual merits of each case.

To be clear: this definition was explicitly designed to limit the number of people who would fit within it. "By carefully establishing the hallmarks of refugeehood, it was hoped that assistance could be afforded to those in the greatest need without risking the serious domestic political problems likely to result from continued open immigration" (Hathaway 1984, 349). In other words, in these conversations, the refugee was constructed as the exceptional figure with possible claims on state sovereignty, as opposed to migrants who lacked these claims.

In the end, the Second World War led to the death and displacement of millions of people, some of whom could have been saved if the Western powers had been swifter to act, more generous, more welcoming. As Arendt stated: "The comity of European peoples went to pieces when, and because, it allowed its weakest member to be excluded and persecuted" (1943, 119). But the devastation of the war did not lead Western countries to substantially revisit their immigration restrictionism. Even several years after the war had ended, there were still over a million people displaced within Europe. Since many of them came from Eastern Europe, they would not be allowed to come into the United States, Canada, or Australia in any large number due to the national origins restrictions that were still in place at the time. For example, the United States was still operating under the quota system it had developed in 1924, which made it all but impossible for Eastern Europeans to enter because the quotas for those countries were so low. With the United States politically unwilling to remove those quotas, in order to admit displaced Eastern Europeans Jews, Congress passed the Displaced Persons Act of 1948, which enabled the US to admit refugees as a distinct category without having to change its generally highly restrictive, race-based system (Hamlin 2012b; Bon Tempo 2008).

The International Refugee Organization (IRO), established by the newly formed United Nations in 1946, built upon the ICR definition of a refugee to create its own, which also focused on individual persecution. The IRO worked to resettle people in the United States, Canada, Australia, and the new state of Israel, but by 1951, displaced people remained and the numbers continued to rise as people fled from Eastern to Western Europe (Gallagher 1989, 579). A consensus emerged among the power players of the UN that something new was needed.

1951

Perhaps because so many scholars of displacement are trained in law, many explorations of the concept of the refugee focus on the relatively recent history since the Refugee Convention was adopted. It is certainly true that the legal person of the refugee has gained significant traction since the mid-twentieth century, when it was codified into international law in a particular form. However, by placing too much stock in the idea of collective internationalism underpinning the Refugee Convention, scholars reify 1951 as a major moment of consensus and clarity in which the "problem" of refugee protection was finally fixed. Too often, scholars tell the story as if in 1951 an essentially unique group of people who have existed since ancient times were finally recognized as being particularly in need of protection. Treating 1951 like "year zero" for refugee studies runs the risk of fostering "ahistorical" understandings of the concepts (Long 2013; Elie 2014). Some observers have gone so far as to accuse refugee studies of being "averse" to engaging deeply with historical context (Marfleet 2007, 136).

Refugee scholars commonly focus on 1951 as a pivotal moment in recognizing the long-standing needs of refugees. For example, Malkki justifies this focus by saying that "people have always sought refuge and sanctuary. But 'the refugee' as a specific social category and legal problem of global dimensions did not exist in its full modern form before this period" (1995, 497–98). Similarly, Gatrell argues that the mid-twentieth century marks a major turning point for the concept of a refugee because of the "internationalization of responses to refugee crises" that emerged out of that period (2013, 2). UNHCR and the Refugee Convention are often held up as major advancements over previous attempts to assist displaced people. Early twentieth-century responses to the series of displacements in Europe were very ad hoc and country specific. Multiple international organizations, some more multilateral than others, had been created but had not lasted. And these organizations had failed miserably at the task of protecting victims of the Nazis. Such failures are usually cited as evidence of the inadequate nature of the pre-1951 refugee regime, and of the way in which the legal concept of refugee protection was still half-baked before that moment. This conventional view in refugee studies—an "evolutionary" understanding of the 1951 Convention as a major advancement over previous attempts to establish a refugee regime—is revisionist at best (Nyers 2006, 12).

In contrast to this approach, my retelling of what happened in 1951 reminds us that the moment is only momentous in retrospect. UNHCR and the Convention definition have only grown to their current level of breadth and significance over time in an incremental way. Further, an overemphasis on the postwar moment incorrectly suggests that the concept of a refugee is a product of the international human rights regime that developed in the aftermath of the Second World War. The institutional and political realities of 1951 reveal that the Refugee Convention is not a document of universal rights protection. Rather than representing progress toward postnationalism, a hierarchy of state sovereignties shaped the 1951 refugee definition and the scope of UNHCR's work.

The newly formed UNHCR was limited in its ability to influence state behavior, in part because the agency was conceived in the exact same way as the previous international organizations: as a temporary solution to a specific regional problem. Further, "the UNHCR's start was not auspicious" because neither of the world's superpowers at the time, the United States and the Soviet Union, supported it (Orchard 2014, 189). There was significant disagreement on what UNHCR's role should be and how it should be funded. The International Labor Organization and the United Nations had a plan that would have created a single organization to coordinate migration in a much broader way, but the United States wanted there to be a "temporary refugee agency with narrow authority," not a full-fledged relief agency (Karatani 2005, 519). The US succeeded in limiting UNHCR's scope by making it mandatory for the UN General Assembly to approve all appeals for voluntary contributions. Thus, UNHCR had to operate on a very small budget and emergency fund (Loescher 2001, 44). The original mandate was for three years, and it had very few resources at its disposal.

"The justification for separating migrants from refugees on the basis of whether the movement was forced or voluntary appeared retrospectively" due to these institutional realities and constraints (Karatani 2005, 519). The UNHCR was told to assist refugees and not migrants. However, as Long points out, "in separating the humanitarian from the economic drivers of migration, the question of how to solve many refugee crises now became less clear" (2013, 16). Even after refugees and migrants were legally distinguished, states prioritized people for refugee resettlement when they had particular skills and could easily integrate economically (Zahra 2016; Karatani 2005). Thus, "states continued to blur refugee and migrant identities to meet their own political interests" (Long 2013, 19). In response, the early UNHCR emphasized the ways in which refugees were objects of humanitarian concern, not just people with economic potential (20). It is precisely here that one can see the binary beginning to crystallize. As Vernant put it in his seminal study, *The Refugee in the Post-War World* (1953), commissioned by the UNHCR: "The distinction between ordinary emigrants and refugees which used to seem clear enough is nowadays becoming blurred, or even vanishing altogether" (6). Anxiety about preserving the binary goes back to the earliest articulations of it.

The Refugee Convention laid out a very specific definition of a refugee that linked eligibility for protection to individualized experience. This move was not completely novel. As described above, the entire period from the beginning of the Second World War until 1951 represented a shift toward individualized definitions that focused on the idea of freedom (Hathaway 1984). The 1951 definition was just the most recent iteration. Hewing closely to previous legal definitions, the drafters of the Refugee Convention evidently envisioned a refugee as someone fleeing the recent unrest in Europe, limiting the definition geographically, temporally, and also in scope (Chimni 1998). This definition has become hugely significant in the years since, but at the time, the most prominent feature was continuity with the past. The Refugee Convention definition built directly on the IRO and IRC definitions from previous decades to conclude that a refugee is a person who

[a]s a result of events occurring before 1 January 1951 and owing to well-founded fear of being persecuted for reasons of race, religion, nationality, membership of a particular social group or political opinion, is outside the country of his nationality and is unable or, owing to such fear, is unwilling to avail himself of the protection of that country; or who, not having a nationality and being outside the country of his former habitual residence as a result of such events, is unable or, owing to such fear, is unwilling to return to it. (Article 1, Section A[2])

The biggest difference between the Refugee Convention definition and previous iterations was that in this drafting process, the option of making the definition broader in scope was explicitly considered and dismissed. Some newly independent Global South states were included in the deliberations and drafting process, and "there were extensive discussions about the injustice of having a narrow geographical conception of the right to asylum" (Mayblin 2017, 146). Ultimately, however, concerns about the geographic limitations of the definition were sidelined and ignored. For example, India and Pakistan participated in the multiyear discussions leading up to the drafting of the 1951 Refugee Convention. Initially, they did so enthusiastically because of the massive crisis of displacement involving 14 million people that resulted from the partition between the two countries which had been drawn as part of the decolonization process (Oberoi 2001). These two states showed a remarkable degree of collaboration in their attempts to obtain assistance for the crisis of displacement, especially given the tensions between them at the time. But, in the end, both countries withdrew from the process and did not sign the Convention after they "came to the conclusion that the formalized international refugee regime was largely inimical to their interests" (37).

The interests of the European powers and the United States drove the process almost entirely. First, European powers anticipated the end of empire and independence for colonial holdings, and this perspective affected their approach to the proceedings. The United Kingdom was explicitly worried about any formulation that would extend refugee rights to people in its colonial empire, and that might lead people from current and former colonial holdings in the Global South to more freely immigrate to the UK (Mayblin 2017). Similarly, the United States was opposed to an expansive definition that would create obligations to help displaced people who were not of immediate geopolitical strategic concern (Oberoi 2001, 41). And so the definition was purposefully written not to be global in scope and to apply only to people recently displaced in Europe. As a result, people displaced by the events of the Second World War in Asia, those fleeing the Chinese Revolution, and those displaced by the partition of India and Pakistan were deliberately excluded from protection. Then, after playing such a major role in limiting the scope of UNHCR's work and the definition of a refugee, the United States did not even ratify the Refugee Convention. Instead, the US Congress passed the Refugee Relief Act of 1953, and the Truman administration began to explicitly admit people as refugees with the strategic aim of using them as a Cold War tool, continuing its practice of only recognizing people fleeing communist states (Wolgin 2011; Bon Tempo 2008; Dinnerstein 1986).

Shacknove has pointed out that the drafters of the Refugee Convention assumed that the bond between citizen and state is the basis of society, and focused the definition on people who have had that bond severed (1985, 275). The particular form that severance takes—persecution based on political beliefs, association, forms of expression, and other elements of identity—reveals a deeply liberal worldview at work, one in which political and civil rights are the most sacred. This "exhilic" model in turn reinforces the picture of a refugee as a rarity, a dissident who has been individually targeted, rather than invoking the vast number of people who suffer under oppressive regimes or political instability in more generalized ways (Chimni 1998). Crucially, this framing does not connect the refugee to ideas of universal human rights that exist beyond the state. Instead, it tethers the refugee to the state by making her the antithesis of the citizen and central to the idea of sovereignty, because her powerlessness and lack of rights reveal the ways in which the privileges of citizenship are only possible through exclusion.

The fact that universal human rights were based on the notion of personhood rather than citizenship as the source of rights has sparked a whole literature around the idea of so-called "post-national citizenship" (Soysal 1994; Sassen 2002; Jacobson 1996). Much of this literature is focused on the ways in which noncitizens have invoked international law to make rights claims. According to this logic, the rights of noncitizens are not sourced from the state itself. Rather, the noncitizen draws on notions of universal human rights, the idea that individuals have rights even when they are not members of a state, or when their state has failed to protect them. And yet it is precisely the particularity of the refugee experience, as opposed to the universalized humanity of personhood, that leads the refugee to emerge out of the mid-twentieth century with theoretical rights protection. It is not possible to understand it without the state. While some scholars have argued that it is theoretically possible to read the Refugee Convention in a way that reorients it and makes it compatible with universal human rights, it was explicitly and deliberately not conceived as an instrument of universal human rights (Hathaway 1991; Chetail 2014). Refugee protection was not just another strand in the bundle of universal human rights that were articulated at that time. Rather, it was designed to be a very particular and narrow exception to the rule that powerful sovereign states have the right to tightly control their borders.

Reaffirming Rightlessness

The widespread formal recognition of the right to seek asylum and the right not to be returned to death or danger that the Refugee Convention represents is a major step away from the abject rightlessness of displaced people during Arendt's time. However, the need of asylum seekers to subject themselves to the authority of the state and present their case continues to reaffirm the legitimacy of state power, a power that shows no signs of weakening (Gündoğdu 2015, 111). Walls and other harsh border control measures are proliferating and becoming more effective. The fact that a person's human rights are attached to the question of whether they have accessed the territory of the receiving state serves to "re-consecrate the centrality of territory" (Paz 2016, 8) and incentivizes desirable destination states to become more brutally restrictive. An outward commitment by states to the rights of people seeking refuge provides few answers about what to do about border externalization and "remote control" of asylum seekers, keeping needy people at arm's length, beyond the reach of state responsibility. Some scholars have labeled this trend the "non-entrée regime" to highlight the contrast with the concept of *non-refoulement* (Orchard 2014; Gammeltoft-Hansen and Hathaway 2015). On paper, the protections of international refugee law could save many, many lives. But in practice, as Kaushal and Dauvergne argue, contemporary refugee law "functions to re-inscribe the large-scale political concerns of the day onto individuals . . . the aims of asserting western sovereignty and policing exclusion remain central" (2011, 86). The right to not be forcibly returned to danger only actually exists if states do not actively prevent entry. In practice, this right is violated every day.

Another major element of these politics that scholars do not acknowledge often enough is the highly racialized nature of the regime of deterrence. In particular, as Achiume articulates, "for Third World would-be migrants seeking admission and inclusion in First World nation-states, the project of their exclusion from the latter has reached a fevered, bloody pitch . . . which amount[s] to multilateral projects for the regional containment of Third World persons beyond the First World" (2019, 6–7). The default assumption of the international refugee regime is that people coming from the Global South have no general claim to enter the territories of the Global North because they are outsiders, mere political strangers. This "political stranger exceptionalism" makes no attempt whatsoever to acknowledge the colonial legacies that connect many states to one another, not just historically but in ongoing cultural and economic senses as well (Achiume 2019). As British–Sri Lankan scholar Ambalavaner Sivanandan was famously known for saying in reference to migration from former colonies to the Global North: "We are here because you were there." Instead of highlighting racialized and postcolonial patterns in restrictionism, scholars often take it as a given that popular destination states have the right to keep people out, as long as they do not describe the people as refugees.

When advocates of displaced people talk today about the limitations of the 1951 Refugee Convention definition, and how it is not a perfect document, they are usually referring to its specificity, to the ways in which it is clearly a Cold War relic designed to protect dissidents and defectors. But its perversions extend further. In sum, the contemporary concept of a refugee is deeply linked to the modern colonial state. It is mutually constitutive with and reinforcing of state sovereignty in an ongoing way. State sovereignties were never designed to be equal in this system. It is only relatively recently that the notion of territorial rootedness has come to be understood as a key component of membership in a modern nation-state. As empires crumbled and the global order was reconstituted with the expectation that each person be tied to a territorial state that would be home to a people with a common national identity, the obligation to protect refugees was carved out as the rare exception to the sovereign right of some states to control their borders. The migrant/refugee binary developed to advance the interests of certain states and privilege certain forms of displacement over others.

Knowing this history is central to understanding the international refugee regime as a system that continues to reinforce and reconstitute the sovereignty of powerful and wealthy receiving states, which primarily include European former colonial powers, and those states (like the United States, Canada, and Australia) that were created through European settler colonialism. The legacy of international law's ties to colonialism is that, today, the sovereignty of states in the Global South remains "uniquely vulnerable and dependent" (Anghie 2004, 6). This insight is key to understanding the uneven power dynamics of the international refugee regime that are the subject of the remaining chapters in this book.

3

Academic Study

REGARDLESS OF THE LEGAL CATEGORY or the discursive la-
bel that is eventually assigned to them, border crossers physically embody some of the most pressing questions in the social sciences. They can
symbolize and bring into sharp relief the rampant global inequalities of
wealth, freedom, and safety that make birthright citizenship into a lottery (Shachar 2009). They can represent threats to state sovereignty in a
globalizing world, testing the ability of international law and humanitarian norms to supersede the strategic interests of states (Hollifield 2004;
Dauvergne 2008). They can raise questions about what constitutes legitimate and ethical migration control measures (Carens 2013; Gibney 2004).
They can trigger separation-of-powers struggles over administrative independence and the limits of judicial review, and frequently become the
fulcrum over which larger constitutional questions about the nature of
rights are debated (Hamlin 2014). Because of the diverse range of questions they raise, border crossers also traverse boundaries between academic disciplines and across subfields in ways that are ripe for theoretical
and empirical engagement.

Yet the academic study of border crossers who are conceptualized as
refugees is surprisingly ghettoized, often relegated to nondisciplinary specialist journals, largely invisible in the disciplines that should be most
concerned with the questions they raise. In political science, for example, despite the many obvious linkages between refugee policy and international relations, the topic has been left remarkably understudied (Betts
2009, 15; Betts and Loescher 2010, 3). Castles (2003) has made a similar

point about the lack of attention paid by the field of sociology to forced migration issues, and FitzGerald and Arar (2018) have argued that the insights of refugee studies could do much to enrich the sociological study of migration, which has not fully engaged with that field.

Even the interdisciplinary field known as migration studies has, to a surprising degree, overlooked people who have been categorized as refugees, with standard theories of migration tending to focus heavily on economic push and pull factors, sidelining those whose border crossing is viewed as involuntary and/or politically motivated (Cornelius and Rosenblum 2005; FitzGerald 2014; Massey 1999). In particular, undocumented or "illegal" migration that is cast as economically motivated receives disproportionately high levels of academic (and political) attention. An ambitious recent study attempted to map the topical patterns in the field of migration studies over the past thirty years (Pisarevskaya et al. 2019). The study found that despite an "exponential growth trajectory," the field has experienced a "coming of age" and is fairly stable in terms of topical focus (24). Of the sixty thematic topics the authors found in their survey of the field, one of them was labeled "settlement of asylum seekers and refugees." None of the other fifty-nine had anything to do with refugee status, refugee law, forced migration, displacement, or any other related concept.

This finding of refugees as a niche topic in migration studies is corroborated by a quick look at content in the top migration studies journals. For example, in the 210 issues and thousands of articles it published between 1964 and 2018, *International Migration Review (IMR)* published only 163 articles with the word "refugee" in the abstract. Half of those articles were published during the 1980s, as the field of refugee studies was being founded and *IMR* devoted several special issues to the launching of that field. In the twenty-first century, *IMR* has published only one or two articles about people described as refugees each year. In contrast, *IMR* has published 384 articles with the words "economy" or "economic" in the abstract. Similarly, in the 265 issues it has published since 1971, the *Journal of Ethnic and Migration Studies* has published only 84 articles with the word "refugee" in the title. These patterns are likely due in large part to self-selection by authors, especially as specialist refugee studies journals became more established, as opposed to a bias on the part of migration studies journal editors. And there is no way of knowing exactly what a more "balanced" proportion of articles about people categorized as refugees would look like. Of course, scholars who eschew the binary and talk about border crossers in general terms would not show up in this simple glance at the data. Nevertheless, when this data is viewed as just one point of reference in the larger context of the academic institutional landscape of journals, professional associations, and research centers, it helps to illustrate the point that the empirical study of border crossing has been surprisingly bifurcated into the study of two phenomena that are assumed to be distinct.

While there is some evidence that these barriers are gradually eroding, resistance to such changes remains. Some scholars have critiqued the idea that refugees and migrants are discrete categories of people (Richmond 1988; Zetter 1991, 2007; Crawley and Skelparis 2018). Some have even suggested that the field of refugee studies has actually functioned as a tool of the interests of Western states (Chimni 1998, 2009; Kukathas 2016). However, others have explicitly and vigorously defended the insulation of refugee studies from research on other forms of border crossing, suggesting that to do otherwise would put vulnerable refugees in jeopardy (Hathaway 2007a, b).

Since the early 1980s, the field of refugee studies has developed as a discrete area of study, with its own journals, research centers, conferences, and associations. This refugee-specific intellectual space was deliberately created for the dual purposes of better understanding the experiences of people who have been identified as refugees and better protecting such people. Since its creation, the field of refugee studies has tended to be dominated by legal positivism, an approach that assumes the essential nature, and thus the political neutrality, of the refugee category. Especially in the early years of the field, scholarly work frequently began by providing the definition of a refugee from international law, with the assumption that this information answered the question of who would be included in the topic of study. Studies that use this approach are highly positivist, taking legal definitions at face value and then focusing on how to best protect those who have been so categorized, or how to get people who "are refugees" to be recognized as such by receiving states.

In order to better understand the migrant/refugee binary in the academic study of border crossing, this chapter asks first, how did the study of border crossing become so bifurcated, and in particular, how did the study of refugees become so isolated from other academic inquiry about border crossing? Second, the chapter explores the durability of this binary approach, despite repeated concerns raised by a variety of scholars about the constructed and bureaucratic nature of the categories that drive the division. Scholars can play a useful role in questioning and complicating categorical divides. However, the field of refugee studies has often existed uncomfortably with instances of boundary crossing and categorical confusion, which can partially be explained by the very close relationship between the refugee studies scholarly community and the United Nations High Commissioner for Refugees (UNHCR). The chapter outlines some of the consequences of a binary approach for the study of border crossing, suggesting that the findings of scholars concerned with people who have been, or who advocates believe should be, classified as refugees are often left out of larger academic discussions of migration, and opportunities for insightful connections are missed. In particular, while more attention has been paid to asylum seeking in recent years, it remains a blind spot that can "fall between stools," understudied by both self-identified refugee and migration scholars alike.

The Birth of Refugee Studies

The overlapping relationships between refugee policy-makers, advocates, and scholars predate the birth of the field of refugee studies, and seem to have been built into its foundations. While the separate field was not founded until the early 1980s, beginning in the 1920s, scholars increasingly devoted attention to refugees as a unique form of border crosser, even if there was no consensus on the definition of a refugee, or on what precisely made them distinct (Skran and Daughtry 2007). In the decades leading up to and immediately following the Second World War, the concept of a refugee was codified in international law and the policies of receiving states as a distinct category of migrant. Academic study picked up on the increasing salience of this divide, and followed suit.

The interwar period also coincided with the rise of the intellectual position that has come to be known as methodological nationalism. This lens helped to reify the importance of the state as the unit of analysis in social scientific work. As national identity was clarified and movement was restricted, the social sciences began to inquire into migration as a process (Wimmer and Glick Schiller 2003, 591). Within this framework, the homogeneity of the nation was assumed, and integration and assimilation of immigrant outsiders was the process under study. "People were envisioned as each having only one nation-state, and belonging to humanity was thought to require a national identity. The social sciences neither investigated nor problematized this assumption" during the early to mid-twentieth century (592–93). Instead, the early literature on refugees overwhelmingly took the form of case studies of specific occurrences of displacement, and did not yet have a coherent methodology or theory that conceptualized the particularity of refugee movement. Scholars began to adopt the definitions of a refugee that were becoming more crystallized in international law, and proceeded from there.

When Peterson assessed the growing literature on migration in a 1958 issue of the *American Sociological Review*, he noted this tendency toward legal positivism. He lamented that the terms used by scholars uncritically followed bureaucratic or legal categories, and were not undergirded by any theory of what actually causes people to migrate (1958, 264). Despite this call for theorizing based on observation, the reliance on legal definitions dominated scholarly work on displacement throughout the decades leading up to the birth of refugee studies. Even when scholars critiqued the lack of theoretical heft in the field, they fell back on positivist legal distinctions, revealing their assumption that there is something essentially unique about refugees. For example, Kunz's assessment of the literature in 1973 found that most studies to date consisted of descriptive accounts of particular events. He concluded that there was a real "need to conceptualize refugee phenomena" because the refugee "is a distinct social type," which he then defined using the definition from Article 1 of the 1951 Refugee Convention (127, 130).

In their 2007 survey of academic research on refugees from the 1920s through the 1970s, Skran and Daughtry noted another major trend in the literature. They found that academic studies were disproportionately focused on refugees who were a "foreign policy priority for a Great Power and aided by an international organization" (2007, 19). This political angle was true even as early as Sir John Hope Simpson's 1938 survey of the various major refugee situations that he believed were likely to affect Europe. The survey was conducted in the interests of providing information to the representatives at the Intergovernmental Committee that was slated to meet at Evian. So, the research was explicitly designed and conducted to provide information for policy-makers in the West.

These two trends of legal positivism and prioritizing policy relevance for the Global North coalesced further, leading to the rapid creation of "refugee studies" in the 1980s. The birth of the field took the form of several public calls to isolate and contain the study of refugees, which led to the establishment of centers at Oxford and York universities, and the founding of several specialty journals. The larger and preexisting field of migration studies seemed to support the notion that refugees should be studied separately. For example, in 1981, *International Migration Review*, which had been published by the Center for Migration Studies in New York since 1966, published a special double issue called "Refugees Today." In the forward, the editors lamented that the "lack of scholarly attention" to refugees meant that each new crisis was treated ad hoc (Stein and Tomasi 1981, 6). Thus, in devoting this special double issue to the topic, "the ultimate objective must be the development of a new body of knowledge, the cataloging and evaluation of existing programs, and perhaps, most importantly, the establishment of an institutional memory for policymakers and operational personnel" (7). The policy and advocacy orientation of this new field of refugee studies is explicit in this call.

This kind of boundary-drawing was based on the belief that there was a distinct "refugee experience" that was common across episodes of forced migration, and conceptually distinct from the voluntary decision to migrate (Stein 1981). Stein explained:

It is common to think of the immigrant as pulled to his new land—attracted by opportunity and a new life. The refugee is not pulled out; he is pushed out. Given the choice, he would stay. Most refugees are not poor people. They have not failed within their homeland; they are successful, prominent, well-integrated, educated individuals who fell because of fear of persecution. (322)

While it is not at all clear that Stein was basing this assessment on any systematic observations of people whom he understood to be either refugees or migrants, the characteristics that he associated with both groups in the quote above reveal that the refugee category was explicitly viewed in the minds of some as a way for states to admit desirable people with social and economic capital. The specter of the Cold War also hangs in the background of these discussions, revealing that in many people's minds, a refugee was someone fleeing communism, a dissident in exile whom the West would be advantaged to admit.

The call for more attention to the unique yet universal refugee experience was also explicitly driven by the desire to encourage study of a vulnerable group, to generate empirical accounts of the desperate situations faced by refugees, and to better advocate for their protection. Also in 1981, and also in this vein, *Refugee Abstracts* began as an official publication of UNHCR. The aim was to be a central clearinghouse of information about crises of displacement as they unfolded. It changed its name to *Refugee Survey Quarterly* in 1994, but its focus remained on the publication of information about refugee situations, "in order to promote the protection of refugees" by providing information to those who make decisions affecting refugees (Franco 1994, 2).

The field of refugee studies continued to take shape in 1982, when Barbara Harrell-Bond founded the Refugees Studies Programme at Oxford University. Harrell-Bond was frustrated by the lack of research on how to improve humanitarian service provision for refugees. According to the website of what is now called the Refugee Studies Centre (RSC), "from the beginning, the RSC aspired to bridge the divide between scholarship, policy and practice." The explicit mission was to "build knowledge and understanding of the causes and effects of forced migration in order to help improve the lives of some of the world's most vulnerable people."[1] The program convened a group of sixty researchers and practitioners from around the world for a conference in 1990, which led to the formation of the International Research and Advisory Panel on Refugees and Other Displaced Persons (IRAP), a body that was tasked with advising the program at Oxford and the newly formed *Journal of Refugee Studies* (Robinson 1990). This group eventually decoupled itself from Oxford and became its own separate entity, the International Association for the Study of Forced Migration (IASFM), which continues to meet annually. In 1988 the Centre for Refugee Studies (CRS) was established at York University in Toronto, building off of previous efforts to help facilitate the resettlement of people from Indochina to Canada. Like its counterpart at Oxford, the CRS was founded with the explicit mission of establishing an interdisciplinary network of scholars dedicated to improving the lives of refugees.

While the late 1980s was a key period for establishing an international community of refugee scholars and advocates, of the many forms this institutionalization took, the founding of the *Journal of Refugee Studies* (*JRS*) at Oxford University in 1988 was perhaps the most significant development. In his introduction to the first issue, editor Roger Zetter pointed out that, to date, the academic study of refugees had been constrained by the needs and objectives of policy-makers and service providers, which "often resulted in the blurring of boundaries between consultancy and research" (1988, 3). He further noted that the close relationship with UNHCR and other agencies had compromised researchers' independence and limited their ability to bring a critical lens to the study of refugee service provision. He then articulated that *JRS* would be open to work that critically examined the concept and definition of a refugee, and would not always assume that international legal definitions are definitive.

This critical lens represented a fairly novel attempt to push refugee studies to examine its core assumptions. It was echoed that same year in an article by Anthony Richmond, a sociologist, who boldly argued that "the majority of population movements are a complex response to the reality of a global society in which ethno-religious, social, economic, and political determinants are inextricably bound together" (1988, 20). As a result, he concluded:

The distinction between 'free' and 'forced' or 'voluntary' and 'involuntary' is a misleading one. All human behavior is constrained . . . Many of the decisions made by both 'economic' and 'political' migrants are a response to diffuse anxiety generated by a failure of the social system to provide for the fundamental needs of the individual, biological, economic, and social. (17)

While Zetter (1991) continued to argue in his role as *JRS* editor that the bureaucratic process of labeling some people as refugees is not based on organic identity, he also insisted that it was important for the journal to explicitly "separate and exclude from the agenda of JRS patterns of migration solely or largely generated by voluntary and self-determined decisions" (1988, 5). And, despite some critical voices influenced by Marxism and cultural anthropology, the dominant perspective in the field of refugee studies, especially in the early days, was almost ideologically committed to a binary approach.

This essentialist view is exemplified by works such as Zolberg et al.'s highly acclaimed *Escape from Violence* (1989), which purports to be the first "comprehensive, theoretically grounded explanation of refugee flows" (v). The assumption that refugee movement needs to be conceptualized distinctly from other types of migration is built into the book. However, in the first few pages, this assumption bumps into the difficulty of trying to explain the causes of group behavior when the group is defined by presumed causes. The authors claim: "Within a shrinking world subject to violent upheavals affecting large and very poor populations and resulting in the appearance of all kinds of people on everyone's doorstep in search of assistance, it becomes vital to distinguish refugees from international migrants" (30). What is unclear in this statement is, vital for whom, and why? It is left unstated who is threatened by the idea that it may be difficult to distinguish among large numbers of very needy people in order to establish which ones are worthy of assistance and protection.

By the mid-1990s, refugee studies had established itself as a field to the extent that several disciplines devoted annual review articles to survey the literature. Writing in the *Annual Review of Sociology* in 1993, Hein noted an internal tension in the world of refugee studies, naming the two perspectives "realist" and "nominalist." To realists, refugees are distinct in their motivations for migration, and their identities are defined by the experience of exile. Hein seemed critical of this dominant view, encouraging a nominalist approach that acknowledges the concept of a refugee to be a social and political construction. Refugees are distinct from other migrants, he argued, only insofar as states construct different integration pathways for people with different bureaucratic labels. Similarly, Malkki's 1995 critical review of the anthropology literature on refugees lamented the "essentialist" way in which scholars treat refugees, the "tendency . . . to proceed as if refugees all shared a common condition or nature" (512). Rather, she argued that there is no one kind or type of refugee experience because it is nothing more than a legal category or label that which covers a wide range of people. She also made the important critique that the field of refugee studies was built on a "sedentarist" assumption of human life—that people are "naturally" rooted in one place and that being uprooted is a devastating loss (508). Such an assumption again reveals the deep connection between the refugee concept and the premise of the Westphalian system—that states are sovereign, bounded entities with the power and the right to exclude.

Contemporary Scholarship and the Advocacy Trap

Despite varied critiques from the surrounding disciplines, the self-identified field of refugee studies remains remarkably durable in its resistance to change. In a 2001 article assessing the field fifty years after the 1951 Refugee Convention, and twenty years since the birth of refugee studies, Black made several of the exact same criticisms that were levied by others in the 1980s. He outlined the negative consequences of a focus on policy-making, and the close working relationships between scholars and the big service provision agencies and NGOs. He argued that "the uncritical use of the term in scholarly literature can contribute to the perception of the naturalness of the category of refugees and of differential policies towards those who do and those who do not qualify for the label" (2001, 63). Black even went so far as to conclude that because of its isolation, refugee studies had become "an intellectual cul-de-sac" that was not participating in the "development of social science" (66). While some in the field of refugee studies have continued to point out that research driven by the policy concerns of UNHCR misses many aspects of the worldwide phenomenon of displacement (Bakewell 2008), and that siphoning off the scholarly examination of refugees from the larger field of migration studies has led to confusion about whether refugee status is a sociological category or a purely bureaucratic label (Scalettaris 2007, 40), these tendencies continue to dominate the field. Most recently, Crawley and Skelparis (2018) argued that "categorical fetishism" is still a major limitation in the academic study of border crossing. Because the existence of refugee studies as a distinct area of study is in some ways reliant on a positivist/essentialist/realist approach to the concept of a refugee, that tradition continues to dominate, despite the long-standing pattern of individual scholars raising conceptual concerns.

In fact, over time, resistance to these critiques has become more overt and explicit, revealing a deep commitment to the project of maintaining the binary among many core members of the field of refugee studies. Some very influential scholars have spoken out explicitly against the breaking down of conceptual barriers between refugee and migrant because they insist that the distinction serves a beneficial purpose. For example, in *Refuge: Rethinking Refugee Policy in a Changing World* (2017), Betts and Collier repeatedly insist that refugees are not migrants but rather are a categorically distinct group (1, 30, 117, 199). They state that we "do not need" political philosophers to show us that we have a particular moral obligation to refugees as opposed to migrants, because it is "intellectually lazy" to blur the distinction between the two groups (101). Similarly, Price has cautioned scholars not "to miss the special horror of violence organized and exploited for political ends" that sets refugees apart from other migrants (2019, 172). Using logic that reveals the liberal hierarchy of rights that lies at the heart of the migrant/refugee binary, Price argues that the ability to grant an individual refugee status is an important tool that states can use to send a message of condemnation to the refugee's country of origin, showcasing the origin state's failure to protect the political and civil rights of their own citizens. In *The Ethics and Politics of Asylum*, Gibney argues that it is morally legitimate for states to distinguish and prioritize the claims of refugees over economic migrants because refugees are the most vulnerable: "their very lives might be on the line" (2014, 12).

One of the most vocal and long-standing defenders of the migrant/refugee binary has been legal scholar James Hathaway, who has argued repeatedly that "failure to take account of the specificity of the refugee's circumstances" will lead to the production of scholarship that is less capable of challenging the waning global commitment to protecting refugees (2007a, 349). Because he believes that governments are trying to "render the refugee as much a migrant as possible" (355), he argues that it is the refugee scholar's job to resist that slippage. He explicitly warns that academics "have an ethical duty" not to "play into the hands of those who would subordinate the legal commitment to refugee autonomy to pursuit of broader migratory management goals" (2007b, 388). Adelman and McGrath have pushed back on Hathaway, arguing that the Convention definition is a product of the Cold War, designed to serve the interests of the West rather than representing an "eternal and essential concept" (2007, 377). But in a response to this critique, Hathaway doubled down on his insistence of the essential nature of refugee-ness, arguing that "refugee rights accrue to persons who *are in fact refugees* even when refugees cross borders without authorization, and even when their protection needs are not formally evaluated" (Hathaway 2007b, 387, emphasis added). In other words, a person can be a refugee even if they are never legally recognized as such. It is this logic that leads some scholar advocates to use the phrase "de facto refugees" to describe people who are believed to deserve refugee protection even if they are not recognized formally as refugees (Medrano 2017). But this label is merely a rhetorical tool. It does not confer any protection, since only a *de jure*, official protective status can do that.

Scholars who are dedicated to preserving the binary and the distinct community of refugee studies have the noble goal of protecting vulnerable people. Especially for scholars who are also lawyers, the definition of a refugee is not only a tool that states can use but also a tool that legal advocates can use to argue for protections that will, if granted, potentially save lives. From this perspective, it does not matter if the emperor's clothes are "real," so long as they can be used to circumvent the otherwise closed borders of Global North states, and secure protection for at least some needy people. It is for this reason that scholar-advocates based at UNHCR have consistently insisted that "refugees are not migrants" (Feller 2005). Because of the close relationship between the refugee studies scholarly community and UNHCR, the refugee studies literature has generally supported this claim. And through this approach, refugee studies has been remarkably successful at achieving policy relevance in the international advocacy community, working closely with UNHCR, and linking scholarship to advocacy. For example, the *Oxford Handbook of Refugee and Forced Migration Studies*, published to commemorate the thirtieth anniversary of Oxford's RSC, has a preface by then–High Commissioner for Refugees Antonio Guterres. In it, he wrote that he hopes "the Handbook will be a valuable tool for practitioners in the field" (Fiddian-Qasmiyeh et al. 2014, vii).

Because of this deep connection to the international refugee protection regime, some scholars have critiqued the field of refugee studies for being too focused on helping refugees, and not detached enough to be academically rigorous (Scalettaris 2007; Bakewell 2008). However, these same connections have also led some to levy the opposite critique—that rather than truly being on the side of displaced people, the field has served the interests of the Global North (Chimni 1998). In particular, Chimni has critiqued refugee studies for focusing on the impacts of displacement on the Global North, and not including the voices and perspectives of scholars from the Global South (2009, 18). He has argued that the international refugee protection regime was created as part of the Cold War, and is now evolving toward a broader forced migration frame in order to adapt to the new post–Cold War migration management concerns of Global North states. As I mentioned in the opening chapter, this perspective and ones similar to it have come to be known as "critical refugee studies" as opposed to the more mainstream field of refugee studies (Espiritu 2014).

Chimni's critique has much in common with, but is the inverse of, Hathaway's concern about how refugee studies has expanded over the years to call itself forced migration studies. The new moniker reflects the notion that not all involuntary migrants fit neatly within the international legal definition of a refugee laid out in the Refugee Convention. The umbrella term of forced migration is meant to include internally displaced people who have not crossed an international border, as well as those who have been displaced by "nonpolitical" causes such as climate change. Yet Chimni views this new, broader, interdisciplinary field of forced migration studies as part of a project of neocolonial humanitarianism (2009, 20). With this shift, he argues, the focus of refugee studies has reoriented from an East/West preoccupation during the Cold War to an obsession with movement from South to North (23). Hathaway has also viewed the merger with "forced migration studies" as the first step toward a terrible outcome: total merger with the study of migration more generally. But further evidence of the persistence of the binary in academia can be seen in the fact that, even as refugee studies has expanded to call itself forced migration studies, the expansion has not continued out to its logical conclusion to integrate with migration studies more generally, a merger that it seems Chimni would embrace (12).

Instead, the shift from refugee studies to the broader frame of forced migration studies still bifurcates an imagined spectrum of migration motivations into two categories—forced (deserving) and voluntary (undeserving). For example, Betts (2010, 2013) has argued that because current categories are no longer adequate, instead of narrowly focusing on refugees, scholars should talk about the needs of "survival migrants," those who cross borders in order to survive. While this argument seems at first glance to be breaking down the binary, it soon becomes clear that Betts is still engaged in binary thinking. He depicts his expanded concept of survival migrants in terms of concentric circles instead of a spectrum. In this visual, survival migrants are a subset of all migrants that encompasses, but is bigger than, refugees. So while he believes that the refugee/migrant binary is inadequate, he still describes "dividing lines" and calls survival migrants "analytically distinct" from other migrants, presumably because their motivation for migrating is viewed as involuntary (2013, 25). Here we still see the lingering belief that, while we might need to make the refugee side more inclusive, the majority of border crossers will remain on the voluntary side of the divide.

The Binary in Political Theory

While the bulk of this chapter has focused on the empirical study of border crossing, the uniqueness of refugees has also been widely perpetuated by normative political theorists who write about the ethics of border control and rights of border crossers. Binary logic has led many prominent scholars in this tradition to justify the legitimacy of border control by adding the caveat that refugees must be allowed access. For example, Walzer, in his elaborate defense of the right of states to define membership and refuse access to those they do not wish to include, contends that "the cruelty of this dilemma is mitigated to some degree by the principle of asylum," suggesting that as long as there is a provision for people to claim refugee status, exclusionary laws are just (1983, 50). Similarly, Benhabib insists that a careful distinction between "the moral claims of migrants on the one hand and those of refugees and asylum seekers on the other" is essential for establishing what a just migration policy would be for a liberal state (2004, 1773). Even in Carens's famous "Case for Open Borders," he acknowledges that totally open borders are a politically unrealistic proposition, limited at least for now to the world of ideal theory. He then explains that in a nonideal world, "priority should be given to those seeking to immigrate because they have been denied basic liberties over those seeking to immigrate simply for economic opportunities" (1987, 260–61). In this way, even someone who is dedicated to the principle of open borders falls back on a binary logic as soon as the border is reintroduced.

Several more recent books by prominent scholars on the ethics of immigration have continued this trend. They defend the basic right of states to control their borders, and then bracket the question of refugees as an exception to that rule. As these recent examples illustrate, normative political theory has frequently adopted the binary in ways that make sustaining the refugee exception seem more straightforward than it is in practice, and by extension naturalizes the premise of border control. For example, in Carens's 2013 book on the ethics of immigration, he dedicates a separate chapter to refugees, arguing that states have a particular obligation to help people who they have had a causal role in displacing and to those who are in urgent need. He also suggests that the normative presuppositions of the state system should be taken into account when receiving states are making admissions decisions. In other words, because the world is organized into states, when states fail their people, other states must help in order to maintain the system (196). These are specific and defensible criteria for prioritizing some border crossers over others. However, when Carens suggests later in the chapter that states take a "flexible and expansive reading of the Convention's requirements," he seems to assume that the Convention definition matches well with the protection priorities that he outlined earlier (200). Further, while he critiques "techniques of exclusion" for asylum seekers, he fails to acknowledge that it is often quite difficult to separate these techniques from ordinary border control measures, which he has defended elsewhere in the book as a practical necessity (209). By isolating the topic of refugees in a separate discussion, these difficult realities are not explored as fully as they could be if the topic of border control was addressed in a more holistic way.

Miller's book about the ethics of immigration also has a stand-alone chapter on refugees, which begins by stating that the "familiar distinction between refugees and economic migrants" is based on whether a person's "human rights" motivate their decision to migrate (2016, 77). This is an interesting framing, since it goes beyond the typical prioritization of civil and political rights outlined in the Convention definition. Indeed, later Miller reveals that he does not think the Convention definition is broad enough, and that he prefers to think of refugees in more general terms than the way they are defined in international law (83). Nevertheless, he argues that reluctance on the part of states to admitting refugees stems from a concern that some of them are "bogus"—that in fact they are economic migrants posing as refugees (77). Thus, he concludes that "to combat such skepticism, a clear definition is essential" (78). Miller seems to want the distinction between refugees and migrants to be maintained, so that the border control measures he describes throughout the book can be defended without harming those in need. And yet, he wants to expand the category of refugee beyond the Convention definition to include some, but not all, of the other vulnerable border crossers in the world. He does not provide any specific suggestions to indicate how this line is to be maintained in practice.

Perhaps the most detailed recent exploration of this topic is Song's *Immigration and Democracy* (2019), which sets out the goal of creating a cohesive political theory of what a just immigration policy would look like, based on her articulation of a right to collective self-determination. Like the other books in this vein, Song also treats refugees in a separate, stand-alone chapter, "Refugees and Other Necessitous Migrants." This framing suggests a view that casts refugees as a subcategory of migrant. But as she works through the theory of what is owed to refugees by receiving states, Song concludes that refugees are unique in many key respects. She argues that "what is normatively significant about refugees is not simply that their basic needs are not being met. Rather it is that their basic needs can only be met by allowing them to enter a safe country . . . Refugees are defined by their need for membership itself" (119). For Song, refugees are unique because they cannot be assisted and protected at home, unlike most other people in need of assistance. While she acknowledges that "there is reasonable disagreement about where to draw the line . . . doing away with the distinction altogether would leave us without any way to prioritize truly necessitous migrants" (112). As in the other books, Song does not leave the reader with much insight into how people in moments of dangerous transit should be treated when the answer to whether they are "necessitous" may be a point of some disagreement between the border crosser and the receiving state. The unspoken assumption is that necessity is established in the eye of the receiver, not the border crosser.

While the end result of Song's analysis (that refugees are more deserving of protection than other migrants, who can more justifiably be excluded) is the same as many other works of political theory on this topic, she spends more time explaining precisely why she thinks refugees are uniquely worthy from a normative theoretical standpoint, rather than assuming, as many theorists seem to do, that the reasons are obvious. Further, like Carens but unlike many other normative political theorists, Song also spends a few pages arguing that wealthy receiving states should prioritize taking in people whose displacement was caused by their foreign policies, such as people coming to the United States from Southeast Asia after the Vietnam War. This point about obligation and causality gets closer to one of the key points I am making in this book, which is that the whole conversation about obligation needs to be reoriented to include both colonialism and continuing neocolonial patterns of exploitation and domination. But because so many works of normative political theory rely on the unspoken assumptions that refugees are distinguishable, needy, and relatively rare, they bracket conversations about refugees into separate discussions. This separation marks people classified as refugees with a metaphorical asterisk, suggesting that they are a minor exception to the overarching rule that borders are justifiable.

My reading of this body of work is that the difficulties that arise when applying theories about just immigration policy to "the refugee" can be used to diagnose larger, deeper problems with the theory. If refugees are the exception, but the devil is in the details of how, where, and when to identify them, the whole project of morally justifying border control comes under strain. Ultimately, the embeddedness of binary logic in normative theories of border control leaves this reader highly skeptical of the notion that there is such a thing as a just border control policy in a world with rampant inequalities of wealth and power.

Academic Consequences of Binary Thinking

As I see it, there are three major consequences of the persistence of binary thinking in the academic study of border crossing. First, binary thinking perpetuates the isolation of refugee studies from the major academic disciplines conducting research on migration (political science, sociology, anthropology, etc.). Aside from the conceptual problems inherent in maintaining a separate field of refugee studies, the first direct result of the field's isolation from the rest of migration studies is that generalist migration scholars tend to be more thoroughly integrated into their academic disciplines. Thus, "voluntary" and economically motivated migration is viewed as the general rule (studied by generalists) and other motivations are cast as exceptional. Many detailed and respected scholarly discussions of what causes migration focus exclusively on economic factors, including Massey's detailed chapter for *The Handbook of International Migration* (1999) surveying the literature on the causes of international migration. People migrating for reasons of war, violence, persecution, or who are perceived to be involuntarily leaving their home state are not mentioned at all. This lack of connection to the world of forced migration results in real intellectual losses for the fields in question. FitzGerald and Arar (2108) have articulated some of those losses for the field of sociology in particular.

The separation of refugee studies as its own particular field of study has had some real advantages. It has facilitated advocacy, enabled the development of expertise and specialization, and made visible to many the lives and experiences of extremely vulnerable people in desperate circumstances. I must be clear that I am not critiquing its existence, or advocating that it be dismantled as a field. Rather, I am suggesting that at this stage in its development, a higher level of engagement, communication, and collaboration with the traditional social science disciplines and the field of migration studies could only expand scholarly understandings of border crossing, its causes, and its consequences.

Within work that self-identifies as refugee studies, much of the focus is still on individual case studies and rich description of one particular group or host country, or exploration of specific questions in international refugee law. Often, it is highly normatively driven, taking as a given that states should be more generous to refugees and other forced migrants. This work is not always linked to larger theoretical developments from political science and sociology about how law, political institutions, or immigration policy works. Scholars within law schools who focus specifically on refugee law also tend to shy away from comparisons, preferring to be experts either in the laws and jurisprudence of the country in which they practice or in the international legal guidance emanating from UNHCR.

The second major scholarly implication of binary thinking is that, because it is based on the legal categories adopted by the so-called receiving states of the West/North, this approach makes scholarship vulnerable to focusing on the priorities and perspectives of these states. As both Adamson and Tsourapas (2019) and Natter (2018) have articulated in some detail, the field of migration studies has been predominantly focused on the "Western liberal democracies" of the Global North. For Adamson and Tsourapas, the Global North bias in the migration studies literature, which has focused on the policies and preferences of liberal democracies in the study of border crossing, has left the study of the Global South to the refugee studies literature. They argue that this "bifurcation" has led to a lack of understanding about how Global South states manage migration (2019, 3).

While these authors do not go this far, I would add (with Chimni) that the academic insistence on the migrant/refugee binary leads a significant amount of scholarship to ultimately serve the agendas of those who wish to preserve and protect borders that prevent people from the Global South coming to the Global North. Even if this bias is unconscious and inadvertent, a binary perspective inevitably and implicitly leads scholars to conceptualize people's motivations for border crossing as either forced or voluntary. This tendency seems remarkably resistant to change, despite the increasing evidence that the realities of border crossing are extremely complex. As I discussed in chapter 1 (see, for example, Crawley and Skelparis 2018; Van Hear 2014), so-called "mixed flows" of border crossers are not just people with differing but pure motivations migrating together in the same boat—a genuine refugee sitting next to a completely economically driven migrant. Rather, individual border crossers often embody mixed motivations that combine to inspire migration. Some factors may have more salience in some moments of the journey than others, so that the motivations of an individual border crosser are multiple and fluctuating. A binary perspective might acknowledge this fact occasionally, but on balance it views mixed motivations as the exception rather than the rule.

Because binary logic also assumes that refugees are rare, by default it must assume that the vast majority of border crossers are primarily motivated by something else—a better life as opposed to bare life. If that assumption undergirds our scholarly inquiry into state border control practices, it becomes all too easy to take at face value the idea that what states are engaged in is the task of sorting the wheat from the chaff, of finding the few genuine refugees among the many whose needs are less desperate and to whom our obligations are slim. This logic can blind us to the ways in which states can make refugees appear to be rare by according refugee status very deliberately to only a select few. This logic may also (ironically) harm those who are assigned to the category of refugee. Long (2013) has argued that the insistence by advocates and scholars on keeping refugees separate from migrants has perpetuated the idea that refugees are objects of charity and obligation rather than economic actors. This framing has excluded people with refugee status from accessing integration pathways that could help them attain economic stability after they migrate. It has also obscured the ways in which refugees can contribute to host societies through their skills, abilities, and social capital.

A third consequence of binary thinking in academia is that some topics of study tend to elude notice because they do not seem to neatly fit into one side of the binary or the other, and it is not clear which frameworks to use. For example, Gibney's (2013) exploration of why deportation has been largely ignored by forced migration scholars is a perfect example of the blind spots created by the migrant/refugee binary. He argues that because deportation is unquestioningly deemed a legitimate use of force by so many, people who are deported are not generally considered to be forced migrants and thus not studied by forced migration scholars. Another group of people who are displaced but do not always cross international borders are those whose movement is caused to some degree by climate change. Lister (2014) has observed that until very recently, there has been surprisingly little work within the forced migration and refugee studies field on this kind of displacement. McAdam (2012) has proposed some important conceptualizations about how climate displacement can be dealt with using a combination of international refugee law and international human rights instruments, but in general, because climate is not one of the reasons that can make someone eligible for refugee protection, people displaced by climate change have been given short shrift by refugee and forced migration scholars. Nevertheless, climate change is already having wide-reaching migration consequences in many parts of the world, including within North Africa, sometimes inducing people from both North and sub-Saharan Africa to migrate on to Europe (White 2011).

Forced migration scholars may also not be focused on analyzing developments such as the 2013 discovery of the bodies of ninety-two Niger citizens, mostly children, in the Algerian desert. Nevertheless, the response of John Ging, director of the UN Office for the Co-ordination of Humanitarian Affairs, is instructive. He told the BBC at the time: "They are basically economic migrants. They are in search of work. They are so impoverished that they have to make these hazardous journeys" (Fessy 2013). At the very least, the language around forced and voluntary migration is confused in this statement. There also seems to be a veiled suggestion that the deaths of those cast as economic migrants are less tragic than the deaths of refugees. Scholars who take the two categories as fixed and given will not probe and dissect this type of public discourse. But it is exactly these types of scenarios, where the categories of migrant and refugee are stretched, challenged, or used for political ends, that, while grimly tragic, could illuminate the investments of various political actors in maintaining a binary in order to justify harsh border control measures.

Further, the study of asylum seekers, who are seeking refugee status but vulnerable to categorization as unauthorized voluntary migrants, has historically been under- or inadequately studied in a binary world. Because they are by definition without a long-term legal categorization, asylum seekers are most likely to fall between the stools of forced and voluntary migration studies. They are often portrayed in political discourse and the media as illegal immigrants, particularly in the US context, where the illegal immigration debate is focused almost exclusively on undocumented migrants, who are assumed to be voluntary (and frequently assumed to be Mexican) and tend to be overshadowed (Hamlin 2012b).

Thus, leading histories of American migration policy (Tichenor 2002) and American refugee policy (Bon Tempo 2008) have both devoted little to no discussion to the history of policies aimed specifically at deterring and managing asylum seekers. Similarly, political theorists who write about the ethics of migration have surprisingly little to say about asylum seekers, usually lumping them in with refugees as people who are deserving of protection but without providing any guidance as to how they will be identified as potential refugees instead of being caught up in deterrence policies designed to keep economic migrants out.

The experience of Mexican nationals who seek asylum in the United States forms another example of an understudied but theoretically rich topic. Many of those asylum claims grow out of a fear of drug cartel violence, and the inability of the Mexican government to provide adequate protection. These types of claims fall into a legal gray area; it is much more difficult to gain asylum status under international law when the persecution is not government sponsored and the violence is generalized rather than individually targeted. Nevertheless, under the right circumstances and with the right lawyer, it is possible. However, Mexico has a massive border with the United States, and high levels of undocumented migration. Thus, the incentive to discourage Mexican asylum seekers is very high. Leaders in the US Congress have repeatedly called for investigations of the increasing numbers of Mexican asylum seekers, claiming that they are illegal immigrants (Planas 2013). "Generalist" migration scholars who do not have an expert understanding of the asylum system and standard interpretations of the refugee definition may be underprepared to analyze such developments in American migration control politics. Similarly, forced migration scholars who are not well versed in the American history of migration control and the extremely complicated US/Mexico relationship will also miss important nuances. In all of these examples, the bifurcation of academic study of border crossing serves to silo the insights and findings of scholars from each other.

A huge exception to this trend was Mountz's *Seeking Asylum* (2010), which does a masterful job of examining asylum seekers and state measures to deter them without wading into a debate about whether they are migrants or refugees. Perhaps Mountz's disciplinary background as a geographer helped make this approach possible, but it stood as the exception to the rule for many years. Since I began writing this book, several more books have come out that begin to fill in the hole around the study of asylum seekers as an inherently ambiguous category that I intended to highlight here. For example, Ghezelbash's *Refuge Lost* (2018) and Fitz-Gerald's *Refuge beyond Reach* (2019) both depict the ways in which states actively discourage asylum seekers from accessing their territories. Brigden's *The Migrant Passage* (2018) tracks the experiences of Central Americans trying to access the United States, and Kahn's *Islands of Sovereignty* (2019) chronicles the long-standing refusal of the US to recognize Haitians as legitimate asylum seekers. These works are necessary contributions to the literature on border crossing, and I am hopeful that they indicate a new trend in which migration and refugee policy are not treated separately in the literature. A shift is only possible if generalist migration scholars read the Ghezelbash and FitzGerald books and people who locate themselves in the field of refugee studies read Brigden's and Kahn's.

Embracing Ambiguity

In the process of carving out a protected space for the study of refugees, the fields of refugee studies and migration studies have each worked to reify the migrant/refugee binary, reducing the potential of the academic study of border control. The fact that the study of border crossing has been bifurcated into two relatively distinct camps has shaped and constrained the types of questions that scholars have asked, and the conclusions they have reached. Ultimately, I hope this chapter serves as a call for scholars to move past binary thinking and to deliberately explore instances in which the categories, concepts, and motivations of migration are confused. It will certainly be more complicated to theorize a broader spectrum of migration causes, to more fully integrate previously distinct interdisciplinary fields, and for migration scholars to more thoroughly embrace the study of migration across and within borders in the Global South. However, I believe that it is the only way to actually understand the role that border crossing plays in the world.

A clear theme that has emerged in this exploration of the migrant/refugee binary in academia is the close relationship between the academic field of refugee studies and the international refugee protection regime. In particular, UNHCR, the major NGO service provider, global advocate, and organ of international soft law on the protection of refugees, is openly invested in and committed to the notion that refugees are not migrants but rather are categorically distinct. The next chapter will explore the role of UNHCR in perpetuating and policing the migrant/refugee binary.

4

The United Nations
High Commissioner for Refugees

IN DECEMBER 2007 the cover story of *Refugees*, the magazine published by the United Nations High Commissioner for Refugees (UNHCR), was entitled "Refugee or Migrant? Why It Matters." The cover image accompanying this title is both visually striking and disturbing (see Figure 4.1). It is an aerial shot of an inflatable orange speedboat racing through the green sea, with an orange life-ring buoy trailing behind. In the white froth of the boat's wake is a Black man clinging to the rope while facing the sky, his white shirt flapping open in the wind. Two white men are kneeling in the boat, looking down at him and reaching with outstretched arms. One might be inclined to view this image as a scene of rescue, and the editor's note inside the magazine's cover assures the reader that "whoever he is, he deserved to be saved" (UNHCR 2007b, 2). However, the superimposed question (refugee or migrant?) that is hanging over the encounter gives the picture an ominous tone. Once he is saved from the immediate risk of drowning, the African man will be assessed by the relevant European authorities, and the question of whether he will be granted refugee status will matter very much to him. It will determine whether he risked his life at sea for any hope of a new beginning, or whether he will be returned to where he came from, a place he clearly felt he needed to leave.

This chapter analyzes the role that the major international organization (IO) in the field of refugee protection, UNHCR, has played in the perpetuation of the migrant/refugee binary. Despite the many difficulties with binary logic, UNHCR has been a key player in policing the distinction between refugees and migrants, and promoting the importance

FIGURE 4.1. Cover of UNHCR's organizational magazine. Source: *Refugees* Magazine, Number 148, Issue 4, 2007.

of the distinction to policy-makers, journalists, and the general public. In fact, emphasizing the importance of maintaining the distinction between these categories is a central component of UNHCR's public relations work. The consistency with which a binary perspective on conceptions and terminology has been articulated by UNHCR over the past fifteen years makes clear that advocating for the binary is not the brainchild of one particular High Commissioner or communications officer. Rather, it is an ingrained viewpoint that has permeated every dimension of the agency's work. It is central to how UNHCR "sees like an IO" (Broome and Seabrooke 2012, 4).

It is tempting to assume that binary logic persists simply because it is in the interests of the large and powerful donor states that fund UNHCR to frame border crossing in this way. But constructivist scholars of international organizations have long argued that IOs are not simply agents of the states that create them. Rather, they develop "autonomous values and behavioral predispositions" that form an organizational culture (Barnett and Finnemore 1999, 709). Scholars have found that IOs can play an independent role in global governance when their staff act as policy entrepreneurs for issues that have not been advanced by a member state (Ram 2017). But in order to push the agenda to new areas while still maintaining legitimacy, IOs must fit the new work into a larger context to justify that it is included in the mandate of the organization. In-depth studies of UNHCR have been compatible with these more general theoretical claims about how IOs function. Venzke's (2012) study of how international law evolves through interpretation concluded that UNHCR has played a central role in shaping the meaning of its own statute. Barnett and Finnemore's case study of UNHCR also concluded that it has expanded its scope over time through a series of "incremental deviations" from its original mandate (2004, 75).

Building on these studies of IO behavior, this chapter provides the institutional and political context to explain UNHCR's commitment to the migrant/refugee binary. Others have commented on UNHCR's commitment to this distinction (Carling 2017), but thus far, no one has offered a detailed accounting of what this commitment looks like in practice. Further, the question remains: *why* is UNHCR so committed to the binary as a kind of operational ideology? Broome and Seabrooke's (2012) concept of "seeing like an IO" is useful for answering this question. These scholars argue that it is important to examine "how IOs' activities construct both policy problems and policy solutions" (10) because "the construction of cognitive authority affords IOs a source of indirect political power" (9). IOs draw on their intellectual resources to build and shape a common cognitive framework that they use both to think internally about the issues at hand and to encourage other actors to understand the issues in similar terms.

The explanation that follows provides a detailed case study of the ways in which discourse and categorization can be an important instrument of both legal and political power for an IO. We know from previous ethnographic studies that UNHCR lawyers "share a strikingly uniform image of the international law with which they work" (Kennedy 1986, 2). This chapter looks more holistically at UNHCR to understand the relationship between the agency's legal protection work, which is highly essentialist and formalist, and its public relations work that promotes the binary. It concludes that the legal formalism of the organization is also expressed in its public communications, and the migrant/refugee binary becomes a cognitive framework that ties together multiple agency goals. Among other advantages, the binary helps UNHCR stake out its mandate to assist one specific type of border crosser, thus defining itself out of the much larger "regime complex" of migration governance (Keohane and Victor 2011).

The arguments put forward here are based on a close study of UNHCR's public relations work over the past decade, specifically its social media efforts to promote and protect the migrant/refugee binary. The chapter includes the first comprehensive analysis of the @Refugees Twitter handle from 2014–18, a period in which the growth of UNHCR's social media presence coincided with the dramatic and often tragic peak of arrivals across the Mediterranean Sea and at the US/Mexico border.[1] The analysis also draws on a research trip to UNHCR headquarters in Geneva that included in-depth interviews with thirteen key communications and social media staff, and four separate conversations with the head of the social media team. These interviews provided valuable insights into the global social media and communications strategy of the agency and how it has changed over time.

This fieldwork revealed that promoting binary logic fits into the larger communications strategy of engaging, informing, and reassuring citizens of Global North states. Changes to the media landscape, and in particular the rapid rise of social media, have altered the diplomatic relationships between IOs and donor states by giving IOs much more direct access to the publics of those states. Thus, rather than viewing the interests of donor states as autonomous forces that shape and constrain IO behavior, UNHCR staff view state interests as potentially malleable through direct communication with their publics. Indeed, they view the possibility of influencing public opinion as pivotal for maintaining agency survival and providing refugee protection, at a time when states in the Global North are outwardly hostile to both direct mass arrivals and large-scale refugee resettlement. In particular, binary logic reassures publics in the Global North that they can support admitting and protecting refugees without having to support open borders or massively increased immigration. It reassures people that they can support refugees and still believe in national security, sovereignty, and the rule of law.

UNHCR's Commitment to the Binary

UNHCR has been an active and determined proponent of the binary since about 2005, when Ericka Feller, director of UNHCR's Department of International Protection, published the article "Refugees Are Not Migrants" in *Refugee Survey Quarterly* (Feller 2005). This framing has been consistently used ever since. For example, in the 2016 press release "Refugees and Migrants: Frequently Asked Questions," UNHCR called the distinction between the two terms "crucial" because "refugees are people in a specific predicament which calls for additional safeguards" (UNHCR 2016b). Migration scholar Jørgen Carling (2017) has called this view "residualist" because, rather than acting as an umbrella term that includes all border crossers, it suggests that migrants are the catch-all term for everyone who does not meet the definition of a refugee. Indeed, UNHCR defines migrants as outside of their organizational mandate by describing a migrant as "a person who, for reasons other than those contained in the definition, voluntarily leaves his country in order to take up residence elsewhere" (UNHCR 2019a, 22). Further emphasizing the distinction between migration and refugee movement, UNHCR has also insisted that it "does not consider itself to be a migration organization, nor does it consider its activities to fall within the function that is commonly described as 'migration management'" (UNHCR n.d., 1).

In order to understand how the binary fits into the organizational priorities of UNHCR, we must first be acquainted with two important features of UNHCR's view of the refugee definition. First, UNHCR takes a highly essentialist view of what makes someone a refugee. The agency frequently asserts implicitly and sometimes explicitly that particular individuals have a quality of "refugeeness" that exists within them whether or not it is discovered or recognized. For example, according to the UNHCR handbook, "recognition of his refugee status does not therefore make him a refugee but declares him to be one. He does not become a refugee because of recognition, but is recognized because he is a refugee" (UNHCR 2019a, 17).

The essentialist framing of the concept is a powerful advocacy tool, and it fits neatly with the second element of UNHCR's position: a formalist legal view based on the distinction between law and politics, treating the refugee definition as a neutral legal category. International legal scholar Venzke has concluded that for UNHCR, "asylum has been seen as part of the nasty domestic political business whereas UNHCR walks in the pure beauty of law on the international level" (2012, 133). Similarly, as Forsythe described it, "there is the pretense that if protection is a matter of protecting legal rights, it is therefore strictly non-political. What is legal cannot be political, by definition" (2001, 12). Kennedy's (1986) ethnography of UNHCR lawyers also noted an extreme reluctance to acknowledge the political dimensions of refugee protection, and an insistence on the formal legal work. This position gains legitimacy from the fact that Article 2 of the 1951 Refugee Convention, the founding document of the organization, specifically states that UNHCR is to be nonpolitical. While it has often been very difficult to maintain a nonpolitical stance, UNHCR has been so committed to that position that it has recently come under criticism for presenting "mono-causal and often deeply depoliticized and asocial explanations for movement" (Landau and Achiume 2017, 1184).

Essentialist and formalist articulations of what makes someone a refugee complement and prop up binary logic. While they outwardly depoliticize the work of refugee status determination, they simultaneously confer power on those agents who are tasked with recognizing refugees. This perspective on what makes someone a refugee stands in direct contrast with the legal realist view that people are sorted and categorized into groups according to a complex set of factors that prioritize geopolitical calculations and include gendered and racialized conceptions of persecution. Essentialist and formalist views of refugees can also lead to great organizational anxiety about how to identify and distinguish between people arriving, sometimes literally, in the same boat. For example, while UNHCR recognizes the concept of "mixed migration," it is still insistent that refugees and migrants are distinct individuals, traveling together. At least in its public-facing communications, the agency never imagines that some border crossers are internally motivated by a combination of factors, some of which may come to the fore in particular moments. As UNHCR explains in its 2016 update to the "10-Point Plan of Action" for dealing with "mixed migration," "mixed movements, by definition, involve various categories of persons travelling along similar routes and using the same methods of transport but with different needs, profiles, and motivations" (UNHCR 2016a, 14). It is for this reason that the 10-point plan of action argues that "steps must be taken to establish entry systems that are able to identify new arrivals with international protection needs and which provide appropriate and differentiated solutions for them" (UNHCR 2007a, 2). As such, "UNHCR may, on a good offices basis, assist states in the return of people who are not in need of international protection where this is the most appropriate and agreed solution" (UNHCR 2007a, 4). Thinking back to the *Refugees* magazine cover story, sorting people correctly as they cross borders is a central organizational priority for UNHCR.

While UNHCR is extremely clear in its assertion that refugees and migrants are distinct, it has not always gone into detail about what the agency views as the potential consequences of blurring the distinction. Most frequently, UNHCR spokespeople and official press releases have only gestured at negative ramifications by making statements such as: "The two terms have distinct and different meanings, and confusing them leads to problems for both populations" (UNHCR 2016c). However, the logic behind the position was further elaborated in a 2017 speech by Volker Türk, Assistant High Commissioner for Protection, which is worth quoting at some length:

It has also become common in current debates to muddle language and terminology at the expense of refugees. We have heard too often refugees described as something other than who they are. For instance, they have been called 'undocumented people' or 'vulnerable migrants'. This may have been done with the laudable intention of making a stronger case for the rights of all people on the move. However, this has not had the intended effect. Instead it has created confusion. Rather than advancing the cause of protecting migrants' rights, it has provided fodder for those who wish to undermine refugees' rights. Quite apart from the erroneous legal depiction, it is inappropriate to present refugees as a sub-set of anyone else, migrants or otherwise. A person who is a refugee is a refugee, full stop. There is a clear legal definition of refugees linked to absence of national protection. And there are clear accountabilities for ensuring this protection . . . It would be a huge and costly mistake to be unclear about definitions. Blurring the distinction between refugees and migrants undermines the specific legal protections to which refugees are entitled. It obscures focus on who is accountable for their protection. And it feeds into justifications for restrictive measures towards refugees. If we are not careful about this, we are somehow losing here the very thing that we are trying to achieve. (Türk 2017)

From this explanation it can be inferred that the feared consequence of blurring language is that it will lead the public and politicians to assume that everyone is "just" an economic migrant, and therefore believe that harsh border control measures are justifiable. This fear was articulated even more explicitly by a senior UNHCR official in an interview:

We argue that the distinction matters because this is exactly what people who don't want more people coming to their country say. It plays directly into the Donald Trumps and the Victor Orbans of the world . . . We saw this with Orban in 2015, he kept saying that the Syrians were just coming to economically better themselves. And at first it was just him, but this has spread. And this has massive consequences. Brexit has resulted from this kind of talk.

Binary logic has continued to dominate the most recent efforts at international collaboration and policy-making on border crossing that resulted from the 2016 Global Summit on Refugees and Migrants at the United Nations' New York headquarters. After decades of functioning as a separate entity, the summit was opened with a signing ceremony through which the International Organization for Migration (IOM) joined the UN system. The IOM is the other major international organization tasked with assisting people on the move, and the agreement to put it under the auspices of the UN has brought UNHCR's commitment to the migrant/refugee binary into even sharper relief. Despite the gesture toward consolidation represented by the signing ceremony, binary logic dominated the proceedings and is abundantly clear in both the "New York Declaration" that was issued at the end of the summit, and the two Global Compacts that were produced as a result of it. The "New York Declaration" states clearly that more global cooperation, coordination, and burden-sharing is needed to manage the unprecedented levels of displacement in the world today. It then goes on to discuss refugees and migrants as distinct categories of border crossers in different sections of the document (UNGA 2016). Moving forward from the 2016 summit, two separate groups of diplomats and organizations were each tasked with developing their own document. UNHCR took the lead on the Global Compact on Refugees, and the IOM took the lead on the Global Compact for Safe, Orderly, and Regular Migration. These were developed via "two separate processes" because "migrants and refugees are distinct groups governed by separate legal frameworks" (UNGA 2018b, 2).

Setting aside some of the obvious weaknesses of these documents—they are not legally binding, they have not gained the support of the United States, and yet they claim to be "entirely non-political in nature" (UNGA 2018a, 1)—the compacts also strain to comply with the binary logic that dictates their separation. For example, the two compacts discuss border crossing in completely different terms, with different tones. The Global Compact on Refugees is focused on finding ways to improve "burden sharing" for the protection of refugees, who are cast as a major problem for the world community. In contrast, the Global Compact on Migration (GCM) portrays migration in a positive light as something beneficial to states. Yet the GCM concedes that "these positive impacts can be optimized by improving migration governance" (3). While binary logic portrays migration as a voluntary phenomenon, a core objective of the GCM is to invest in economic development in order to "minimize the adverse drivers and structural factors that compel people to leave their country of origin" (8). Further, advocates for the victims of human trafficking were quick to point out that these compacts complicate protection for trafficking victims, because, since some will qualify for refugee status and some will not, they are governed by two separate regimes (Oberoi 2018).

In the aftermath of the New York summit, as the two Global Compacts were being negotiated, UNHCR issued a statement on "migrants in vulnerable situations" (UNHCR 2017). That statement takes great pains to emphasize that there are two types of vulnerability that should not be confused. On the one hand, some migrants are very vulnerable in a situational way because the process of migration has made them vulnerable, and in contrast, some are actually vulnerable because they are refugees, which would trigger international protection obligations. This statement reads as an effort to hold the line on the distinction between migrants and refugees in order to prevent the Global Compact on Migration from commenting too extensively on matters that fall within UNHCR's mandate.

UNHCR's Mandate

UNHCR has a long history of resiliency and adaptation that has enabled its ongoing survival and fostered a reputation for being the definitive source of information about refugees. Most studies of UNHCR devote significant attention to the ways in which the agency has widened its scope and expanded its mandate over time (e.g., Barnett and Finnemore 2004). Writing as early as 1975, Holborn in her study of UNHCR commented on how it had already expanded dramatically, and this trend has generally continued in the years since. UNHCR began in 1950 with a staff of 99, a budget of $300,000, and a mandate to help only the people who had been displaced as a result of events occurring in Europe before its creation. Seventy years later, it has grown to an organization of 16,803 staff in 134 countries with an annual operating budget of over $6.54 billion.[2] In the words of a leading scholar of the agency, it has become a "principal actor" in world politics, with its own interests, capabilities, and agenda (Loescher 2001, 6). Even critical studies of UNHCR have found it to be a "resilient agency with a capacity for significant, and occasionally semi-autonomous, legal and bureaucratic innovation" (Cuellar 2006, 653).

The success and longevity of UNHCR "was not ordained" (Orchard 2014, 202). By all accounts of the organization, it was able to survive, unlike the other international refugee organizations that had been created in the first half of the twentieth century, because it was quickly able to establish itself as a moral authority and an expert actor that did not threaten the interests of the West. It acted as a key norm entrepreneur, pushing for more global recognition of and concern for its cause. Crucially, it eventually gained the support of the United States. UNHCR was not created with a general mandate to assist refugees and other displaced people of the world. Nevertheless, the agency almost immediately began to go beyond its limited agenda (Barnett and Finnemore 2004). After the Hungarian Revolution of 1956, it seemed on its face that the 1951 Convention did not cover Hungarian refugees, because the Convention said that it applied only to "events occurring before 1 January 1951." However, UNHCR got around this by arguing that the displacement crisis in Hungary was a result of earlier political changes (Loescher 2001, 86).

UNHCR handled the Hungarian crisis well and, as a result, "expanded its mandate and gained considerable autonomy" (Orchard 2014, 192).

In the late 1950s, the UN General Assembly recognized UNHCR's growing authority by passing a series of resolutions that allowed UNHCR to have a more flexible role (Gallagher 1989). In the early decades of its operation, the agency learned how to respond quickly to unfolding displacement events, and how to raise money beyond its annual allocations from the United Nations (Holborn 1975). By the 1960s, displacement crises in China, Tibet, India, Nepal, and Algeria led many powerful actors, including the US government, to conclude that UNHCR had to reorient from Europe to the "third world" (Loescher 2001, 91).

Much of the legitimacy UNHCR gained in the early decades seems to have been generated by the skill and creativity of a series of savvy High Commissioners. In particular, Prince Sadruddin Aga Khan of Iran became the fourth UN High Commissioner for Refugees in 1965. Under Khan, UNHCR expanded into an established global player, becoming involved in refugee emergencies "on all continents . . . [in] proportions hitherto unknown to UNHCR" (Loescher 2001, 39). Kahn strategically focused on relief assistance rather than legal protection, and "competed" with "rival" NGOs in order to establish the agency as the global authority for responding to mass displacement (140–41). Under his leadership, the UN General Assembly passed a series of resolutions expanding the power and the discretionary funds of the High Commissioner, giving the person in that role more discretion and flexibility to respond to emerging situations (Barnett and Finnemore 2004).

UNHCR significantly expanded its mandate in 1967 when it added a Protocol to the Convention, which officially removed the geographic and temporal restrictions on who the agency could serve. High Commissioner Kahn pushed for the Protocol because he believed the narrowness of the Convention definition was "contrary to the universal spirit of the Convention itself" (quoted in Davies 2007, 720). This move was also designed to maintain UNHCR's dominance in the area of refugee protection, as various newly decolonized states had expressed frustration with the Convention, were reluctant to accede to it, and had even discussed alternative regional definitions (720). The Protocol only addressed some of these concerns, however, since it enabled UNHCR to act in refugee situations all over the globe, but maintained the individualized and Eurocentric definition of a refugee that had been outlined in 1951.

Nevertheless, after the Protocol was added in 1967, UNHCR continued to expand dramatically, and by 1980 it was a massive organization, playing a pivotal role in the management of people fleeing the conflict in Vietnam (Orchard 2014, 201). UNHCR's Orderly Departure Program, which helped facilitate the exodus of over 650,000 people without engaging in any individualized refugee status determination, "occupied a kind of middle ground between refugee resettlement and ordinary emigration" (Kumin 2008, 117). This was by far the most creative and ambitious undertaking the agency had managed in its forty-year history. Despite its contemporary insistence to the contrary, UNHCR of the 1980s was most certainly a migration management agency.

Once the Cold War ended, however, UNHCR had to reinvent itself once again. Increased ease of travel and the lifting of emigration restrictions, combined with conflicts in the Balkans and East Africa, led to a rapid increase in the number of people seeking asylum in the Global North. Unlike people fleeing communism during the Cold War, admitting these so-called "new asylum seekers" of the late 1980s and 1990s had little geopolitical strategic value for wealthy liberal democracies (Martin 1988). Issues of sovereignty made many countries defensive, and UNHCR became more marginalized (Loescher 2001, 239). As the agency struggled to maintain leverage, it "sought to operationalize the vision of containment of the powerful donor countries" (Chimni 1998, 367; Barnett 2001). This operationalization took two forms. First, UNHCR expanded its mandate to include people who had been displaced within their state and had not crossed international borders. Global North states accepted the expansion of UNHCR's mandate to include internally displaced peoples (IDPs) as refugee protection and intrastate peacekeeping began to intertwine and the agency took on more of a security focus (Adelman 2001). While this expansion technically threatened the sovereignty of states in the Global South, it protected Global North sovereignty because it enabled UNHCR to give assistance to people while keeping them contained within borders (Barnett 2001, 267). It also added over 40 million people to UNHCR's annual total "persons of concern," which has allowed the agency to make a stronger case when seeking funding from donor states.

The second prong of the containment strategy was the development of what Cuellar (2006) has called the "grand compromise" of the global refugee regime. Northern states pay UNHCR to provide services in, and contain the vast majority of refugees within, the Global South—in other words, to keep them at arm's length. Meanwhile, donor states are free to express a firm commitment to the concept of refugee protection for the fraction of people who are granted resettlement in the Global North. As the terms of the compromise make clear, the resulting system again "prioritizes the sovereignty of states in the Global North at the expense of sovereignty in the Global South" (Arar 2017, 300). Global South states host millions of displaced people on their territories while balancing their needs against domestic development priorities. Meanwhile, vulnerable people are left in protracted and often dangerous situations that can last generations, with little hope of return to their home country or integration into the host country, and few opportunities to build a meaningful life via education or work. Ironically, because its operational scope has grown so much, UNHCR has become even more dependent on donations from the states of the Global North. This dependency has put the agency in somewhat of an advocacy bind because, as its capacity to provide relief has expanded, its diplomatic ability to criticize the refugee status determination and border control policies of the Global North has contracted (Cuellar 2006, 675).

Many observers of UNHCR over the years have pointed out the ways in which the agency has always been pragmatically sensitive to the interests of the powerful states that fund it, and has been careful not to criticize them or push agendas that will alienate them (Adelman 2001; Barnett 2001; Chimni 1998; Forsythe 2001; Loescher 1993). Specifically, while the mandate of the agency is now officially global in scope, it focuses on some displacement crises much more than others due to the realities of global power politics, and is therefore not truly international in its operations (Loescher 2001, 349). UNHCR is limited by state sovereignty concerns that prevent intervention in domestic affairs that have shaped the meaning and practice of humanitarianism (Barnett 2001, 251). Arguably, the agency is more constrained today than ever before. If the United States, which under President Donald Trump has expressed unprecedented hostility toward both refugees and the UN system, decided to pull financial support for UNHCR, it would wipe out 38 percent of the agency's annual government contributions.[3] As one UNHCR staffer put it, the "constant realpolitik" is frustrating. As UNHCR staffers plan their work, they must contend with significant limits on what the agency can say and do, and they have to be strategic about who they criticize. As another UNHCR staffer explained:

I know people want us to call things a crisis and be more critical, especially of the EU and the US. But this is diplomacy. We are not an NGO. People don't think of us as a government organization but we are. We're a 190-government organization. We cheer on Amnesty and Human Rights Watch, but we aren't them and we can't do the same things. We don't want to criticize the EU directly on Libya, so we say things like, "No one should be returned to Libya." And in the US case we say, "Everyone has the right to asylum."

In some ways, the story outlined above of UNHCR's remarkable expansion sits in tension with the idea that UNHCR actively holds the line on defining who is a refugee. But a closer look at UNHCR's relationship to donor states reveals that these two facts are compatible. UNHCR's devotion to the binary is a contemporary example of the agency's long-standing flexibility. UNHCR has come under criticism for expanding its mandate strategically and entrepreneurially in order to ensure long-term institutional survival (Cuellar 2006). However, UNHCR has never expanded its mandate completely to cover all vulnerable border crossers. Instead, it insists on the particularity of the population it views as falling under its mandate. Especially in this political moment, an emphasis on the binary reinforces UNHCR's institutional legitimacy and enables its survival. Reminding receiving states that refugees are special has become an important part of that work in a world in which deterrence and border control are the default stance.

Binary logic has also shaped UNHCR's treatment of climate change displacement. By some estimates, climate change could displace 140 million people by 2050, a number that is double the current number of UNHCR's persons of concern (Thompson 2018). Yet climate change displacement is not a major area of focus for the agency. As one staffer explained it, "UNHCR has really not embraced the reality of how climate change will affect the work. Ex comm [UNHCR's Executive Committee] has expressed that it does not want to talk about it." Another senior staffer said in regard to climate change, "It doesn't come into my work." On its website, UNHCR is very explicit in resisting the notion of a "climate refugee," thus defining people displaced by climate change outside of their mandate unless climate change leads to instances of persecution and targeted violence, which then cause people to leave their countries. UNHCR states: "the term 'climate refugee' is often used in the media and other discussions. However, this phrase can cause confusion, as it *does not exist in international law*" (emphasis in original). The website goes on to make clear that "the term 'climate refugee' is not endorsed by UNHCR, and it is more accurate to refer to 'persons displaced in the context of disasters and climate change.'"[4] Expanding the mandate to include people who are undeniably displaced by climate change is not currently an expansion that serves the interests of UNHCR. For now, the victims of climate-related displacement are squarely placed by the agency onto the migrant side of the migrant/refugee binary.

Social Media and the Binary

Communications scholars have identified several features of humanitarian public relations that shape the content IOs produce. First, rapid changes to the media landscape over the past two decades have posed significant challenges to the big traditional humanitarian organizations, who worry that they are losing their standing as the definitive and authoritative sources on the issues. Agencies are very aware that new media facilitates the spread of disinformation, and can make publics unsure of what information to believe about situations unfolding far away (Bunce 2019). IOs increasingly accept that they must brand themselves in order to compete in a crowded market and maintain their authority as a trusted source of information (Cottle and Nolan 2007). Compounding this challenge, research has shown that an overload of depressing images and stories from war zones, disaster areas, and other humanitarian crises can lead to a sense of helplessness and disaffection among privileged publics in the Global North. Disturbing images and stories can have a backlash effect known as "compassion fatigue" as media consumers become overwhelmed with the magnitude of problems (Moeller 1999). Human rights organizations must navigate the "dueling incentives" of calling public attention to the dire needs of the people for whom they advocate, and maintaining trust and credibility in the public mind (Cohen and Green 2012). Producers of media content for humanitarian organizations are very aware of this phenomenon, and put an extraordinary amount of effort into combatting and guarding against donor public apathy.

A particularly promising strategy from the perspective of big humanitarian IOs is the rise of social media, because it allows humanitarian subjects to speak with their own voices directly to people in the Global North. Within the past decade, social media has allowed for a qualitative shift in the representation of suffering and the moral agency of the spectator-witness, which some scholars believe is "fostering a cosmopolitan public" who feels closer to subjects of suffering than ever before, even when they are located far away (Madianou 2013, 250). Agencies like UNHCR have recognized the potential of social media to democratize communication and reduce compassion fatigue, enabling organizations to foster a much more immediate relationship with publics in donor states.

When one steps into the Geneva headquarters of UNHCR, it is immediately obvious that social media is growing rapidly and featured prominently in the organization. It has been well integrated into the conceptual frameworks of the organization. During my 2019 visit, there was a huge banner in the main lobby above the information desk that said #withrefugees, the hashtag associated with a recent UNHCR social media campaign. The current High Commissioner Filippo Grandi is on Twitter and tweets regularly from his personal account. Ten years ago, UNHCR headquarters only had one social media person on staff; today there are eight. As one senior staffer explained the rationale for investing heavily in a social media presence for the agency:

Around 2014–15, we gained an awareness that we have a different role to play. We have always done quiet advocacy, diplomacy with governments. But we realized we needed to be more present at the grassroots level, to be a trusted voice. We don't have a presence in the West on the ground like we do in some countries, so this was a way to have presence.

In 2015 UNHCR issued a report that described the first major attempt to consolidate and coordinate a global communications strategy for the agency, with a focus on social media. A stated goal of UNHCR is to lead the narrative by providing vital information and making authoritative statements about refugee situations as they unfold. Beyond a coordinating team in Geneva, staff in regional offices and out in the field are also strongly encouraged to share content. The 2015 report announced that "more than 500 staff have received in-person and online training on the use of social media, helping to ensure that timely, high-quality content is regularly shared from the field" (UNHCR 2015a, 6). By coordinating content production to ensure a consistent message, while simultaneously sharing unique content directly from the field, UNHCR aims to build and cultivate a "brand identity, enhancing the Office's authority and reputation" (3).

This agency-wide investment in social media has paid dividends. UNHCR's Facebook page has 3.65 million followers, and on Twitter, @Refugees has 2.4 million followers. It has tweeted over 70,000 times in its first decade, increasing in frequency each year. By comparison, the International Organization for Migration (IOM) has only 136,000 followers on Twitter. While UNHCR's social media strategy states that its target audience includes "digital influencers," it now functions as a digital influencer itself, shaping online narratives about who refugees are, what they look like, and what they need (UNHCR 2015a, 3).

One of the goals that the social media and communications staff at UNHCR are most passionate about is building empathy for refugees among voting publics in the Global North. In interviews, multiple staff at UNHCR referred to a 2016 study by Katwala and Somerville as being extremely influential on their approach. In their study of public opinion about migration in the UK, Katwala and Somerville refer to the "anxious middle," not the far right or the far left, but people who have concerns about migration without being openly hostile. Crucially, this group makes up the majority of the population in donor states and is not hardened in its position on migration and refugees. Thus, this group can theoretically be swayed by information that frames migration so as to assuage their fears of its consequences. As one staffer put it:

We know that about 15 percent on the far right are just hateful and xenophobic, we know about 15 percent on the far left are totally supportive. And that leaves a lot of people. We call them the conflicted middle. We need to be understanding about why they are afraid. We need to show them that people like them are befriending refugees.

Another staffer explained how the agency frames stories to appeal to this group:

We do a lot of really strategic outreach based on a lot of research . . . A huge part of it is dispelling stereotypes with stories. So, we know that there is hostility and xenophobia and so we want to tell stories about how refugees are integrating, working, learning the language, getting involved in their communities.

Another staffer explained that social media is very good at first-person stories, humanizing stories, and stories of resilience:

We want to find examples of humanity all over the world and shine a light on them. This is how we are going to counter the ugly, hateful language on social media. By putting out a different narrative.

On its face, using social media simultaneously to build empathy toward refugees and to promote the migrant/refugee binary seems like two distinct parts of UNHCR's communications strategy. In interviews, staff certainly did not draw many connections between these two aspects of the work. But a closer look at the social media efforts to promote the binary reveal the two forms of communication to be deeply linked, two prongs of the larger strategy to reach and reassure the "anxious middle." Taken together, these efforts are designed to illustrate the humanity of refugees while defining refugees as a distinctive group, not the hordes of migrants that Global North publics may be worried about.

In keeping with their long-standing efforts in public relations communications, UNHCR currently makes extensive use of social media to promote and protect the migrant/refugee binary. International relations scholarship tells us that IOs work to develop expertise and authority on particular topics in order to establish themselves as the definitive source in their area of focus. One way of carving out areas of expertise is to rely on classifications, which take on meanings that are "not only political and legal but also discursive" (Barnett and Finnemore 1999, 711). For example, the classification and meaning of the word "refugee" is central to the work of UNHCR and directly affects the scope of its mandate. UNHCR has used social media to establish clear ownership of the term refugee (as suggested by the Twitter handle @Refugees). The comprehensive cognitive framework of UNHCR is well illustrated by this integration of the legal protection and public relations elements of the agency.

The first major effort to use social media to promote the binary came in 2015, as large numbers of mostly Syrians were coming to Europe across the Mediterranean Sea, and European media outlets were using the word migrant to describe these arrivals. As a senior UNHCR staffer put it in an interview:

We spoke out about that and the BBC defended it, saying it [migrant] is an umbrella category, and we disagreed with them about that. Al Jazeera then called them all refugees, and all the other outlets basically just switched around the terms for variety of language, using them interchangeably. So, we decided to do a campaign about the language.

The #wordsmatter campaign used celebrities such as Academy Award–winning actors Cate Blanchett (also a UNHCR Goodwill Ambassador) and Colin Firth, and supermodel Helena Christensen, to promote the distinction between the two terms. The video accompanying the hashtag campaign had each of these celebrities and others look somberly into the camera and say "words matter" with great gravity. The video goes on to explain that "a migrant chooses to leave their country, often to improve their life" and can return home at any time. In contrast, "a refugee is running for their life."[5] Significantly, this language glosses over the specific legal definition of a refugee in order to emphasize the binary nature of border crossing.

As the situation with people attempting to cross into Europe unfolded further and was constructed in the media as a "migration crisis," UNHCR stepped up its social media efforts (Maddaloni and Moffa 2019). Especially in late 2015 and early 2016, the @Refugees Twitter account tweeted regularly about the binary, sharing explainer pieces with titles such as "Refugee or Migrants—What Is Right" (September 3, 2015), or "There's a crucial difference between refugees & migrants—learn more" (March 25, 2016), or "Confused about who is a refugee and who is a migrant? Our FAQs will help" (July 18, 2016). UNHCR has continued to release these types of explainers in the years since the initial flurry of activity on this issue. Consistently, this content does not go into detail on the legal definition of a refugee, and does not explain why the distinction matters, but instead maintains its importance by warning that there will be negative consequences if the terms are confused. For example, in 2018 UNHCR launched a cartoonish slideshow campaign across all social media platforms including stick figures of various different colors looking awkward and confused (see Figure 4.2). The slideshow asks the question that may be in many media consumers' minds, "What is the difference between a migrant and a refugee?" and then goes on to say, "Mixing these terms can cause problems."

In interviews about why UNHCR consistently emphasizes the binary, UNHCR staff frequently returned to the topic of the mandate. As one staffer put it, while there may be many different kinds of vulnerable people on the move, "our job and our mandate is to focus on refugees who have specific rights that are under threat." They also insist that they are helping to counteract disinformation and provide people with the knowledge they are seeking. A UNHCR staffer explained that they carefully track trending issues on Google and on social media in order to discover what terms people are searching for and what questions they have. "We know we need [explainers] because of the questions that come in on the comments. There is a lot of confusion about definitions. We think a lot about the anxious middle, which was such a helpful study, and about reachable audiences." Another staffer explained how they strategically

FIGURE 4.2. Images from UNHCR's Instagram feed, February 18, 2019. Source: https://www.instagram.com/p/BuCbo7NgLRD/

work to maintain UNHCR's status as the authoritative voice on refugee issues:

We also did a great job of reorganizing the website around what we know to be common queries . . . We do all of this in part so that when people search for terms and queries, we are the top hit. We have to think about terms like crisis and immigration, which we know people search alongside "refugees" but which are not terms we use on our website. We have to think about how, when we don't use words, we potentially miss a chance to be the top hit. So, we are thinking about ways we can use those terms subtly and without compromising.

Perhaps because of the essentialist outlook about what makes someone a refugee, UNHCR often uses the term to describe people who have not officially been granted refugee status. This approach to language may seem like it is in tension with an insistence on the binary distinction between refugees and migrants, but it is compatible with an essentialist view because many refugee advocates believe they know them when they see them. As one staffer put it, "In terms of how I use the definition, the definition is codified, and that definition gives us our mandate, but I'm not going to wait until someone has the stamp to use the term. I use the term liberally." Another staffer confessed, "When there is a situation where it is not clear-cut, I don't feel like I have to run my language by a lawyer every time. I'm in lots of meetings on these issues, so I feel really close to it." A third staffer explained: "We are pretty liberal with the term refugee. I tend to use it in more of the sociological way. We use it to describe people who we know are going to be given refugee status. Like Syrians are going to get it, they just have to file the paperwork, so we call them all refugees." In each of these accounts, there is the assumption that there is something intuitive about who is a refugee and who is not.

In sharp contrast to UNHCR's approach, IOM's social media output persists in using a different conception of the relationship between migrants and refugees, consistently using the term migrant as an umbrella term to describe all border crossers, including refugees. Despite the potential for more coordination that could arise from bringing two behemoth agencies closer together organizationally as parts of the UN system, IOM has managed to resist the binary logic and framing that UNHCR uses. For example, in the fall of 2018, @UNMigration tweeted: "Safety. Dignity. Human Rights. For all migrants. Regardless of their status. At all times." A few weeks later they followed up with, "All migrants must be respected, regardless of their migratory status." IOM also implicitly treats migration as an umbrella term by tweeting about all kinds of non-voluntary movement, including displacement as a result of natural disasters, migration due to environmental factors, internal displacement, human trafficking, and often, stories about people in refugee camps. As a UNHCR staff member put it in an interview: "The IOM sees refugees as a subcategory of migrant. We do not. I have never talked to them about it. It's just hard when one part of the UN is not being consistent with another part of the UN." Another high-level UNHCR staff member expressed frustration about this inconsistency: "We use both terms in contexts of mixed flows. We say refugee AND migrant. And we encourage the IOM to do that but they don't. They take a BBC approach that refugee is a subcategory of migrant, and we strongly disagree with that."

This interagency rivalry may be frustrating to UNHCR staff, but there is no contest as to which agency's message is having a bigger impact. UNHCR's social media presence dwarfs that of the IOM in terms of followers, likes, and shares on every platform. Further, there is some evidence that UNHCR is having influence over IOM communications about climate change. In July 2019 @UNMigration tweeted: "Human mobility is complex. Seeing climate migrants as refugees could weaken legal protection for people seeking safety from persecution and ongoing conflicts." Conceding the ground that people displaced by climate change will not usually qualify for refugee protection is not openly playing into the migrant/refugee binary because it sidesteps the question of whether refugees are a subcategory of migrant. However, the phrasing reveals an assumption that is highly compatible with binary logic: while there may be many, many migrants in the world, refugees are relatively rare. The further implication is that if it seems to some unnamed audience that there are too many people who might qualify for protection in the world, protection will be weakened.

Left Unchecked

The migrant/refugee binary has become a central component of the cognitive framework of UNHCR. This feature originally stems from the essentialist and legally formalist logic of the protection side of the agency. But it has also emerged as a key aspect of the agency's public relations work because it helps UNHCR carve out a specific institutional mandate and maintain moral and legal authority in the face of various threats to its dominance. Ultimately, promoting the binary facilitates agency self-preservation. As IOM joins the UN family, UNHCR views that agency as something of a threat, not simply because proximity makes turf wars more likely, but because IOM is undermining the legally formalist position that is central to how UNHCR sees like an IO. A commitment to legal formalism and the distance from politics that comes with it is key to maintaining legitimacy for UNHCR, and it is becoming more difficult for the agency to achieve.

UNHCR staff are extremely worried about the populist turn in the politics of many Global North states, and the rampant xenophobia that can be found both in the electoral realm and online. They are also motivated to enhance and maintain the authority of UNHCR because they believe that if UNHCR continues to be respected as the authority on refugee issues, it will be empowered to help more people. In order to stay relevant, UNHCR has had to become social media savvy, and promote its brand as the leading IO on refugee issues. To do so, the agency has decided to insist on the particularity of the refugee. This particularity is appealing—it reassures the majority of voters in these donor states that refugees are not a threat because obligations to refugees do not extend to every border crosser. Calls by the IOM to remember that refugees are just one flavor of migrant, and that all migrants have rights, work to undermine UNHCR's central cognitive framework.

This chapter has shown how pathologies can stem from the institutional and political realities that shape IO behavior. As IOs specialize and compartmentalize, their work becomes routinized in ways that "limit the bureaucrats' field of vision" (Barnett and Finnemore 1999, 719). Proponents of the binary within UNHCR genuinely want to protect vulnerable people and believe that the binary is the most effective way to do so. However, leaving the migrant/refugee binary largely unquestioned has consequences for which type of people receive help when they are on the move, which agendas are served, who represents which types of need, and how noncitizens are treated within states. These consequences are not necessarily intended. In fact, there is an irony to the fact that the goal of UNHCR's social media strategy is to push against donor state reluctance and restrictionism. Building empathy for refugees by insisting that they are uniquely deserving of concern, and emphasizing the importance of sorting them from other border crossers, runs the risk of unwittingly legitimating harsh border control measures. Even if that is far from the goal of UNHCR's support for binary logic, reluctant receiving states can take this logic and run with it, using it to justify measures that limit access to their territories.

The next section of the book will explore three specific examples of this legitimation: power struggles between the Global North and South over obligations to displaced people (chapter 5), debates over how to respond to arrivals across the Mediterranean (chapter 6), and contestation over how to classify people at the US/Mexico border (chapter 7).

5

The Global South

THE SOCIAL SCIENCES have come startlingly late to the realization that global power dynamics have marginalized knowledge about and by people living in the Global South, centering the perspectives and problems of the North (Connell 2007). The migration studies literature has not been immune to this feature of knowledge production. Migration policy in the Global South has been significantly undertheorized in a field that has been predominantly focused on liberal democracies of the Global North, and thus has a very limited conceptualization of the role of postcolonial state formation and economic development in migration policy-making (Adamson and Tsourapas 2019; Natter 2018). Further, as this chapter will demonstrate, the existing migration studies literature has not adequately theorized the interactive dynamics between host states and UNHCR in situations of mass displacement, even though these delicate agreements represent a significant aspect of migration policy in the Global South (Abdelaaty 2021).

This lack of theorization of Global South hosts as migration states is ironic, since the vast majority of displaced people in the world today reside there. According to official UNHCR statistics, 84 percent of people who are classified as refugees live in developing countries, and nine of the top ten host countries for displaced people who have crossed borders are in the Global South (UNHCR 2019b). Global South host countries have particular pressures on them, which can be conflicting and highly politicized. For example, displaced people often live among host communities that are equally poor and vulnerable. Further, many displaced people live beyond the reaches of the international protection regime, or even formal domestic law (Landau and Amit 2014). Thus, rights protection may have to be negotiated horizontally at the local level rather than with the state government (Kihato and Landau 2017).

This chapter breaks free from the dominant trend in the migration studies literature focusing on wealthy Western receiving states and examines the life of the migrant/refugee binary in the Global South. It is worth noting that the North/South distinction has been subject to critiques of "binary essentialism" not unlike the ones I outline in this book about the distinction between migrant and refugee (Go 2016, 12). Critics of a North/South frame have asked: What is the essential character that makes something Northern or Southern? What about the ambiguous or hard-to-classify parts of the world? What about privileged people in the South and subjugated people in the North? As dominant as many Global North states are, not all of them are equal. There are certainly hierarchies *within* Europe, for example. But this is not a book about the complications of the North/South binary. There is a rich and diverse literature devoted to the conceptualization of the South, and what a turn to the South means for the production of social knowledge (Patel 2018). While the overall goal of that literature is to dismantle the monopoly of the European perspective, there is less consensus and clarity among these scholars about what should be built in its place (Go 2016). Some believe that a total radical reorganization of the social sciences is needed in order to build alternative theories that are not Eurocentric, while others focus on critiquing existing theories and making them more inclusive and pluralistic (Patel 2018).

This chapter proceeds from the premise that the Global South is not a "directional designation" but a symbolic one (Grovogui 2011, 177). It lacks the cohesion of a region; rather, it refers to the formally colonized peoples of the world and to a recognition that even after empire, "former colonial powers relapsed in the tendency to mistake their injunctions to others for international morality" (182). This has certainly been the case with the moral imperative that has been granted to the 1951 Refugee Convention definition, and the opprobrium that has been leveled against Global South countries that do not embrace it and all of the obligations it brings.

The view from the Global South that I attempt to put forward in this chapter is not the same as the trend in Global North–based refugee studies to include "refugee voices" in the work. Rather, the "Southern standpoint" is a turn toward the global in a radical reorientation that considers the uneven sovereignties which still govern our world (Go 2016). It is

[A] social position of knowing akin to a feminist standpoint but one that is rooted not necessarily in gender but rather in geopolitics and global social hierarchy. It captures the position, and hence the activities, experiences, concerns and perspectives, of globally peripheral (e.g. colonized and postcolonized) populations. (14)

In this sense, the South is a metaphor that is interchangeable with the concept of the peripheral (Connell 2007). Thus, there is not one but many Souths, places where (as I discussed in chapter 2) the extraction of resources occurred under circumstances in which "sovereignty and the public good were construed at the expense of the colonized and for the benefit of the colonizer" (Grovogui 2011, 184). B. S. Chimni famously made an appeal for such a turn in his 1998 article "The Geopolitics of Refugee Studies: A View from the South," in which he advocated for an approach to studying displacement that would "take cognizance of the history of imperialism, in particular the role this has played over the centuries in the forced displacement of people" (369). Over twenty years later, the field of refugee studies has a long way to go to fully realize the extent of his call.

A Southern standpoint on the migrant/refugee binary that I attempt to develop below helps to contextualize what is often characterized by scholars and advocates in the North as noncompliance by Global South states in the international refugee regime. Many host states or adjacent states to conflict and displacement are not signatories to the Refugee Convention, notably Lebanon, Jordan, Iraq, Saudi Arabia, India, Pakistan, Indonesia, Malaysia, and Thailand. Much of the debate in the refugee studies literature focuses on how these countries are not fully complying with the Refugee Convention, assessments that can border on the paternalistic. Such studies sometimes acknowledge that Global South states may be dealing with the sensitivity of critiquing one's neighbors that is inherent in recognizing refugee status, and some studies point out the economic burden of processing refugee claims and providing refugee benefits. However, these works do not tend to include the story of systematic exclusion of Global South perspectives in the development of the refugee concept, and they do not tend to acknowledge the political context of decolonization that occurred simultaneously with the period of UNHCR's dramatic expansion.

Too much of the literature on the politics of compliance does not use a geopolitical or a postcolonial lens to explore the power dynamics of the international refugee regime. Examining perspectives from Global South states denaturalizes dominant understandings of the "refugee" category as essentialist and universal. Instead, it is revealed to be a construct driven by the interests of the Global North.

Global South Resistance

Global South resistance to UN refugee projects predates the creation of UNHCR, because it initially emerged in the context of UN intervention to assist displaced Palestinians in the Middle East. In late 1947, the UN had committed to a partition plan that drew up separate states for Israel and Palestine, but instead of partition, war broke out in 1948, and eventually 800,000 people were displaced. The UN then created a special regime based on the idea that because the Palestinians had been directly displaced by the actions of the UN, the obligations were unique and deserved special consideration (Akram 2014). Thus, the UN created the United Nations Relief and Works Agency (UNRWA) in 1949, and then explicitly excluded Palestinians from the 1951 Convention, which says that it "shall not apply to persons who are at present receiving from organs or agencies of the United Nations other than the United Nations High Commissioner for Refugees protection or assistance."

Much like the League of Nations in the 1920s, UNRWA quickly became a vehicle for Global North intervention into the Middle East (Robson 2017). Even as the United States refused to sign the 1951 Convention, it became UNRWA's largest funder by far, driven not by humanitarian concern but by Cold War motivations. The US State Department viewed "refugee relief as a mode of preventing Communist feeling among the Palestinian dispossessed" (636). Nevertheless, UNRWA ran into serious opposition and resistance, both from the Palestinians themselves and from the host governments of Egypt and Jordan. These and other newly independent Arab states actively resisted the international intervention of the UN in the Middle East during the 1950s. Some of this tension can already been seen in the proceedings that document the drafting of the 1951 Convention.

As was alluded to in previous chapters, Global South resistance to the refugee definition in the 1951 Convention was articulated both during the drafting and in the aftermath of passage when UNHCR was attempting to achieve widespread adoption. Unlike previous international refugee definitions, the one cemented in 1951 was the result of a process that actually did formally include representatives from some newly decolonized Global South states. These states were not silent about the limited nature of the definition that was being created. For example, at one point during the drafting, the Pakistani delegate commented that the Convention definition "covered European refugees only, and completely ignored refugees from other parts of the world" (quoted in Oberoi 2001, 40). The Indian delegate reiterated that "the United Nations should try to help not only special sections of the world population, but all afflicted people everywhere" (quoted on 41). The Chilean delegate made a similar point, that "it was the duty of the United Nations to extend protection to every person" who needed it (41). Lebanon, Egypt, and Saudi Arabia issued a joint resolution, arguing that the definition of the term refugee was "unduly restrictive, because it was limited in time and space and omitted certain categories of refugees" (Janmyr 2017, 442). Yet the Convention was adopted despite the objections clearly raised by Global South states about how the Convention deliberately excluded their needs. During the discussions over the wording of the definition, European states explicitly defended the limitations that kept the focus on displaced people in Europe, because of their desire to address their own priorities first (Davies 2006). Much like the uneven sovereignties of the past, the drafting of the Refugee Convention operated to protect the interests of the powerful among the drafters.

Global South concerns about these power dynamics did not disappear after the Convention was finalized. Newly decolonized states did not accede to the Convention in the way UNHCR hoped they would. In the first ten years, only twenty-seven states had ratified the Convention, most of which were European (Holborn 1975, 182). Throughout the 1950s and 1960s, Asian states in particular resisted attempts by UNHCR to get them to accede to the Refugee Convention, frequently citing the fact that they were not involved in its drafting (Davies 2006). The first time a Global South state asked UNHCR for assistance was in 1957, when the Algerian War of Independence from France caused people to flee to Tunisia and Morocco (Davies 2007). UNHCR provided some material assistance but was reluctant to declare the people to be refugees because that label would imply that France, a member of the UN Security Council, was producing refugees through its suppression of an anticolonial uprising. This example makes explicit the notion that pressures to maintain a limited conception of a refugee were deeply connected to European anxieties about decolonization.

Decolonization also directly contributed to increased displacement in the Global South in the 1960s. Violent decolonization struggles and the reconfiguration of colonial boundaries led many people to move. Further, newly independent states—whose boundaries were set by colonial powers with little to no input from the people haphazardly enclosed or separated by them—were often, not surprisingly, prone to civil wars. It soon became clear that UNHCR wanted to expand the scope of its work so it could intervene to provide humanitarian assistance in these unfolding displacement situations without expanding the legal concept of a refugee. In response to this desire, in 1961 the UN General Assembly passed a resolution that allowed the High Commissioner to use its "good offices" power to assist large groups of displaced people without giving them full refugee status. Throughout the 1960s, UNHCR used this good offices power to provide aid to people in Africa and Asia. UNHCR repeatedly referred to these people as "new refugees" who required material aid, as opposed to the "old refugees"—Europeans who required the legal protections of citizenship (Davies 2007). This distinction was a direct product of the continuing limitations of the 1951 Convention. UNHCR archives reveal that states in Africa, Asia, and Latin America all expressed doubts about the relevance of the Convention during the first half of the 1960s (Davies 2007). Specifically, states often raised the concern that the definition was very individualized, and did not cover people fleeing generalized violence and unrest. In particular, UNHCR became quite worried about losing the support of African states, which had been the most supportive in the Global South, as Africa turned its attentions toward developing its own regional refugee instrument. By the mid-1960s, UNHCR decided that it needed a change that would satisfy the concerns raised by Global South states, while at the same time remaining generally acceptable to Global North states by not creating too many new obligations.

For this reason, UNHCR chose to create a Protocol instead of a full new Convention because it would be faster and easier. The proposed Protocol would remove both the geographic and temporal restrictions on the 1951 Convention, but the definition itself would remain intact. In an eerie parallel to the dynamics of the 1951 Convention, several Global South states raised strenuous objections to the contours of the Protocol, concerns that were again ignored. Because many of the concerns that Global South states had raised about the 1951 Convention had to do with the limited nature of the refugee definition, the fact that the Protocol intended to leave the original definition intact was viewed by them as inadequate. For example, when the Protocol was debated by the UN General Assembly in 1966, the representative from Nigeria complained that it did not go "far enough to solve the problems" of displacement in Africa, which "had not been of their making," and the representative from Uganda also spoke up in support of this objection (Davies 2007, 725). Delegates from the United Arab Republic, Afghanistan, Madagascar, Jamaica, and the Philippines all objected that the Protocol had been written too quickly and without enough global consultation (725). Based on her research in the UNHCR archives, Davies concluded that "what is apparent from the drafting procedures of the 1967 Protocol is that developing states had little role in the process of creating this instrument but were, nonetheless, expected to adopt it" (727).

Davies's detailed account about the failure of UNHCR to improve upon its exclusionary process from 1951 is troubling. During the second iteration of drafting an international refugee instrument, despite sixteen intervening years of decolonial struggle and its professed desire to draw newly postcolonial states into the fold, UNHCR, led by European states, repeated its mistakes almost exactly. This context calls into question the tendency in many accounts of the Convention and Protocol to suggest that the 1967 addendum fixed the limitations of the original version. As Davies puts it: "In commending ourselves on the creation of these instruments it is, perhaps, easy to forget that they were promulgated at the cost of excluding alternative forms of refugee experience" (728). The fact that the Protocol did not resolve the concerns raised by many Global South states helps to explain why its addition to the Convention did not lead to a rash of new signatories in the 1970s, as UNHCR officials had hoped.

Global South reluctance to embrace the international refugee regime in the 1950s and 1960s is not just a relic of the past. It is a key element for understanding the geopolitics of contemporary displacement crises, one that is tellingly neglected in the literature. This history helps to contextualize the condescension with which Global North states, advocates, and media often discuss Global South states' lack of ratification.

The Organization of African Unity Convention of 1969

In May of 1963, representatives from the newly independent states of Africa met in Addis Ababa, Ethiopia, to found a pan-African league of nations, the Organization of African Unity (OAU). A specific goal of the OAU was to end all forms of colonialism in Africa. Soon after its founding, the OAU formed a commission whose task was to draft a refugee convention to address the issue of displacement on the continent. The original idea was to create a completely separate convention for Africa that would address the fact that Africans were officially not covered by the 1951 Convention because of the temporal and geographic restrictions, as well as the strictures of the definition itself.

In stark contrast to the 1951 Refugee Convention drafting process, whose proceedings were exhaustively documented, there is very little background history on the drafting of the refugee definition in the OAU Convention of 1969 (Rutinwa 2017; Sharpe 2018). However, the existing information makes clear that the OAU Convention was a direct product of decolonization. Many OAU delegates believed that the UN definition, even if its temporal and geographic restrictions were to be ignored, did not cover people who were freedom fighters working to overthrow oppressive colonial regimes, because the 1951 Convention definition excluded people who had engaged in so-called "political" crimes (Rutinwa 2017). OAU wanted to create a way to protect people who had fought for African liberation. Over half of the refugees in Africa in the 1960s were people fleeing continuing colonial repression in the face of independence movements in places such as Angola, Mozambique, and Portuguese Guinea, or white domination in South Africa and Rhodesia (Arboleda 1991). The remaining refugees were displaced by conflicts between ethnic groups who were cohabitating newly independent states that had been clumsily, if not callously, configured under colonialism.

The original draft of the OAU Convention was met with serious consternation from UNHCR. In particular, UNHCR was concerned about language stating that the new convention would supersede all preceding agreements about refugees (Sharpe 2018). In a 1965 letter, High Commissioner Aga Khan expressed his concern that the "present draft would seriously jeopardize protocol or other instrument to extend effects 1951 Convention to post dateline refugees" (*sic*, quoted in Sharpe 2018, 25). In fact, archival documents reveal that UNHCR moved faster on the 1967 Protocol because of the 1965 OAU draft, which they believed was in competition with the 1951 Convention (Sharpe 2018).

UNHCR convinced OAU to allow it to consult on the process, and the UNHCR Legal Division ended up working closely with OAU during the later stages to make sure that the Convention was complementary, not competitive, with the 1951 Convention and 1967 Protocol. Thus, the scope of the OAU Convention shifted significantly during the drafting process due to UNHCR's involvement, and to the speed with which the 1967 Protocol was moving forward. The Protocol "contributed significantly to the OAU's decision to abandon its initial intention of elaborating a completely independent African instrument" (Arboleda 1991). Instead, OAU began to focus on "the specific aspects of the refugee situation in Africa" so that it could be a complement to the geographically and temporally unrestricted Convention (Sharpe 2018, 31). From this contextual history, it is clear that while the existence of the Protocol dissuaded OAU from superseding the UN definition altogether, the OAU did not think the Protocol would be sufficient, or that its existence would make an OAU Convention unnecessarily redundant as the UNHCR leadership may have hoped.

The final version of the OAU Convention of 1969 is broader than the 1951 Convention definition in several key respects. First, it includes two parts. Article 1.1 replicates the 1951 Convention definition. Then, Article 1.2 defines refugees as people displaced by "external aggression, occupation, foreign domination or events seriously disturbing public order in either part or the whole of his country of origin." Rather than deliberate, targeted, individualized persecution, this definition allows people to be protected if they flee their homes due to the randomized violence and instability that arises in times of conflict. It also allows external causes of disorder to be considered. Second, not only is this definition broader in scope than the language of the 1951 definition, the OAU Convention also allows for refugee status to be granted en masse, which is sometimes referred to as prima facie recognition. In this way, "the OAU Convention marked the beginning of a refugee protection system which directly addressed the causes of mass refugee influxes" (Arboleda 1991, 189). Rather than the assumption of the 1951 Convention definition that each individual should be assessed for fit, the OAU Convention assumes that individualized refugee status determination would be impractical and unnecessary in many circumstances. Third, because the member states drafting the Convention realized that they would be accepting people crossing borders separating neighboring member states, they took measures to ensure that the act of granting asylum to a displaced person would not take on the weight of political condemnation that the UN definition implies.

Instead, the OAU Convention states that "the grant of asylum to refugees is a peaceful and humanitarian act and shall not be regarded as an unfriendly act by any Member State." Such provisions are the reason why scholars such as Okoth-Obbo describe the OAU Convention as an attempt at "depoliticization and humanitarianization" when compared to the UN definition (2001, 90).

Commentators on the OAU Convention have noted that there is a wide gap between the aspirations of the document and the reality of implementation (Rutinwa 2017; Okoth-Obbo 2001; Sharpe 2019; Crisp 2010). No supervisory system was established when the Convention was created, and it did not provide guidance to states as to how to actually carry out mass influx, prima facie adjudication, leaving it to individual state variation based on capacity and political will. Thus, "systemic" problems with refugee protection "abound" in Africa despite widespread adoption of the OAU Convention (Sharpe 2019, 262). Further, domestic courts have had difficulty interpreting and applying the broad definition (Wood 2019). And the actual lived experience of displaced people in Africa may have little to do with refugee law and policy, and may be determined by all kinds of other factors, which tend to be much more local and connected to social networks (Landau and Amit 2014).

Despite the practical limitations related to implementation, the OAU Convention has significant and ongoing political meaning. The broad aspirational language has taken on a "mythical" character for many people interested in refugee protection (Okoth-Obbo 2001, 109). While UNHCR initially was threatened by the potential of the OAU Convention, over time it has come to embrace it. For example, in a 2009 speech marking the fortieth anniversary of the OAU Convention, a UNHCR spokesperson noted: "Over the past four decades, the Convention has made it possible for millions of Africans to reach safety and receive protection and assistance. Its importance and vitality remain undiminished today" (UNHCR 2009). Perhaps most importantly, the postcolonial context of its creation gives the OAU Convention particular meaning as a form of resistance against European imperialism. Newly independent states rejected the notion that they had to adopt the 1951 Convention definition alone, despite its limited applicability in Africa. They later continued to develop a definition that not only built upon the 1951 Convention definition but also expanded upon it in key ways that undermine its central premise of individualized persecution. Implicitly, the OAU definition resists the essentialism of the 1951 Convention definition because it creates room for the idea that forced displacement can occur as a result of colonial oppression and its destabilizing after-effects. In other words, refugees are produced by large global structural forces, not by the qualities of the individual being displaced. The OAU Convention also inspired the states of Latin America to mimic and build upon its wording in the 1984 Cartagena Declaration, which cites the OAU Convention as an important precedent.

The 1984 Cartagena Declaration on Refugees

Latin America has a long-standing tradition of providing diplomatic asylum for political, academic, and artistic elites fleeing government persecution (Reed-Hurtado 2013; Arboleda 1991). This concept of the political asylee is distinct from the European concept of a refugee, and had been codified through a series of seven regional conventions dating back to 1889 (Fischel de Andrade 2019). Because of this history, there remains an enduring distinction in Latin America between the concepts of political asylum and refugee, with the former carrying much more political significance and regional resonance. After 1951, Latin American countries were reluctant to sign the Convention, viewing mass displacement as a European problem and reflecting concerns about subjecting themselves to international control (Cantor 2018). Brazil, Colombia, and Venezuela were the only Latin American states that participated in the 1951 Convention drafting, and only Argentina, Brazil, Colombia, and Ecuador had become signatories in the first decade after its creation (Reed-Hurtado 2013). For these reasons, as more displacement occurred in the region during the 1960s, Latin American states were reluctant to look beyond the traditionally narrow concept of asylum and view people fleeing *en masse* as qualifying for international protection. In 1965 the Inter-American Commission on Human Rights issued a statement saying that international and domestic law was not adequate to address the increasingly dire situation with displacement in Latin America, and thus new efforts were needed. Nevertheless, individual states continued to be reluctant to engage with international law (Reed-Hurtado 2013).

Two main factors help explain a shift that occurred in Latin American migration politics during the 1970s and 1980s. First, the phenomenon of mass displacement increased dramatically. Rather than one particular source or host country, the issue was widespread, affecting many parts of the region. Second, in response to this reality, UNHCR became much more involved in Latin America, establishing some regional offices and providing humanitarian support to displaced people (Arboleda 1991). In 1981 UNHCR was involved in convening a meeting in Mexico of academics and representatives from some states, an event that became known as the Mexico Colloquium. Conclusion No. 4 of that colloquium's Conclusions and Recommendations identified a need for a broader regional refugee definition because circumstances had surpassed the limits of the existing legal framework (Arboleda 1991). In the years following the Mexico Colloquium, Cubans, Haitians, Guatemalans, and Salvadorans continued to flee their countries to destinations within the region and beyond, driven out by oppressive regimes and violent civil wars. Whole villages from Guatemala and El Salvador fled together in some instances. During this period, UNHCR continued to advocate for the broader conception of a refugee that had been articulated at the Mexico Colloquium (Fischel de Andrade 2019).

UNHCR's efforts to draw attention to the issue, and the pressing nature of displacement in the region, eventually led in November of 1984 to the Colloquium on the International Protection of Refugees in Central America, Mexico, and Panama, held in Cartagena, Colombia. Representatives from ten states attended: Belize, Colombia, Costa Rica, El Salvador, Guatemala, Honduras, Mexico, Nicaragua, Panama, and Venezuela. UNHCR helped organize and was present at the conference, including High Commissioner Poul Hartling, whose remarks opened the colloquium (Fischel de Andrade 2019).

This background helps to contextualize the main differences between the OAU Convention and the Cartagena Declaration. While the texts of the two documents have many obvious similarities, and, as mentioned above, the Cartagena Declaration references the OAU Convention as an inspiration, the contexts of the two regional refugee definitions are quite distinct. First and foremost, UNHCR was much more involved and supportive in the Latin American case, partially because the postcolonial political moment had passed, and UNHCR had become more open to the possibilities of regional refugee definitions for creating buy-in for humanitarian assistance in the face of mass displacement. The second major difference between the two regional refugee definitions is that one is a legally binding Convention that emerged from a pan-African politics, and the other is a nonbinding statement of support for a more internationalist approach to protection that was promoted by the norm entrepreneurship of UNHCR (Fischel de Andrade 2019). UNHCR's influence can be seen in Articles 3.1 and 3.2 of the Cartagena Declaration, which articulate the importance of wider ratification of the Convention and Protocol in Latin America and emphasize the need for collaboration and cooperation with UNHCR, and the complementary nature of the expanded definition in Article 3.3.

Nevertheless, the Declaration departs from the Convention and Protocol in several key ways. First, the expanded language defines refugees as "persons who have fled their country because their lives, safety, or freedom have been threatened by generalized violence, foreign aggression, internal conflicts, massive violation of human rights or other circumstances which have seriously disturbed public order." This language is even broader than the OAU Convention because it uses terms like "generalized violence" and "massive violations of human rights," which are not defined in international law. Second, the influence of the OAU Convention can be seen in Article 3.4, which reiterates the point that the granting of asylum is "non-political" and shall not "be interpreted as an unfriendly act towards the country of origin of refugees." It is highly significant that the Declaration emphasized the nonpolitical, humanitarian aspect, given the traditional concept of political asylum in Latin America. In this way, the Declaration can be seen as articulating a need for coordination to solve a totally distinct problem. The nonpolitical nature of the situation is also emphasized in Article 1, which makes clear that the displacement situation in Central America has been exacerbated by the economic crisis. Based on his interviews with the drafters of the Cartagena Declaration, Reed-Hurtado concluded that the process was "less concerned with individual refugee status determination procedures[;] the main purpose was to offer a point of reference that justified humanitarian engagement" (2013, 12).

UNHCR's position on the concept of a refugee in Latin America during this period is an interesting window into the agency's behavior before its more extreme essentialist turn. UNHCR advocated support for a broader definition in Latin America prior to the Declaration, and "skillfully promoted" the Declaration after it was drafted to Latin American governments who had not been present at the meetings to encourage their endorsement (Fischel de Andrade 2019, 83). In 1985 the Executive Committee of UNHCR adopted Conclusion No. 37 on Central American

Refugees and the Cartagena Declaration, which stated that the agency "welcomed the use of regional approaches in resolving refugee problems of regional scope." It is clear that in this context, UNHCR saw a broad regional definition as a way to gain a foothold in a region that had resisted the international refugee regime.

Experts on Latin American displacement seem to agree that the Cartagena Declaration represented a major turning point in the relationship between states in that region and international norms of refugee protection. Even though it is not legally binding, it has become "the established norm throughout Central America" (Arboleda 1991, 190). Seven Latin American countries adopted wholesale the language of the Declaration into domestic statutes, and six others have done so with slightly altered wording (Reed-Hurtado 2013). As a result, it "was a crucial instrument for the protection of refugees from Central America in the 1980s" (Castillo 2015, 90). Perhaps more enduringly, it has cultivated a culture of cooperation and at least a rhetoric of solidarity in managing regional displacement (de Menezes 2016; Cantor 2018). At the tenth, twentieth, and thirtieth anniversaries, there have been conferences that brought together states, NGOs, academics, and displaced people, resulting in further declarations committing to continued cooperation and principles. Thus, it "encapsulates the capacity and will of a whole sub-continent to periodically analyze the humanitarian challenges ahead" (Castillo 2015, 91) and is "a unique and intriguing model for humanitarian cooperation among states in the Global South" (Cantor 2018, 435).

On the other hand, many of the main "states of first asylum" that are currently hosting large numbers of displaced people in Latin America have not adopted the language of the Cartagena Declaration (de Menezes 2016, 132). Further, some states, such as Ecuador, that originally adopted the language of the Declaration in its domestic statute have revised their asylum policy as the backlash against mass arrivals has created political tension (de Menezes 2016). The Declaration has also only had a minor impact on the development of refugee law in Latin America. According to legal analysts of the current state of Latin American refugee law, the Declaration's expanded definition is "seldom applied in practice, guidance on its interpretation is undeveloped and national authorities rarely consult its provisions when providing international refugee protection" (Reed-Hurtado 2013, 5). Like the OAU definition, it includes a lot of terms that are not defined in international human rights law, and so are difficult to actually interpret in individualized refugee status determination decision-making. In practice, the broad definition is not applied consistently in domestic RSD procedures and there has been very little doctrinal development. And because it has been so inconsistently adopted by states, "there is no common, harmonized regional broad definition of "refugee" adopted and used in Latin America" even when compared to the incomplete adoption of the OAU definition in African law (Fischel de Andrade 2019, 84).

The stories of these regional definitions are complex. Neither the OAU Convention nor the Cartagena Declaration has been a panacea for the problems of displacement in their regions. However, both are fascinating examples of how regional solidarity can develop and lead states to think creatively about solutions.

Contemporary South–South Displacement

This section turns to the rhetorical treatment of border crossers in the two largest contemporary displacement crises, which also happen to be the largest situations of mass displacement since the 1940s: Venezuelans in Latin America and Syrians in the Middle East. The burden of hosting millions of displaced people in both of these situations has overwhelmingly fallen on neighboring states in the Global South, with the possible exception of Turkey, which is a state that resists categorization in the North/South binary. The neighboring host states of the Middle East and Latin America bear no overt responsibility for causing the displacement in their regions, and they have limited capacity to provide muchneeded humanitarian assistance or permanent resettlement opportunities (Achiume 2015). Accidents of geography have placed many Global South states in the difficult position of providing safe haven for fleeing neighbors while balancing the equally pressing needs of their own citizens. The stakes of striking this delicate balance can sometimes be as significant as the continuing legitimacy of host state governments and the stability of their economies. According to the norms of the international refugee regime, neighboring host states are obligated to provide some level of support for displaced people who cross into their territories, physically presenting themselves for protection. Meanwhile, wealthy and more geographically removed countries are under no similar obligation to assist (Hathaway and Neve 1997). In both examples below, the historic ambivalence of Global South states toward the Eurocentric concept of a refugee is a surprisingly central aspect of the politics of response to displacement.

Syrians in the Middle East

The Syrian Civil War began in 2011 after protestors, inspired by the Arab Spring uprisings, were brutally suppressed by the regime of Syrian president Bashar al-Assad. Over the past decade, the conflict has grown and morphed into a multitude of conflicts on many fronts, involving the Syrian government, various opposition groups, and the Islamic State of Iraq and the Levant (ISIL). Widespread armed warfare and destruction is ongoing, and as the situation has unfolded, the infrastructure of the Syrian state has essentially disintegrated, and lawlessness abounds. International human rights organizations have chronicled rampant human rights violations and war crimes, particularly but not exclusively on the part of the Assad regime, which include attacks on civilians and the use of internationally banned weapons (Amnesty International 2019). UNHCR estimates that more than six million people have been internally displaced within Syria, and another six million people have fled beyond Syria.[1] Taken together, more than half of the prewar Syrian population has been displaced by this conflict. Especially as the war drags on, with little hope of resolution in sight, people are beginning to leave the region in larger numbers, sometimes seeking more permanent resettlement in Europe. However, the neighboring states of Turkey, Lebanon, and Jordan continue to host the vast majority of the people who have left the country. Turkey is currently hosting about 3.5 million people, Lebanon over 900,000, and Jordan 650,000.[2] I will speak more about Turkey and the 2016 EU-Turkey deal for managing refugees in chapter 6. Below, I discuss the reception context for Syrian arrivals in Lebanon and Jordan, including government rhetoric and UNHCR responses in both places.

Syrians who flee their country are crossing borders in a region which, since the time of the Ottoman empire in the nineteenth century, has experienced significant internal movement and repeated instances of local communities providing refuge and hospitality to displaced populations from other parts of the region (Chatty 2016). Distinct states with a border between them did not exist during the Ottoman empire and were only created during the French mandate of the early twentieth century

(Dionigi 2017). While neither Jordan nor Lebanon has ratified the 1951 Refugee Convention, for more than seventy years both countries have hosted Palestinians, Iraqis, and now Syrians in large numbers. Jordan has had historically open borders for citizens of other Arab states who wish to come and work or trade in Jordan (Stevens 2013). Similarly, there has traditionally been a very loose border between Syria and Lebanon because of close cultural ties and long-standing patterns of economic exchange and labor migration. In short, there has been "a robust pattern of interdependence that has inhibited restrictions on border crossings, while the physical boundary also facilitated the quick transfer of people and goods" (Dionigi 2017, 28).

Both Jordan and Lebanon have had similar trajectories in terms of their national-level responses to Syrian arrivals. Both states were initially welcoming, with a turn toward closure in 2014 due to security concerns and economic strain (Betts, Ali, and Memisoglu 2017). More recently, both states have made strong appeals to the global community for financial assistance, leveraging the European desire to contain Syrians in the Middle East as a way to receive significant new influxes of development aid (Arar 2017). Jordan has contained the vast majority of Syrian arrivals in a series of camps in the desert areas that border the two countries. In contrast, Lebanon has refused to set up any camps, assuming that people will absorb into kin networks and find ways to be self-sufficient, so Syrians live among the general population with no permanent resettlement plan and limited access to employment opportunities (Carpi and Senoguz 2019). Despite this major difference in the reception context, both countries have similarly strained relationships with UNHCR, and the issue of terminology is an extremely fraught point of contention between the refugee agency and both host states.

The Jordanian government reluctantly allows both UNRWA and UNHCR to assist displaced people and conduct refugee status determination in its territory. In conducting RSD, UNHCR uses an expanded mandate definition that includes people who have fled "for reasons arising from a situation of generalized violence or serious public disorder" (UNHCR, *Guidebook for Asylum Seekers on UNHCR's Refugee Status Determination Procedures in Jordan,* quoted in Stevens 2013, 14). This broad interpretation on the part of UNHCR has caused tension, because "the very evident anathema that Jordan has towards the term 'refugee' is striking" (14). As Stevens observed based on fieldwork in Jordan, "labelling is clearly politicized" (17). The government prefers to refer to non-Palestinian displaced people as guests, and so "the tension between efforts by the (I)NGO community, on the one hand, to have an inclusive label, and by the state, on the other, to exclude is also very evident" (20).

Lebanon has an even more ambivalent attitude toward the concept of a refugee. Most basically, it rejects the notion of itself as a country of refuge: the 1926 Lebanese Constitution seems to prohibit permanent settlement of foreigners, it has not ratified the Refugee Convention, and there is no domestic asylum legislation, so foreigners must live there illegally (Janmyr 2017, 440). Yet it is the country that is hosting the largest per capita population of displaced foreigners in the world, and has been a member of UNHCR's ExComm since 1963 (Janmyr 2017). Like in Jordan, Lebanon allows UNHCR to operate and conduct RSD on its territory, and as the numbers have gotten larger, the agency has taken on a bigger and bigger role (Janmyr 2018). In part due to Lebanese government reluctance and UNHCR's attempts to accommodate that reluctance, Syrians are received into a complex and somewhat ad hoc system in which some are registered as official refugees, some are not, and many occupy ambiguous in-between statuses (Janmyr and Mourad 2018).

Based on her interviews with both Lebanese government officials and UNHCR staff, Janmyr concluded that for years, "most disagreements appear to have concerned the employment of the 'refugee' label" (2018, 397). A Lebanese government official told Janmyr: "For us, they're not refugees. Officially speaking . . . we realize whether under the Convention, or international law, or whatever, they're acknowledged refugees, they're not [only] displaced. But because of the specificity of Lebanon in particular they are not considered as refugees" (Janmyr 2017, 455). Similarly, the UN Convention on the Rights of the Child Committee, which has been pushing Lebanon to ratify the Refugee Convention, received this response from the Lebanese government in 2015: "The characterization 'refugee' does not apply to displaced Syrians who came to Lebanon as the Lebanese State does not grant them such characterization and considers their presence temporary and for purely humanitarian grounds" (quoted in Janmyr 2017, 454). Instead, communications by local government aimed at the Lebanese population refer to people using terms ranging from "*nazih* [displaced], to '*ammel* [labourer], while others are more particular to local dynamics, such as '*ajaneb* [foreigners] and in some cases even '*ikhwa* [brethren]" (Janmyr and Mourad 2018, 554). Part of the issue is the value of good neighborliness and not wanting to denounce Syria by calling it refugee-producing. As a senior government adviser explained to Janmyr, "the Lebanese government not only avoided labeling those who have fled to Lebanon as people escaping from persecution, it avoided acknowledging that there is a war in Syria" (Janmyr 2017, 460).

Despite Lebanon's refusal to call Syrians refugees, in all public-facing communications UNHCR unequivocally refers to them as refugees. High Commissioner Filippo Grandi has called it "the biggest humanitarian and refugee crisis of our time, a continuing cause of suffering for millions which should be garnering a groundswell of support around the world."[3] The "Syrian emergency," as UNHCR calls it, has been the subject of the largest-ever funding appeal by UNHCR, asking for US$4.4 billion from the international community to assist people displaced by the war.[4]

While this rhetorical frame is a key part of fundraising, it has an impact on the domestic politics of the host states. A Lebanese government official told Janmyr that "because Lebanon long has hosted a considerable number of Syrian laborers, the 'Syrian migrant', unlike the 'Syrian refugee', is perceived by many as less of a threat to Lebanon's social fabric. This re-labelling of refugees as economic migrants would therefore be 'easier to manage' since 'by saying [that the Lebanese government has] 700,000 economic migrants in Lebanon . . . the pressure of refugee settlement . . . will decrease'" (Janmyr 2018, 410). Other scholars have concluded, based on extensive fieldwork in the region, that "the humanitarian-promoted hospitality discourse in Lebanon has rather (maybe ephemerally) produced a new form of Lebanese nationhood vis-a-vis the new Syrian 'Other'" (Carpi and Senoguz 2019, 138). In other words, the framing of Syrians as refugees has created conceptual distance between Syrians and Lebanese people that had not previously existed. Because Syrians have been framed by UNHCR as people seeking Lebanese citizenship via permanent settlement, local populations are more likely to view them as a threat. Thus, it is not clear that labeling Syrians as refugees is the obvious way to ensure their good treatment, as some might assume.

Venezuelans in Latin America

The crisis in Venezuela has sparked the largest-scale displacement in the history of the Western Hemisphere. An estimated 4.6 million people had been displaced by the end of 2019, representing 16 percent of the total

Venezuelan population (Bahar and Dooley 2019). The situation escalated after Nicolás Maduro took over the Venezuelan presidency following the death of President Hugo Chávez in 2013. Since that time, Maduro's presidency has been characterized by corruption, suppression of dissent, political instability, and generalized violence. It has also led to massive economic collapse, severely limiting access to food, water, electricity, and medical care. While many countries around the world have severed ties with the Maduro government and have recognized opposition figure Juan Guaidó as the leader of Venezuela, neither the humanitarian crisis nor the mass displacement that stems from it shows sign of abatement (Specia 2019). In fact, estimates project that another million or more people could leave Venezuela in 2020 (Bahar and Dooley 2019). At this stage, the vast majority of displaced people remain in Latin America, with seventeen states in the region hosting some, but Colombia and Peru hosting the largest numbers of people, with official counts at 650,000 and 550,000 respectively, although many estimates are much higher.[5] Given the scale of the displacement, it is somewhat surprising that the situation has received such little international aid or attention. There is far less media coverage in Global North outlets on the plight of the Venezuelans and far less scholarly work on the reaction of host states to their arrivals than there is about displaced Syrians and their host states. In terms of funding, the international community has spent ten times as much on humanitarian assistance per displaced person from Syria, and has even spent proportionally more on the Rohingya and South Sudan crises, which also have not received the same level of media attention as the Syrian war (Bahar and Dooley 2019).

Rather than a global crisis, then, Venezuelan displacement has become a profoundly Latin American issue, with massive political and humanitarian consequences for the region. Especially since the leftist turn in Latin American politics around the turn of the twenty-first century, many states have passed migration laws that are generous, expansive, and embrace the rights of free movement. Some analysts have interpreted this shift as a reaction to the increasingly harsh treatment of Latin American arrivals by the United States (Freier and Parent 2019, 58). Whatever the motivation behind it, until very recently "in South America, the right to regularization is the expected rather than exceptional state response to irregular migration" (Bauer 2019, 11). The Venezuelan crisis has put that commitment to the test. Asylum claims by Venezuelans have skyrocketed across Latin America, but "the institutional infrastructure for processing asylum requests and applying the Cartagena Declaration in practice is very weak, leading to long backlogs in refugee processing and a resulting disincentive to claim such status even among those who qualify under applicable law" (Camilleri and Hampson 2018, 15). Latin American host and transit states have tended to avoid classification of Venezuelans as refugees, despite the expansiveness of the Cartagena definition, and instead have adopted alternative methods for regularizing arrivals that are quicker and less expensive (Freier and Parent 2019).

Peru is a party to the Convention and Protocol, and uses the expanded definition of a refugee outlined in the Cartagena Declaration in its domestic legislation. It also has several other generous legislative provisions for the protection of vulnerable irregular migrants, which leads to a multifaceted, if fragmented, migration policy landscape in Peru (Blouin and Button 2018). In 2018 Peru changed its law to allow Venezuelans without legal status temporary work permits, but in 2019 it added a visa requirement for the first time (Bauer 2019). President Vizcarra explained the change: "Peru has a long tradition of humanely welcoming citizens of other countries, but also has the obligation to ensure the security, tranquility and peace of all Peruvians" (quoted in Bauer 2019, 10).

Much like the Syria-Lebanon border, the Colombia-Venezuela border has historically been "dynamic," as citizens from both countries have moved back and forth over the years to seek safety from armed conflict and better economic opportunities (Ordóñez and Arcos 2019, 158). Thus, the recent exodus from Venezuela has included within it a substantial population of Colombian return migrants, who had been living in Venezuela until the crisis hit. Perhaps because of this close connection between the two states, Colombia has had a more progressive response than Peru, letting Venezuelan people enter and work, and giving them access to basic services. Since 2017 Colombia has been issuing arriving Venezuelans a special stay permit that allows them to work and go to school. In 2019 Colombia changed its citizenship law, which previously granted birthright citizenship to any baby born to a parent with legal status, to include children born to Venezuelans without status (Forero 2019). The Colombian government has not called the Venezuelans refugees, "since doing so might exacerbate a bureaucratic backlog in the asylum system and risk a political backlash in a country where anti-immigrant rhetoric is growing in the border regions" (Betts 2019, 128). Instead, the Colombian government refers to the arrivals as "nuestros hermanos venezolanos" (our Venezuelan brothers) (Ordóñez and Arcos 2019, 160). Colombia has not been conducting refugee status determination on any scale, or granting group-based prima facie refugee status. So, despite a reluctance to formally label or legally classify Venezuelans as refugees, the Colombian government has been remarkably welcoming, even in the face of potential economic and political costs.

The mixed response of Peru and Colombia, hosting many people while resisting the refugee label, is strangely similar to that of Lebanon and Jordan. The stance of UNHCR, however, has been much more complicated. Despite the regional Cartagena definition that seems on its face to cover the vast majority of Venezuelans, the agency referred to them as migrants for the first several years of the displacement. My interviews with UNHCR communications staff in spring of 2019 revealed that there had been very high-level internal debate within the agency at that time about which terms to use, and UNHCR had come under pressure from outside groups to use the term refugee. For example, Dany Bahar, a fellow at the Brookings Institute, wrote an October 2018 article in *Foreign Affairs*, "Why It Matters That We Call Fleeing Venezuelans Refugees, Not Migrants." He argued:

As with other refugee crises, the millions of Venezuelans who have left their homes are not migrants searching for better opportunities but rather refugees fleeing for their lives. Recognizing fleeing Venezuelans as refugees would be an acknowledgment of a reality that can no longer be ignored. (Bahar 2018)

Using a binary logic, Bahar had argued for Venezuelans to be categorized on the side that he clearly believed would bring more attention to the plight of the displaced. In May 2019 UNHCR issued a public statement on the matter of terminology. The statement noted that "the majority of Venezuelans are in need of international refugee protection, based on the wider criteria of the 1984 Cartagena Declaration applied in Latin America. This is because of the threats to their lives, security or freedom resulting from circumstances that are seriously disturbing public order in Venezuela."[6] Ultimately, the UNHCR communications staff and High Commissioner Grandi agreed to use the phrase "refugees and migrants" to cover their belief that the situation involved what UNHCR likes to call "mixed flows."

The latest phase of the crisis has inspired a striking degree of coordinated response, suggesting a shift in frame. For example, in September

2018, representatives from eleven host states plus UNHCR and IOM met in Quito, Ecuador, to coordinate a regional response to the Venezuelan situation. Since then, the group has met three more times, continuing what has come to be known as the "Quito Process." These meetings fit within the spirit of the Cartagena regime, which pledged a regional approach to addressing Latin American displacement issues. They also represent a fairly unusual example of UNHCR/IOM collaboration. UNHCR and IOM have appointed a joint special representative, Eduardo Stein, former vice president of Guatemala, to coordinate a regional Refugee and Migrant Response Plan that includes the two UN agencies and many regional governments.[7] In December 2019 the Inter-American Commission on Human Rights adopted a set of Principles on the Rights of All Migrants, Refugees, Stateless Persons, and Victims of Trafficking (Inter-American Commission on Human Rights 2019). It is an extremely broad statement of support for the rights of all migrants, for the principle of *non-refoulement* as it extends to people beyond narrow definitions, for the Cartagena Declaration, and for regional coordination to address migration. The broad language of the Cartagena Declaration, and the regional outlook on displacement that it has fostered, has laid the groundwork for an inclusive and humane response by Latin American states to the Venezuelan crisis. However, without more resources to assist displaced people, these states will be limited in their practical response.

A Global North Construct

Attention to the development of alternative refugee concepts and their application to contemporary migrations in the Global South helps to illustrate the ways in which the strict nature of the migrant/refugee binary emerges as a Global North construct. The case studies of contemporary displacement outlined above demonstrate that the migrant/refugee binary is a source of tension and conflict between host states and UNHCR. Now, as in the past, many Global South states view the UN refugee definition as being foisted upon them externally, or as inapplicable to unfolding displacement scenarios, or as unwieldy and expensive, politically fraught, and not necessary for the generous provision of safe haven. While it is true that individuals who are granted refugee status would theoretically have rights to more extensive resettlement options, and access to more benefits in their host state, in practice things are much more complex.

To be clear, it is not my intention to paint UNHCR as a villain. The agency should not be caricatured as a nefarious force of Global North oppression. UNHCR employs thousands of Global South citizens, and its leadership works with great diplomatic care to foster conditions that they genuinely believe are most conducive to the humanitarian protection of vulnerable people. In many instances, the refusal of host states to recognize border crossers as refugees is a naked attempt to avoid assisting them. And yet, as this chapter has shown, framings of displacement crises that focus predominantly on host state noncompliance miss some important contextual background.

First, the Global South is not simply a producer of refugees and migrants but also a producer of international law. Of course, there is only so much that law can do to solve major displacement problems, but the existence of broader regional definitions has, for many decades, existed as a reminder of the narrow scope of the 1951 Convention definition. Global South resistance to that definition has at times stood as a proxy resistance against framings and narratives that place the sole blame for displacement on Global South states, and that continue to blame them for not declaring the people they host to be refugees. These narratives neglect to appreciate the fact that Global South states have done the vast majority of the hosting, and they neglect to acknowledge the history of colonial exploitation and state boundary-drawing, as well as ongoing Global North military and economic intervention that plays a role in creating displacement crises.

It is also worth noting that, today, UNHCR seems less set on a narrow definition of a refugee when it comes to South–South displacement. It never encourages Global North states to consider broader conceptualizations of a refugee in the face of arrivals at its borders, but is currently doing just that in both the Syrian and Venezuelan contexts, while maintaining a robust communications platform based on a narrow migrant/refugee binary when facing Global North publics. Finally, there seems to be a huge disconnect in Global North public perceptions of displacement. This disconnect stems from the logical tension between the assumption that refugees are not being helped in the Global South and the assumption that the people who come to the Global North from the Global South are not really refugees, which is the subject of the next two chapters.

6

Arrivals in Europe

BY THE SUMMER OF 2019, the "crisis" of people attempting to cross the Mediterranean Sea to Europe had receded in its immediacy, enough for some to decide it could be artistically commemorated. A ninety-foot-long fishing boat was hoisted onto an Italian dock as part of the Venice Biennale exhibit, realizing the vision of the controversial installation artist Christoph Büchel (Tondo 2019). It was the same boat that had launched from Garabulli, Libya, on the morning of April 18, 2015, carrying 800 people, most of whom had been packed down into its hull. It did not get far before it ran into trouble, issued a distress call, and then collided with a massive cargo ship loaded with containers. It capsized, sinking in a matter of minutes. At least 700 of the passengers drowned in what the media labeled a "migrant tragedy" (Miglierini 2016). The Italian government had recently suspended its search and rescue program, Mare Nostrum (Our Sea), under criticism that the program had become a pull factor encouraging more people to make the risky journey. The cargo ship had been the only vessel available to respond to the boat's distress call, inadvertently destroying it in an attempt to help (Taylor 2015a).

In the five years between 2014 and 2018, almost two million people crossed the Mediterranean Sea and landed in the European frontier states of Italy, Cyprus, Malta, Spain, and Greece. During that same period, an estimated 18,000 people died attempting the crossing.[1] The Venice Biennale exhibit, entitled *Barca Nostra* (Our Boat), in many ways embodies the duality of the European response to those arrivals. Most Italians would presumably understand the title as a reference to the Italian search and rescue program, which had been named for the ancient Roman term for the Mediterranean. They would also probably know that the program had been discontinued and that the Italian government was criminalizing humanitarian groups for taking search and rescue operations upon themselves (Denti and Pantaleone 2019). While the artist left no other contextual statement with which to interpret his intended message, it may have inspired a sense of shame or collective responsibility in some viewers. And yet, the placement of the boat/coffin next to a café, where Italians sat and chatted in its shadow, was eerily (perhaps intentionally) callous and decontextualized.

Europe's response to mass arrivals, which peaked in 2015 but continues despite reduced media attention, has moved beyond a "migrant crisis" or a "refugee crisis" to verge upon an existential one. In the fall of 2019, the newly elected European Commission president Ursula von der Leyen created a new position of Vice President for Protecting Our European Way of Life, whose portfolio includes migration management and security (Noack 2019). This move is a stark example of the many ways in which "the political consequences [of the 2015 crisis] changed Europe forever" (Betts 2019, 122). To put it as Arendt might, the "comity of Europe" is at risk of going to pieces again over the question of what to do about and for people who continue to arrive, despite the risks (1943, 119). French scholar Didier Fassin called it a "moral crisis" in 2016, since it has led Europeans to grapple with the questions of what Europe is and what European values are.

There is a lot of talk in contemporary Europe about European values, and the concept of Europe seems to have simultaneously become more salient and more ambiguous (De Genova 2016). In a legal sense, those values were specifically laid out in the preamble of the 2000 Charter of Fundamental Rights of the European Union: "respect for human dignity, freedom, democracy, equality, the rule of law and respect for human rights, including the rights of persons belonging to minorities" (European Union 2010). But the term is also invoked and mobilized for a variety of different political ends "in reaction to the major threats currently affecting European democracy" (Foret and Calligaro 2018, 1). "European values" are cast as universal, yet somehow also particular when set in contrast to the values of foreigners, and the concept of Europe itself has become "deeply contradictory and fundamentally incoherent" (De Genova 2016, 77). Borders were invented in Europe (Torpey 2000). So were refugees, and the concept of universal human rights, and colonial empire. Today, the ways in which these inventions sit in tension with one another is becoming increasingly clear, and more inescapably problematic.

Recent mass arrivals into Europe have triggered an identity crisis, part of which includes an unprecedented public interest in the terminology of migration. Compared to other reception contexts, the "the use of different categories to describe those on the move has become deeply politicized" in Europe (Crawley and Skelparis 2018, 49). Public debate about the proper terms to use to describe people on the move is now a common aspect of the politics of response to arrivals. Politicians, advocates, and media outlets have all taken positions on the matter, and these positions are associated with a whole host of other policy preferences. Even though the terminology debate is explicit in Europe, there has not been as much discussion of the "categorical fetishism" that leads politicians, advocates, and sometimes even academics to use these terms as if people were easily distinguishable (a major exception is Crawley and Skelparis 2018, who coined the phrase "categorical fetishism").

This chapter consists of a detailed analysis of reactions to Middle Eastern and African arrivals at Europe's southern and eastern borders since 2014. This chapter draws on a massive and highly dynamic set of data: public rhetoric about border crossing into Europe. It is impossible to digest in its entirety because it is constantly being produced on a plethora of different outlets. Even the secondary literature by European migration and media scholars on the topic is a seemingly unmanageable challenge to anyone seeking to keep up with it. As a way of limiting the analysis, this chapter is particularly focused on the choice to refer to people as refugees, asylum seekers, or migrants, and the moments in which speakers or media outlets choose to defend or explain such choices. Based on this analysis, I conclude that the migrant/refugee binary functions as a tool for maintaining an outward commitment to European values, while protecting European sovereignty.

Fortress Europe

While immigration is one of the most contentious political issues in Europe today, European countries were not always desirable destinations. Instead of receiving people, for much of the nineteenth century and the first half of the twentieth century, Europe was a continent of emigration.

People left Europe in large numbers fleeing persecution, wars, and in search of a better and more prosperous life in the United States, Canada, Australia, and a host of other places. The transition occurred in the period after the Second World War, when many European countries went through a major identity crisis as they became reluctant "migration states" (Hollifield 2004). In order to build back their postwar economies, these states recruited foreign workers who were expected to return home once the jobs dried up. To the surprise of policy-makers, many of these people stayed. In the famous words of Swiss novelist Max Frisch, "we asked for workers, but human beings came" (quoted in Hollifield 2004, 896). These human beings often decided to make lives, build families, and settle in their new homes, diversifying Europe in unprecedented ways.

Another feature of postwar migration to Europe was the "context of decolonization and the movement of darker citizens to the metropole" (Bhambra 2017, 403). Public resistance to the migration of colonial subjects from the periphery to the cities of Europe led many states to institute new immigration controls in the 1970s and 1980s (Karatani 2003; Fassin 2016). A combination of racism and selective memory led to "the emergence of the category of the 'migrant' as referring to populations that would, historically, have been part of the body politic, that is, as subjects or citizens" of colonial empires (Bhambra 2017, 403). In other words, people who were colonial subjects of European empires, or people who were citizens of newly independent postcolonial states, were cast as political strangers when they attempted entry into Europe despite long-standing and ongoing political, economic, and social ties.

While European borders were somewhat hardened to people from outside Europe in the 1970s and 1980s, the concept of "fortress Europe" was not realized until well after the Schengen Agreement of 1985. The agreement is named for the town in Luxembourg in which representatives from five Western European states met and decided to gradually abolish controls at their shared borders, allowing for free movement within the so-called "Schengen zone." Since that time, the zone has expanded to include twenty-six countries and 450 million people. By 1995, when the Schengen regime had progressed to where internal controls were virtually nonexistent, European governments became more nervous about unauthorized immigration into Europe from the outside, and concerned about the quality of border control at the frontier of Europe, which tended to be made up of less wealthy states with a lower capacity for border control than the wealthiest states of northern and western Europe. Thus, the emphasis shifted from promoting the Schengen open borders system to clamping down on Europe's external borders in order to "compensate" for the freedom of movement within the continent (Carr 2012, 28). If someone could enter a porous border in Greece or Italy, they had access to almost all of Europe.

In this way, even under the open borders Schengen system, uneven sovereignties were highlighted within Europe, creating tensions between the core and peripheral member states. These hierarchies serve to further complicate the notion that the Global North and South are a strict binary. Rather, the frontiers of Europe constitute a liminal borderscape, which can seem like neither North nor South. Pioneering border studies scholar Gloria Anzaldua described this phenomenon when she referred to the US/Mexico border as an open wound, "where the Third World grates against the First and bleeds. And before a scab forms it hemorrhages again, the lifeblood of two worlds merging to form a third country—a border culture" (1987, 3). As the cases of the Mediterranean and US/Mexico border make plain, these "meta borders" between the Global North and South have become sites of violence and death.

The European powers managed concerns about vulnerability at the borders with two complementary strategies. First, in 2003, the member states agreed on the Dublin II Regulation, which required people to apply for asylum only in the first European Union member state in which they were fingerprinted (European Union 2003). This agreement protected the wealthier countries of northern and western Europe from becoming destination states by keeping refugee status determination tied to the frontier states where the vast majority of people enter Europe. For asylum seekers who choose not to wait in the backlogs of Greek or Italian refugee status determination systems, or who are rejected by those processes, "the European asylum system operates as a regime for the production of migrant illegality" and "becomes a space of rejection and marginalization for most asylum seekers" (De Genova 2016, 88).

In addition to the Dublin II Regulation, which deflected much of the asylum burden to the peripheries of Europe, the second strategy was simply to invest in fortifying Europe's boundaries. In the twenty-first century, Europe has developed "the most sustained and extensive border enforcement program in history" involving over 400,000 border guards, a plethora of different coordinated agencies, naval patrols, detention centers, biometric databases, thermic cameras, and other technologies (Carr 2012, 3). The hardening of the continent's external borders began with visa requirements for North Africans in the 1990s. And it was around this time when unauthorized North African migration to Europe began to use maritime routes, albeit in small numbers (De Haas 2007). Since 2005 the face of European border control has been Frontex, the European Border and Coast Guard Agency. The demands of Frontex as well as the US Department of Homeland Security drive a massive industry of surveillance tools and border control technology (Frontex 2020).

Critical studies of Frontex operations have made two key observations. First, the agency uses a dual discourse of securitization and humanitarianism through which the "irregular migrant" is always cast as a threat who must also be saved (Vaughan-Williams 2015). Vaughan-Williams argues persuasively that because Frontex policies and practices embrace both a humanitarian rhetoric and a security-oriented reality, Europe has experienced a "crisis of humanitarian critique" (4). In other words, humanitarian arguments are difficult to use as a critique of the border violence committed by Europe, because they have been co-opted by the very actors committing the violence—Frontex argues that its deterrence measures, such as using dogs, tear gas, rubber bullets, and pushing back boats to prevent them from reaching European waters, save lives by making people less likely to risk dangerous journeys.

The second line of scholarly critique points out that Europe's border control measures are not just repressive, they are also productive. Frontex's efforts have inspired an "illegality industry," a seemingly endless cycle through which popular migration routes are closed or subject to crackdowns, leading people to take much riskier ones (Andersson 2016, 1056). As Frontex defends its tightening of borders in terms of saving lives, the closures and crackdowns have a dual effect: they push people into more dangerous border-crosser situations and create new markets for further security-oriented solutions. Based on extensive fieldwork studying irregular migration routes through North Africa and across the Mediterranean, Andersson observes:

Given that smuggling is a market driven by rampant demand, punitive measures only tend to drive business further underground while new risks are transferred downwards, from provider to client. . . . Today flimsy vessels, boats without proper captains and predatory smuggling networks are the rule rather than the exception. (2016, 1061)

There is no evidence to support the arguments that deterrence measures work and that search and rescue programs lead to increased crossings. Rather, deterrence measures combined with cutting search and rescue programs seem only to lead to increased deaths. Nevertheless, "European authorities have capitalized on the 'migrant crisis' discourse to legitimize deterrence measures that are legally questionable" but meanwhile have only "increased mortality risks and stimulated the smuggling economy, without achieving their stated objectives" (Steinhilper and Gruijters 2018, 529–30).

Even though Europe has a continental-level agency that manages border control, there has not been an equivalent European-level, systemic effort to deal with this issue beyond mere deterrence. Instead, the latest phase in the escalating intensity of European border control is the criminalization of humanitarian rescue groups (Sigona 2018). Today, those who facilitate the entry of people into Europe are at risk of being prosecuted under laws that were designed to stop smugglers and traffickers, leading human rights groups to raise serious concerns about the reduction of humanitarian space (Fekete 2018). Organizations such as Human Rights Watch have also raised the alarm about the degree to which the EU is now working closely with the Libyan government to enhance their ability to conduct maritime interceptions, despite extensively documented human rights abuses in Libyan detention facilities (Human Rights Watch 2019). These measures make a mockery of the norm of *non-refoulement*.

A major, often unspoken factor in the European response to Mediterranean arrivals is race. While North Africans had been coming across in smaller numbers since the 1990s, what is new in the twenty-first century is the rise in sub-Saharan Africans using the same routes out of North Africa (De Haas 2007). The Blackness of the people arriving stands out in Europe, and seems to trigger the belief that there is a whole continent of people planning to come north as soon as they can. The number of sub-Saharan Africans who attempt entry into Europe is actually dwarfed by the number who migrate north but stay in North Africa, a region that includes many states that are destinations in their own right (De Haas 2007). Nevertheless, African people are framed in European political discourse as a threat to European sovereignty, "as misguided wards dazzled by false promises of better lives far from home" (Landau 2019, 172).

Europe has exported these hostilities, leading to crackdowns in the North African states such as Libya that host both regional migrants and people in transit to Europe. And critics have observed a new mode of "containment development" through which, "across Africa, development aid is increasingly framed as addressing the root causes of migration" (Landau 2019, 172). It is for this reason that Achiume (2019) argues that Africans and Europeans are still closely linked in ongoing neocolonial relationships of subordination that make their casting as political strangers highly disingenuous. There is a shocking lack of discussion of colonialism in the current conversation about Europe and migration. This collective amnesia about the past "enables the dismissal of the postcolonial and multicultural present of Europe and the associated populations—whether they come as migrants or as people seeking refuge and asylum" (Bhambra 2017, 396).

The "Crisis" of 2015–16

The term "crisis" in relation to border crossing situations is frequently deployed not in relation to the human suffering that is being experienced, but in relation to the reaction of citizens and politicians in wealthy receiving states. Specifically, the word is often used to express fears among receiving state publics about threats to security, or about the economic implications of the mass arrival of unauthorized people (Nawyn 2019). This phenomenon is certainly true of the events of 2015 in Europe. The war in Syria had been ongoing for over four years, and neighboring states within the Middle East had been hosting displaced Syrians that entire time. But it did not become a "crisis" in the eyes of the Global North until about a million people tried to enter Europe in one year, quadruple the number from the previous year (Andersson 2016, 1058).

The shipwreck that killed 700 people in April 2015, combined with another major sinking a few days later, marked the beginning of a long summer full of similar tragedies. As the waters of the Mediterranean warmed in the summer months of 2015, more boats started coming. In 2015 the focus was on boats in the so-called central route across the short stretch of sea between North Africa and Italy. As the numbers of people grew, so did the death toll. The rhetoric of Italian government officials in 2015 was very clearly binary, with many of them speaking about the importance of protecting refugees while deporting economic migrants (McMahon and Sigona 2018). For example, in June 2015 Italian prime minister Matteo Renzi said that "asylum seekers should be welcomed, economic migrants should be repatriated" (Kington 2015). The EU-level response identified each person as originating from a "refugee producing country" or not, and processed them accordingly (McMahon and Sigona 2018).

At the end of the summer, on September 2, 2015, the world was shocked by the image of a Syrian toddler named Alan Kurdi, lying dead, facedown on a beach. His family had fled Syria when ISIL attacked their town, and after some time in Turkey, had paid smugglers to take them in a small overcrowded boat across a short stretch of ocean to the Greek island of Kos. Kurdi, along with his brother and mother, drowned when the boat capsized, and he became an "iconic victim" when his image "captured people's attention and generated immediate empathy" (Adler-Nissan, Andersen, and Hansen 2020). The empathy, however, did not translate into a uniform response from European political leaders. Just a few days later, German chancellor Angela Merkel famously stood alone among European heads of state when she pledged that Germany would open its borders to people seeking refuge from Syria without requiring people to file for refugee status in the first EU member state in which they set foot. Breaking from the long-standing Dublin regulation, she declared that "if Europe fails on the question of refugees, its close connection with universal civil rights will be destroyed" (*The Guardian* 2015). With this statement, Merkel linked the protection of refugees to the idea of human rights as an implicitly European value.

Merkel's move sparked criticism from various political leaders. Slovak prime minister Robert Fico declared that "95% of these people are economic migrants" (*The Economist* 2015). Hungarian prime minister Viktor Orban expressed a similar sentiment when he announced that "people now seeking sanctuary in Europe should be seen as immigrants, not as refugees . . . because they are seeking a 'German life' and refuse to stay in the first safe country they reach" (Mackey 2015). In September of 2015, Hungary began to erect a razor-wire fence along its border with Serbia to keep people out. "We are protecting Europe according to European rules," he said (Shields 2015). Here, Orban also invoked the values of Europe in defending a sovereignty-oriented response quite opposite to the one Germany was proposing. The leader of the British far-right UKIP party, Nigel Farage, invoked a binary logic when he said, "If you allow large numbers of people in—like Mrs. Merkel did—what you find is that most people aren't refugees, they're young males, effectively economic migrants." He also noted that Merkel's decision to publicly welcome refugees to Germany was "the biggest foreign policy mistake any Western leader has made since 1945" (Worrall 2017). Criticisms of Merkel were not limited to politicians on the right of the political spectrum. Even the Socialist prime minister of France, Manuel Valls, criticized Merkel's move: "Europe cannot take in all migrants from Syria, Iraq, or Africa . . . It has to regain control over its borders, over its immigration or asylum policies" (quoted in Fassin 2016).

Even though the general sentiment in Europe was not one of welcome in the fall of 2015, the political climate regarding mass arrivals soured significantly in light of the terrorist attacks across Paris on the night of November 13, 2015 (Lyman and Smale 2015). One hundred and thirty people were killed in the attack, which ISIL claimed responsibility for days later. While most of the perpetrators were French citizens, some of them were found to have entered Europe among the throngs of people who had recently been crossing. These events heightened the security framework that had already been part of the discourse around mass arrivals.

By 2016, despite continuing arrivals on the central route, media attention shifted to the eastern Aegean Sea route, as very large numbers of people (mostly Syrians) were crossing from Turkey and arriving on the islands of Greece. In March of 2016, a deal was announced between the EU and Turkey, whereby Turkey agreed to help close off the Aegean route into Europe in exchange for 3 billion euros in financial support for hosting people. The deal was the result of a series of meetings "dedicated to deepening Turkey-EU relations as well as addressing the migration crisis" (European Council 2016). It stipulated that people arriving on Greek islands would be held there and forced to apply for asylum in Greece, rather than be allowed to travel anywhere in Europe. Anyone not able to demonstrate in an initial screening that they had a reasonably founded asylum claim would be deported to Turkey. While Turkey is a signatory to the 1951 Refugee Convention, Turkey is one of the few states to retain the geographic limitation to its ratification, only recognizing people from Europe as refugees (Carpi and Senoguz 2019). The Turkish government has refused to let UNHCR play a major role, instead developing its own government response to the situation (Chatty 2016). The EU-Turkey deal has been criticized as "reminiscent of pre-Convention modes of refugee protection, which understood refugees as a subset of migrants rather than falling under a discrete category of their own" (Mourad and Norman 2019a, 12). The Turkish government, for its part, is aware of the leverage it has gained by hosting so many people who are undesirable in Europe. In order to gain further diplomatic concessions from EU leaders, it has threatened on multiple occasions to cancel the deal and send large numbers of people into Europe (Toksabay 2017).

The EU-Turkey deal did not completely prevent people from using the eastern route into Europe, but it slowed things significantly. Crossings via the central route and the western route into Spain both increased, but to nowhere near 2015–16 numbers. The intensity of that period had waned, but had left a lasting impact on the entire continent. The next section looks back on the role of the media in framing the "crisis" of 2015–16, and particularly the function that the migrant/refugee binary played in that framing.

The Terminology Debate

The academic literature on framing has consistently found that how the media discusses a certain issue, including the particular terminology that is used, has a profound impact on public perception of the issue, and on which aspects of the issue are deemed most salient (Iyengar 1987; Entman 1993; Druckman 2011). Studies have also shown that the mainstream media can play a particularly powerful role in shaping public opinion about minorities, since it is a topic about which majority-group media consumers may not have many other sources of information (Boomgaarden and Vliegenthart 2009; Bleich et al. 2015; Chavez 2013). Further, framing experts have noted that "the selection and use of labels is a crucial and important instrument in the process of framing particular events and individuals" (Lee and Nerghes 2018, 2). Taken together, these studies make clear that the terms used by the media to describe border crossers can shape public attitudes about whether they are deserving of protection, or even sympathy.

The terms "asylum seeker," "refugee," and "migrant" had already been politically loaded and the subject of highly charged political debates in Europe for some time before the mid-2010s (Goodman and Speer 2007). The term "migrant" had been found to have a close association with illegality and criminality in Europe prior to the events of 2015 (Allen and Blinder 2013). Hostility toward immigrants in general had been growing in Europe for well over a decade, linked to the rise of far-right populist parties in multiple European countries (Berry, Garcia-Blanco, and

Moore 2015). However, media watchers have noted that divisive public discourse has crystallized since 2015, and some have argued that the European mainstream media has been complicit in helping to stoke the flames of a moral panic around migration that the far-right in Europe has used to further its nationalist comeback (Matar 2017). An in-depth report produced for the Council of Europe concluded that the European media was generally unprepared for the fast-paced, complex unfolding of the situation in 2015, and reporting was generally not of a high quality (Georgiou and Zaborowski 2017). The report's authors also concluded that the media played a central role in framing these events as a crisis. Two-thirds of all articles during the period "strongly emphasized" the negative consequences of arrivals (9). The authors also found that the people arriving were rarely described on an individual level. The press almost never reported on the names or professions, and did not tend to ask border crossers about their opinions or experiences (9).

Media coverage of the events of 2015–16 has already been the subject of a number of scholarly studies. While these studies reveal that coverage varied both over time and by European member state and news outlet, a consistent theme of these studies is their finding that the term migrant was widely used as a pejorative, whereas the term refugee tended to surface in more sympathetic contexts. For example, Crawley and Skelparis (2018) point out the parallels in binary framing by newspapers across the British political spectrum. The right-of-center tabloid *Daily Mail* ran the headline "The Tragic but Brutal Truth: They Are Not Real Refugees! Despite Drowning Tragedy Thousands of Economic Migrants Are Still Trying to Reach Europe" on May 28, 2016. Eerily similar (though slightly more euphemistic) was the left-of-center *Guardian*'s February 6, 2016 headline: "To Help Real Refugees, Be Firm with Economic Migrants."

A more systematic study of coverage of the crossings in major UK news outlets found that the media began to use the word crisis right after the large-scale boat disasters of April 2015, but that the modifiers accompanying the term varied over time (Goodman, Sirreyeh, and McMahon 2017). The situation was initially referred to as a "Mediterranean migrant crisis," implying some distance from the United Kingdom. By August, newspapers were calling it a "European migrant crisis," bringing it closer to home. By September, the image of Alan Kurdi lying dead on a beach had shaken the world, and the media began calling it a "refugee crisis." The report's authors observed that, "rather than the negative and undeserving category of migrants, there had now been a shift to a much more deserving and morally acceptable category" of refugee (110). After the November 2015 terrorist attacks in Paris, however, the media went back to the phrase "migrant crisis," suggesting that the sympathies aroused by a toddler's death on a beach had been both temporary and contingent (Goodman et al. 2017). Another study of the European media that examined coverage country-by-country found that the Swedish press was the most positive toward refugees and migrants, and the United Kingdom was the most negative and the most polarized by news sources. They also found that Germany and Sweden were most likely to use the word refugee and the UK, Italy, and Spain predominantly used the word migrant (Berry et al. 2015). Thus, positive coverage was associated with the word refugee and more negative coverage associated with the word migrant. Yet another study found that the Hungarian press was most likely to focus on people's economic motivations, and that the Greek press was most sympathetic, giving the people a voice (Georgiou and Zaborowski 2017).

Terminological choices were made quite self-consciously, especially after the summer of 2015, when every major media outlet ended up taking a stand on the terminology they were using. With the notable exception of *Al Jazeera*, every European outlet concluded that "migrant" is a more general umbrella category, and thus, presumably, more politically neutral. For example, in 2015 the *BBC* published an article on its website musing over the various terms used to describe border crossers. The article concluded that while some people found the term migrant to be objectionable "because it implies something voluntary but that it is applied to people fleeing danger," in the end, it is a "neutral blanket term" (Ruz 2015). In contrast, *Al Jazeera* editor Barry Malone wrote a column explaining that paper's editorial choice, saying that the term migrant "has evolved from its dictionary definitions into a tool that dehumanizes and distances, a blunt pejorative." He went on to say that if the media does not take a stand on such matters, "We become the enablers of governments who have political reasons for not calling those drowning in the Mediterranean what the majority of them are: refugees. We give weight to those who want only to see economic migrants" (Malone 2015).

Malone's essay was shared widely on social media and garnered a lot of response. The *Washington Post* wrote a sympathetic reaction piece suggesting that maybe it is time to "ditch the word migrant," much as many news outlets in the United States had abandoned the term "illegal immigrant" in 2013 (Taylor 2015b). A Change.org petition asking the *BBC* to follow *Al Jazeera*'s lead and use the phrase "refugee crisis" instead of "migrant crisis" garnered more than 72,500 signatures in a brief period. In explaining why this issue was important, the petition states:

The term migrant does not properly describe the horror currently unfolding in the Mediterranean. Nor does it properly describe these people's motivation for risking their lives to cross the sea or try to pass under the channel tunnel. It dehumanizes. Only by saying what it really is, a Refugee Crisis, can we have any hope of understanding the issue and finding a real, long-term and humane solution.[2]

It was during this exact period that UNHCR decided to step into the fray, releasing its #wordsmatter campaign and explainer articles focused on the distinctive needs of refugees. For its part, UNHCR recommended that media outlets use the phrase "refugees and migrants" to accurately convey the point that both distinct types of border crossers were included in the mix of people who were arriving in Europe.

Existing studies of media framing and my own analysis of the terminological debates suggest that rhetorical treatment of border crossers in Europe is dominated by binary logic. Further, it seems that there is a big difference among the European public in how they view the deservingness of each group. A study that conducted textual analysis of comments on social media videos about arrivals in Europe found that "the concept of perceived agency is employed to suggest the idea that such labels as 'migrant' and 'immigrant' carry an inherent meaning that these individuals have more freedom of choice and suffer from relatively less duress when deciding to leave their countries" and that "commenters are least sympathetic toward those perceived to have a choice when crossing borders" (Lee and Nerghes 2018, 12).

A large-scale public opinion survey about openness to granting people refugee status found remarkably consistent results across Europeans of all nationalities and backgrounds. Survey respondents clearly articulated their preference for granting asylum to people who had employable skills, who had suffered and were particularly vulnerable, and who were Christian (Bansak, Hainmuller, and Hangartner 2016). The survey revealed a willingness to accept refugees alongside a clear preference for the ability to select, and fear of a mass invasion of poor, economically motivated, and culturally different people. The researchers concluded that "the public has partially internalized the central pillars of international refugee law" but still holds some beliefs that are at odds with it (221). These survey findings also suggest that, to the extent that the binary rhetoric of politicians and the framing of border crossers in the media plays into public concerns about the economic drain of refugees, it could harm support for granting people refugee status. Even when publics are more inclined to feel sympathy for people they believe to be refugees over people they believe to be migrants, the survey results suggest that emphasizing the potential economic contribution of people who are being resettled as refugees softens their attitudes about them. Binary rhetoric often casts migrants as economic actors and refugees as people in need, which could reduce public support for admitting people even within the category for which they feel some sympathy.

Despite their passionate advocacy, appeals such as the Change.org petition, the #wordsmatter campaign, and the *Al Jazeera* position are binary essentialist. They play into the notion that some people truly are refugees while others are merely pretending. As such, they can have the inadvertent effect of perpetuating the dehumanization of the term migrant. By arguing that arriving people are refugees and therefore deserve our compassion, they implicitly suggest that if they had not been refugees, and when they are not refugees, it is less of a tragedy if they suffer or die. As active and robust as the conversation around terminology in Europe has been, these implications of binary rhetoric have not been adequately discussed.

A Tug of War

The European approach to colonialism is a bit like the Barca Nostra installation: it looms large, but the context is narrow and collective memory is short. As a result, the meaning and legacy of European colonialism are left ambiguous. Many of the people coming to Europe today, whether their point of origin is in South Asia, the Middle East, North Africa, or sub-Saharan Africa, have parents or grandparents who lived under European colonial rule. That is why so many of them speak English or French, or maybe Portuguese. In some senses, their arrival is not just about finding safety or opportunity. Even though it is very rarely articulated as such, arrivals from former colonial holdings also signify a reclaiming of a small part of the wealth that their ancestors produced, and in doing so, articulate a shared inheritance to that prosperity. This perspective is not currently part of the European conversation about migration, but remains an unspoken undercurrent. In this sense, De Genova has argued that "the European question is as much about this struggle over the future as it is about accounting for the colonial past and postcolonial present" (2016, 91).

Reading the current politics of exclusion in the EU as a continuation of long-standing uneven power dynamics, rather than simply a recent retreat from European values, is a difficult but important reframing. For example, Mayblin (2017) argues that British attempts to limit the reach of the Refugee Convention in recent years have been portrayed as a "U-turn on commitments made in 1951 which have become the totemic markers of high moral aspirations" (145). She suggests that this version of events obscures the ways in which Britain has historically and systematically excluded "large portions of the world's population from rights and justice" and therefore should be seen as continuing to protect its privilege, not abandoning a record of generosity (146).

Rather than having that difficult reckoning, Europe has pushed forward with protecting the fortress, whatever the costs. Both the Schengen and Dublin systems are in jeopardy, likely to be completely replaced by a new European approach to asylum that is launching in the fall of 2020. The United Kingdom has left the EU, and other member states may well follow suit. European bordering practices now extend well into the continent of Africa, taking on neocolonial dimensions. The EU is currently spending billions of euros on efforts to keep African people from migrating in the first place, without much evidence that this strategy is actually working (Landau 2019). And after spending billions of euros to close Europe's borders to the east, the deal with Turkey rests on very tenuous grounds. Turkey has recently threatened to release the 3.6 million people it hosts into Europe if Europe opposes its operations in Syria (Baboulias 2019). The results of the deal mean that significant numbers of people are now trapped in Greece in a seemingly never-ending limbo, living in poor conditions with few job prospects due to the closing of Greece's northern border (Kuschminder and Koser 2016).

The migrant/refugee binary is a central aspect of European discourse about mass arrivals. Its prevalence allows debates to become a tug-of-war between those who argue that European values support assisting refugees and those who argue that European values require keeping out migrants. A more nuanced continental conversation is not possible until the binary framework is eschewed and the full complexity of the dilemma is exposed.

7

American Public Discourse

IN THE EARLY DAYS of the Trump administration, it quickly became clear that beyond the iconic wall at the US/Mexico border, a more generalized opposition to immigration would be a major theme of the Trump presidency. Once he was inaugurated in 2017, President Donald Trump continued to push for the wall that had been the centerpiece of his campaign, while also issuing two Executive Orders and then an ultimately successful Proclamation banning arrivals of all statuses from a list of predominantly Muslim countries.[1] Next, the Trump administration slashed the annual admissions numbers for resettled refugees to their lowest levels since the passage of the 1980 Refugee Act, called for the end of Temporary Protected Status (TPS) for several national groups, threatened to end the Deferred Action for Childhood Arrivals (DACA) program, and pushed for a comprehensive immigration reform that would reduce the number of immigrants entering the United States overall, particularly in the area of family reunification (so-called "chain migration"), which is the core of the current American immigration system (Weiss 2018; Romo, Stewart, and Naylor 2017; Diamond 2017). In its second and third years, the Trump administration slashed refugee resettlement numbers once again and declared an all-out war against asylum seekers, instituting a series of restrictions that ultimately made it close to impossible for people to receive asylum (Meissner, Hipsman, and Aleinikoff 2018; Wong, Bonilla, and Colemana 2019). It is difficult to conceive of a more anti-immigrant president, at least in modern American history. By consistently expressing hostility to border crossers of all categories, President Trump seems to have broken free from the migrant/refugee binary in many respects.

Concern about this blanket hostility has led some observers to critique it explicitly for the way that it could harm potential refugees. For example, on February 11, 2019, historian Rachel Ida Bluff wrote an op-ed in the *Washington Post* accusing the Trump administration of collapsing a "crucial linguistic distinction" by casting refugees and migrants as "equally threatening and undesirable." She wrote: "To the Trump administration, almost all migrants belong in the 'illegal alien' basket, no matter what their reasons for migrating" (Bluff 2019). As outlined briefly above, there is a lot of evidence to support this assessment of the president. Even while candidate Trump emphasized the need for a wall at the US/Mexico border, suggesting a focus on unauthorized, economically driven migration, it was not always clear that he understood the concept of a refugee, or the ways in which the terms refugee and migrant carry different legal meanings. For example, before he was elected, in November of 2015, he tweeted, "13 Syrian refugees were caught trying to get into the U.S. through the Southern Border. How many made it? WE NEED THE WALL!" (Trump 2015). By ignoring the fact that people entering without authorization would by definition not already have refugee status, and neglecting to acknowledge that it is never illegal to seek asylum, Trump definitely seemed to be tweeting refugees into the "illegal alien" basket with reckless abandon.

Despite the above evidence, in this chapter I explore and ultimately reject the suggestion that the Trump presidency has in fact collapsed the migrant/refugee binary. To do this, I examine the ways in which law operates in society by asking: how does this category of a refugee that has a very specific legal meaning get deployed in public discourse? I analyze the moments in which public figures or media outlets refer to people as refugees or migrants, how they defend or explain such choices, and the assumptions about border crossing that are revealed by the way that they speak. After providing some historical context for understanding current arrivals, I focus on American public discourse about immigrants and refugees since the summer of 2014. During this period, there have been ongoing large-scale direct arrivals at the US/Mexico border as well as significant controversy over the question of refugee resettlement from Syria and other conflict zones. This period includes the end of the Obama years, the 2016 election, and the Trump presidency. By examining rhetoric about people on the move across two presidential administrations that have vastly different reputations on immigration and humanitarianism, and several different "migration emergencies" (Ramji-Nogales 2017a), I can thoroughly explore the durability and persistence of a legal construct ("the refugee") that is made possible by policy ideas and institutions alike.

This fight about who can be labeled a refugee is a long-standing one. It has consistently been shaped by a reluctance on the part of government officials to recognize the United States as a country of first asylum for displaced people in the region, and in particular people arriving at the US/Mexico border. America's southern border has been constructed over the past century as a highly fraught symbol of state territoriality and the site of illegal migrant entry (Ngai 2003). Over a hundred-year period, the US government has steadily increased its presence in the border region, building a massive border control apparatus (Kang 2017). The American media fuels public fears about the threat of a Latinx invasion, the mass arrival of people who do not want to assimilate and therefore need to be kept out at great expense (Chavez 2013). Harrowing evidence that walls and fences and rivers and deserts do not deter people from crossing, that people would rather risk death than stay home, has not yet dissuaded the American public from these beliefs (De Leon 2015). It is thus incompatible with the development of the American state to acknowledge the US/Mexico border as a place of refugee arrivals, because that acknowledgment would undermine narratives about what the border is, and why it looks the way it does.

Previous Controversies

Even though this chapter focuses on the most recent period of controversy, it is important to understand the contemporary moment in its historical context, since this is certainly not the first time that there has been an active discussion of whether the US/Mexico border is a site of mass refugee arrival. Despite semi-regular incidents of large-scale asylum seeking at its borders over the past half century, the United States has consistently failed to recognize itself as a destination for direct refugee movements. Instead, presidential administrations across the political spectrum have cast unwanted arrivals as undocumented economic migrants and devised elaborate deterrence policies to prevent them from accessing the refugee status determination procedures of the United States. This pattern of refusal to acknowledge the United States as a refugee destination can be explained as resistance among many lawmakers and the general public to embrace the concept of international human rights obligations, and this resistance seems to have grown more intense the longer these obligations have been entrenched in American law. However, the resistance also stems from a reluctance to fully grapple with the sordid US history of interventionism and corporate imperialism in Latin America and the Caribbean. Acknowledging that history would spur discussions of the US role in destabilizing the very countries that are sending people northward in large numbers.

With the exception of Cubans fleeing the communist Castro regime during the Cold War, no large-scale direct arrival of asylum seekers to the United States has ever been treated with the presumption that the group of arriving individuals may qualify for refugee protection under international and domestic law. Throughout the 1980s, the Reagan and first Bush administrations demonstrated a consistent pattern of resistance to viewing any non-Cuban direct arrivals as refugees, portraying them instead as economic migrants. The Refugee Act, which established the current statutory regime for seeking asylum in the United States, was passed after much struggle in 1980 (Anker and Posner 1981–82). It codified the UN standard for determining refugee status into US law for the first time, officially creating a refugee status determination system for asylum seekers based on the language of the 1951 UN Refugee Convention (Hamlin and Wolgin 2012). However, despite this official commitment to international legal principles, the process of its implementation revealed a deep systemic resistance to providing a fair process for unwanted asylum seekers, both from Haiti and from the so-called "Northern Triangle" of Central America. Throughout the decade of the 1980s, both the Reagan and Bush administrations exhibited deterrence-oriented responses to spikes in asylum-seeking from those regions. These responses included the reintroduction of the widespread use of immigration detention, a practice that had fallen out of use for decades before the 1980s, but which is now a cornerstone of US immigration policy (Lindskoog 2018). These responses did not succeed in deterring people from attempting to seek asylum in the United States, but did result in widespread human rights abuses and a systematic denial of protection (Hamlin 2012b).

Haitian arrivals served as the first true test of the new legislative standard outlined by the Refugee Act. Their treatment revealed the deep determination of the US government not to recognize people from Haiti as refugees under any circumstances, and the great lengths to which US authorities went in order to cast the Haitians' motivations as economic, not political, in nature (Kahn 2019). In the class action case *Haitian Refugee Center v. Civiletti*, 503 F. Supp. 442 (S.D. Fla. 1980), the Immigration and Naturalization Service (INS) was ordered to stop deporting Haitians until it could develop an "orderly, case-by-case, non-discriminatory, and procedurally fair reprocessing of the plaintiffs' asylum applications." However, the Reagan administration continued to actively deter Haitian arrivals, introducing a Coast Guard interdiction program that turned boats around at sea (Loescher and Scanlan 1986; Lindskoog 2018). Those who made it to the United States had their asylum claims rejected so consistently that their treatment eventually spurred a much larger class action lawsuit that made its way to the Supreme Court in *Jean v. Nelson*, 472 U.S. 846 (1985). The class action brought closer scrutiny to the existing INS process, but was unsuccessful in its larger goal of having the asylum procedures declared unconstitutional (Lindskoog 2018). The federal courts consistently found that Haitian asylum seekers possessed procedural rights to have their cases heard, but protecting those rights did not guarantee a successful asylum claim.

In some ways, events of the 2010s have stood in eerie parallel to the early 1980s, when hundreds of thousands of people from El Salvador, and smaller numbers from Guatemala, Honduras, and Nicaragua, arrived at the border after fleeing violent civil wars or attempting to escape extreme poverty. While there had long been people coming in some numbers from the region, the violence of the 1980s spurred a huge increase in migration from Central America, the majority of whom arrived by crossing through Mexico and into the United States without inspection (Garcia 2006). The United States was implicated in the conditions that led people to flee. Across Central America, repressive regimes were aided by American military funding and training, ostensibly to help them put down leftist insurgencies (Abrego 2018). People from Central America arrived into a new legal landscape created by the passage of the 1980 Refugee Act. However, that landscape was still overshadowed by the anti-communist geopolitics of the time. The Reagan administration, through the mechanism of advisory opinions from the US State Department, consistently rejected the overwhelming majority of asylum claims from Central American countries that were formally US aligned, and publicly portrayed the asylum seekers as economic migrants, not potential refugees. INS spokesperson Duke Austin remarked at the time, "if all they wanted to do is flee violence, they would have stayed in Mexico" rather than continuing northward to the United States (King 1985). This attitude was reflected in acceptance rates that hovered around 2 percent for asylum seekers from US-backed Northern Triangle countries (Zucker and Zucker 1991, 240).

The 1980s was a period of "conflict and disjuncture" for the politics of asylum in the United States (Hamlin 2015a, 8), because the resolute refusal of the Reagan administration to recognize the protection needs of people arriving from Central America was met with staunch opposition and outrage in the advocacy community. The INS "regularly rejected asylum petitions of individuals that UNHCR officials, church workers, and legal counsel commonly regarded and referred to as refugees" (Garcia 2006, 89). Resistance to the mass rejection of Central American asylum claims inspired what became known as the sanctuary movement, which helped an estimated 2,000 people in the early 1980s, and raised public awareness of the situation much more broadly (Garcia 2006, 108). However, the Reagan administration was relentless in refusing to acknowledge that anyone from Central America should qualify for refugee status. The INS brought all of its power to bear on this issue, both through aggressive enforcement and prosecution of sanctuary movement workers, and through forceful legal defense of their exclusionary policies. This effort was expended at a time when asylum applications in the United States were at a low point, less than a third of what they had been in 1980 (Immigration and Naturalization Services 1996).

Government refusal to acknowledge Central Americans as refugees again spurred several class action lawsuits (Coutin 2006). Unlike in the Haitian case, however, legal advocates saw a significant victory in the case of *American Baptist Church v. Thornburgh*, 760 F. Supp. 796 (N.D. Cal. 1991), in which hundreds of thousands of Salvadoran and Guatemalan people were granted new asylum hearings. This ruling resulted in some asylum seekers being granted refugee protection after remaining in limbo for almost a decade. The landmark victory in the so-called *ABC* case illustrates the growing willingness of the judicial branch to hold exclusionary policies in check to some degree, when strong cases are brought by organized advocacy groups.

Similar strategies and debates resurfaced a decade later when President Clinton referred to Cubans arriving in the Gulf of Mexico as "illegal refugees," and defended the right to interdict them at sea rather than fully consider their asylum claims (Hamlin 2012b). In the early 1990s, a new influx of Haitians spurred President Bush to reintroduce and expand the Coast Guard interdiction policy with an Executive Order that called for the return of all boats without any on-board assessment of asylum claims (Bush 1992). President Clinton continued this policy once in office, and its constitutionality was upheld by the Supreme Court in *Sale v. Haitian Centers Council*, 113 S. Ct. 2549 (1993), despite the active intervention of UNHCR, which argued that the policy was in violation of international refugee law (UNHCR 1992). Further, when Congress passed immigration reforms in 1996, it expanded these practices by creating a new Expedited Removal program that screens people via interview at all ports of entry and land borders (INA §235(b)(1)(A)(i); 8 U.S.C. §1225(b)(1)(A)(i)). If no fear is explicitly expressed and their documents are otherwise invalid for entry, the individual is summarily removed. The program survived a legal challenge because the DC circuit court ruled that advocacy organizations lacked standing to file suit on behalf of the asylum seekers who were being removed, and asylum seekers could not sue because they were outside the territory of the United States (*American Immigration Lawyers Association, et al. v. Janet Reno*, Attorney General of the United States, et al., 199 F.3d 1352 [D.C. Cir. 2000]).

In sum, throughout the 1980s and 1990s, presidential administrations from both political parties expressed little desire to comply with international refugee protection standards when responding to large-scale direct arrivals. The legal advocacy community developed its capacity to assert claims on behalf of vulnerable asylum seekers, based both on the statutory commitment to international protection introduced in the 1980 Refugee Act, and on domestic Constitutional protections such as due process and equal protection. These efforts were met with some success in court, but always matched against innovative new deterrence measures introduced through legislation and executive order. This historical context makes clear that the United States has always been extremely reluctant to acknowledge itself as a country of first asylum—that is, a place where people hoping to find refugee protection come directly to file a claim rather than waiting overseas in a camp to be resettled.

Obama's Reaction to Central American Arrivals

In the summer of 2014, after a period of relatively few large-scale direct arrivals, tens of thousands of predominantly women and children from the Northern Triangle began to arrive at the US/Mexico border. These vulnerable people were a living example of the difficulties with classifying the motivations of border crossers into binary categories. Contemporary displacement from Central America is clearly multi-causal, making people arriving from this region difficult to classify into reductive categories such as "forced" or "voluntary," "political" or "economic." Many people are motivated by extreme poverty and the hope of better economic opportunity in the North. However, the region is still suffering from the after-effects of long and violent civil wars and dictatorships, many of which were fueled by aggressive US interventionist policies (Abrego 2018). Government corruption is rampant, and gang violence is widespread. In fact, in many parts of the Northern Triangle, the drug cartels are the most powerful governing body, dominating or controlling local government (Medrano 2017; Martinez 2018). Many people arriving in the United States reported crime victimization as a major motivating factor in their decision to leave their homes (Hiskey et al. 2018). To complicate matters further, Central America has been experiencing a significant increase in extreme weather events caused by climate change. These shifts have led to crop failure and malnutrition, which compounds the economic strife, political corruption, and gang violence (Blitzer 2019a).

Compared to previous large-scale border arrivals, the people crossing beginning in 2014 were disproportionately women with small children, or unaccompanied minors, often preteen or young teenagers. These circumstances led UNHCR to issue special reports on the needs of these populations, called "Children on the Run" and "Women on the Run" (UNHCR USA 2014; UNHCR 2015b). These reports outlined the ways in which drug cartels were threatening children in order to recruit them into gangs, and using sexual violence to terrorize women who were associated by marriage with police or rival gangs.

In addition to the increased complexity of people's home country conditions, the legal landscape into which border crossers arrived in the United States had been complicated by thirty more years of law and politics since the controversies of the 1980s. The anti-communist bias had faded from view as an admissions priority, and the jurisprudence around who could qualify for refugee status when their persecution is at the hands of a nonstate actor, or gender-based, or related to gang violence, had grown more complex. In a fascinating coincidental turn of events, in the fall of 2014, just after the number of arrivals from Central America began to climb, the Board of Immigration Appeals (BIA) issued a decision called *Matter of A-R-C-G* (26 I&N Dec. 388 [BIA 2014]).

In that decision, the BIA ruled that Guatemalan women who are trapped in physically abusive marriages might qualify as a particular social group under the refugee definition. The question of whether domestic violence could be grounds for receiving refugee status had been a matter of major legal uncertainty for many years prior to that ruling. The outcome represented the culmination of tireless legal advocacy by lawyers in the United States, particularly the Center for Gender and Refugee Studies at University of California, Hastings, in San Francisco. While it did not settle the question automatically for any individual asylum seeker, this precedent-setting decision did make it easier for women from Central America to articulate how their situation at home might fit within the refugee definition.

Despite all of these factors that distinguished the new arrivals from the past, the reaction of the Obama administration was strikingly similar to that of previous presidents facing unwanted large-scale arrivals from the Western Hemisphere. That is, both the rhetoric and policy proposals coming out of the White House were focused mainly on deterrence, and cast the arrivals as voluntary migrants whose main vulnerability stemmed from their decision to make a dangerous and fruitless journey (Abrego 2018). President Obama issued a letter calling for "aggressive steps to surge resources to our Southwest border to deter both adults and children from this dangerous journey, increase capacity for enforcement and removal proceedings, and quickly return unlawful migrants to their home countries" (Obama 2014). In the tradition of innovation in deterrence policies, the Obama administration did not just limit its response to increased use of detention and other border enforcement measures. It also introduced a media campaign within Northern Triangle countries designed to discourage people from making the journey by emphasizing its dangers and the unlikelihood of success (Hiskey et al. 2016).

The American news media, including *Al Jazeera*, which had been so adamant about the damaging effects of the word migrant in the European context, predominantly used the word migrant to refer to the unfolding crisis, most frequently as part of the term "child migrant" (Cengel 2015). Soon, however, advocates began to go on record arguing that the people arriving were refugees, not economic migrants. The *National Journal* chastised President Obama for calling the Central American children migrants, asking "Why Won't Obama Call These Kids Refugees?" (*National Journal* 2015). UNHCR also issued a press release asking the US government to "recognize that this is a refugee situation, which implies that they shouldn't be automatically sent to their home countries but rather receive international protection" (Arce 2014). The Center for American Progress think tank in Washington, DC, issued the policy report "They Are Refugees" (Mathema 2016). Two immigration law professors wrote an op-ed for the *Los Angeles Times*, arguing that, while the situation of Syrians was distressing, we should also be paying attention to the "refugee tragedy in our own backyard" (Cooper and Srikantiah 2015). Author Sonia Nazario published an op-ed in the *Sunday New York Times* arguing that "many Americans, myself included, believe in deporting unlawful immigrants, but see a different imperative with refugees" (Nazario 2014). Nazario's piece made explicit what was implied by some of the other advocates: deterrence and deportation measures would be acceptable, even desirable, for migrants but unacceptable for refugees.

Calls by advocates to treat the arrivals as presumed refugees did not seem to influence the US government's response. Instead, Congress made several attempts to remove protections for Central American children that had been in place since the 2008 passage of the Trafficking Victims Protection Reauthorization Act (Wolgin 2016; O'Keefe and Costa 2014). While these rollback measures were ultimately unsuccessful, they received substantial congressional support. Meanwhile, widespread human rights violations occurred as a result of a deterrence-oriented policy response. Most basically, these violations included people being denied entry and returned to home country situations where they were likely to face death or persecution, which is a violation of the Convention Against Torture. Evidence of further human rights failures were extensively documented, including examples of children not being monitored once in the United States and being released to unsafe trafficking situations (Wolgin 2016). In a binary world, the Central American arrivals had been squarely categorized as migrants in the public mind, despite the fact that a small number of them did eventually gain refugee status after being allowed to go through the asylum application process.

Reactions to Central American arrivals revealed the durability of the migrant/refugee binary, which was reaffirmed by the American media a year later, when, in the summer of 2015, there was a surge of arrivals in Europe from Syria and other Middle Eastern and North African countries.

American media coverage differed dramatically from the coverage a year earlier during the first set of Central American arrivals. Rather than portraying the European situation as a tense political controversy, American news outlets produced a flurry of explainer articles in which they attempted to outline the difference between a migrant and a refugee. The tone of these articles was more measured, taking a step back to examine the concepts of migrant and refugee more abstractly, even academically. After some head-scratching about how difficult it is to identify whether people are migrants or refugees when they arrive, literally, in the same boat, these articles all provided the definitions of a migrant and a refugee from international law, and then usually concluded that the arrivals in Europe consisted of some from each category (Jensen 2015; Kent 2015; Martinez and Marquez 2014; Sengupta 2015).

None of these articles challenged the notion that there are two distinct types of migrants that theoretically could be correctly identified through a process of regularized inquiry. Further, none of them drew a connection between the crisis in Europe and the situation at the US/Mexico border. While this type of media coverage is inadequate to the task at hand, it is significant that even this low level of categorical questioning was spurred by events in Europe, not by disputes over how to describe direct arrivals at the US/Mexico border. American public discourse has consistently compartmentalized these two border crossing situations and very rarely, if ever, engaged in any kind of comparison of the parallels between the two.

In the lead-up to the 2016 presidential elections, focus shifted heavily toward the question of how many people displaced by the Syrian war the United States should admit under its refugee resettlement program. This public debate revealed some confusion about the legal meaning of the term. Discussions in American politics about whether or not to admit Syrian refugees seemed to conflate people awaiting resettlement, who had all been officially designated as refugees by UNHCR and who had been thoroughly screened and vetted by the US government, with Syrians arriving *en masse* in Europe, most of whom had not yet received this type of screening and had not been granted official refugee status. This confusion became especially problematic when it was suggested by then–Indiana governor (later to become vice president) Mike Pence that "refugees" had committed the Paris attacks of November 2015, leading to a series of promises by US politicians at every level of government that Syrian refugees would not be admitted (Zezima 2016). Ultimately, thirty governors made public statements saying that they did not want to resettle Syrian refugees in their states (Seipel 2015).

The two political parties in the United States quickly staked out different positions on this issue. Candidate Hillary Clinton stated that she would be open to increasing the numbers of Syrians resettled in the United States, and the Obama administration announced that the US would resettle 110,000 refugees from overseas in fiscal year 2017. In responding to that increase, Republican House Judiciary Committee chairman Bob Goodlatte stopped short of withdrawing support for the notion of refugee resettlement. He stated that "for generations, the United States has been a safe haven for people fleeing persecution. We must remain compassionate toward refugees but we also need to make sure that we use common sense" (Eilperin 2016). This position represented a course-correction away from the momentary frenzy of anti-refugee rhetoric among Republicans. The position of support for the concept of refugees in the abstract, just not these particular ones, was restored. Notably, Goodlatte had also called for an investigation of the increasing numbers of Mexican asylum seekers at the US/Mexico border in 2013. He claimed the investigation was necessary because illegal immigrants were exploiting the American asylum system by making illegitimate claims (Planas 2013). This anxiety about preserving protection opportunities for the real refugees in the face of rampant fraud illustrates the earlier roots of what was to become a powerful theme of the Trump administration's position on refugees.

Trump and the Migrant/Refugee Binary

On April 6, 2019, during an address to the Republican Jewish Convention in Las Vegas, Nevada, US president Donald Trump remarked on the topic of people who file asylum applications at the US/Mexico border. "The asylum program is a scam," he told the crowd. The asylum seekers, according to Trump, are "some of the roughest people you've ever seen, people that look like they should be fighting for the UFC [Ultimate Fighting Championship] . . . They read a little page given by lawyers that are all over the place—you know lawyers, they tell them what to say. You look at this guy, you say, wow, 'that's a tough cookie.'" In a stunningly callous display, President Trump then went on to mock asylum seekers, much as he has mocked the physically disabled in previous public appearances. "'I am very fearful for my life,'" he whined in a high-pitched voice. "'I am very worried that I will be accosted if I am sent back home.'" Then, he dropped his pitch and warned ominously: "No, no. He'll do the accosting" (Trump 2019a).

Trump's remarks highlight the logical consequences of the continuing belief held by many about the US/Mexico border, and the people who try to access the United States by crossing there. Most fundamentally, the belief is that the US/Mexico border is not a place where refugees arrive, and therefore the people who claim to be refugees at the border are lying. There are several logical consequences of the assertion that refugees do not exist at the US/Mexico border. First is the obvious and troubling suggestion that people who present themselves as refugees are frauds, and worse, are the perpetrators rather than the victims of violence. This fear has been a major theme when politicians express concerns about the American asylum system since the 1990s (Hamlin 2015a). The second suggestion is about the role of law in facilitating and perpetuating the fraud. Trump's remarks assert that people who are not deserving can use the law to access the United States by invoking magic words. By this logic, law serves only as a tool to manipulate and cheat the system, which is designed to protect real refugees, who come from somewhere else.

For example, in May of 2019, when Trump declared a national emergency at the southern border, he invoked many of these long-standing tropes. He began with a reminder that the invasion is economically motivated: "Remember, our great country has been the 'piggy bank' from which everybody wants only to TAKE. The difference is that now we are firmly and forcefully standing up for America's interests" (Trump 2019b). The bulk of the remaining statement drew on themes of sovereignty and the rule of law. "Mexico cannot allow hundreds of thousands of people to pour over its land and into our country—violating the sovereign territory of the United States . . . I will not stand by and allow our sovereignty to be eroded, our laws to be trampled, or our borders to be disrespected anymore" (ibid.). In this way, Trump reminds the public that securing the southern border is a matter of the very statehood of the United States.

Refusal to acknowledge the US/Mexico border as a place of asylum has also played out in the way that the Trump administration has presented its reductions in refugee resettlement numbers to the American public each fall. For example, in September 2018, the State Department announced that its refugee resettlement numbers for fiscal year (FY) 2019 would be 30,000, even lower than the 45,000 that had been pledged for FY 2018, and close to the number of refugees resettled annually by the Bush administration in the first few years after September 11, 2001 (Pompeo 2018; Department of State 2015). This was a significant crackdown on refugee admissions, especially given the fact that the administration did not actually meet its resettlement goal for the previous year. The actual number resettled was closer to 25,000, just over half of what had been pledged. However, the State Department's framing used in announcing the numbers was very revealing. Then–secretary of state Mike Pompeo issued a press release that was published as an op-ed in *USA Today*, which began:

I am proud that one of America's greatest qualities is our steadfast generosity and willingness to welcome families who have faced circumstances most of us cannot fathom, including war and ethnic cleansing. Refugees are among the world's most vulnerable people, and America has embraced about 3 million of them since 1980. (Pompeo 2018)

The statement went on to explain that the reduction to 30,000 spots for refugees in FY 2019 was required to offset the extensive cost of processing many hundreds of thousands of asylum cases, and the cost of helping refugees overseas. Pompeo concluded with a reminder that the United States is "the most generous nation in the world" (ibid.). This statement is a subtle reminder that arrivals at the US/Mexico border are not only unjustly claiming refugee status, but by doing so they are diverting resources that could have been used to help a genuine refugee.

In the fall of 2019, the administration announced that the resettlement numbers for fiscal year 2020 would be 18,000, the lowest annual cap in the history of the refugee resettlement program. In the press release accompanying the report to Congress, the State Department again asserted that "the United States is the most compassionate and generous nation in history" and again framed the lowered cap as a necessary step because "the current burdens on the U.S. immigration system must be alleviated before it is again possible to resettle large number of refugees" (Department of State 2019). In addition to parroting the same talking points, in the Presidential Determination announcement, the administration revealed that many of the slots for FY 2020 were being set aside for people who had experienced religious persecution as opposed to any of the other grounds of persecution outlined in the refugee definition (Trump 2019c).

This narrowing of the definition suggests that the Trump administration views religious persecution as the most pressing form of suffering worth protecting, and may be an appeal to the Christian members of Trump's Republican base, who might wish to assist persecuted Christian minorities around the world.

Evidence of this sleight of hand emerges when one tries to pinpoint exactly where the refugees who can come to the United States are waiting. In the aftermath of the first Trump Executive Order restricting Muslim arrivals in January of 2017, CNN identified a clear pattern among people who spoke up in support of the travel ban. All of them emphasized their support for refugees alongside the concerns about dangerous people exploiting the system. As one supporter put it: "We love refugees, but we want only those coming here who love us and want to assimilate into our culture and way of life" (Levenson and Ellis 2017). This kind of public opinion data suggests that Americans do not view Central Americans as refugees and do not believe that Syrians are deserving of protection either. Similar to the findings of public opinion surveys in Europe, the majority of the American public wants to help refugees in the abstract. But it is not clear who they actually have in mind as the truly deserving.

At Trump's first State of the Union Address, he showcased the story of a young man who had defected from North Korea, calling his experience of seeking refuge "a testament to the yearning of every human soul to live in freedom" (Trump 2018). By emphasizing this example, which harkens back to the "exhilic" (Chimni 1998) vision of a refugee that predominated during the Cold War, while simultaneously raising concerns that terrorists are using the refugee program to gain access to the United States, Trump implicitly reinforced the migrant/refugee binary. Such moves suggest that as hostile as he is to most immigration, there are, at least theoretically, people who could be exceptional cases. This Trump strategy highlights one of the troubles with the distinction between migrants and refugees: exclusionary policy-makers and their supporters do not care if they are accused of restricting refugees because they are capitalizing on the notion that genuine refugees are extremely rare—that is, they are dissidents and freedom fighters resisting the oppression of our enemies, or persecuted Christians in majority-Muslim countries. The Cold War roots of binary logic are exposed by this perspective.

Meanwhile, vulnerable people are made far more vulnerable when the US government insists that it is prevented from being generous toward real refugees because it is saddled with the costs of managing an illegitimate invasion. The Trump administration has repeatedly made such claims, even in the face of evidence that undermines the narrative. In 2018 mainstream news outlets such as *Time* magazine published extensive stories about the harrowing ordeals facing Central Americans coming up through Mexico to the American southern border. The *Time* article focused on the violent conditions at home and emphasized that no deterrence policies would stop people from fleeing such conditions. The article was titled: "'There Is No Way We Can Turn Back': Why Thousands of Refugees Will Keep Coming to America despite Trump's Crackdown" (Grillo 2018). The Trump administration has been impervious to these appeals.

Instead, the administration has used legal tools to aggressively push back on interpretations that conceptualize refugees in expansive terms. For example, on June 11, 2018, then–attorney general Jeff Sessions issued his decision in the *Matter of A-B-*, an asylum decision that he had assigned to himself (27 I&N Dec. 247 [A.G. 2018]). The decision began by overturning the four-year-old precedent decision *Matter of A-R-C-G*, which had expanded the legal interpretation of the refugee definition to include victims of domestic violence. The *A-B-* decision goes on to conclude that people seeking refugee status based on persecution at the hands of nonstate or private actors such as gangs or powerful and abusive domestic partners must "show that the government condoned the private actions or at least demonstrated a complete helplessness to protect the victims" (ibid.). This is a much heavier burden of proof than the previous standard, which was that the asylum seeker's home country was "unwilling or unable" to protect them. The opinion goes on to state that generally, "gang violence perpetrated by non-governmental actors will not qualify for asylum" (ibid.). Immigration attorney organizations have asserted that the *Matter of A-B-* decision is plagued by legal and procedural flaws, and have had some success limiting its scope in federal court (*Grace v. Whitaker*, 344 F. Supp. 3d 96 [D.D.C. 2018]). Nevertheless, in the tug-of-war over whether or not Central American asylum seekers should be classified as refugees, this decision represents a staggering legal setback for people making claims based on gang violence and sexual/domestic violence. This attempt fits with a long-standing practice since the 1980s in American legal interpretation of the refugee definition to consistently regard people from Central America as not included within its scope. Such "definitional borders enabled adjudicators to continue to disavow responsibility" for people arriving on foot from states within the Western Hemisphere (Gorman 2017, 8).

In 2019 the Trump administration ramped up its war on asylum at the southern border, unveiling a series of ever more draconian policy proposals. Included in this onslaught was the so-called Migrant Protection Protocols, which require non-Mexican asylum seekers to remain in Mexico for the duration of their asylum process instead of being given access to the territory of the United States while they await their refugee status determination (Wong et al. 2019). Subsequently, there have been several disturbing reports of asylum seekers being kidnapped or murdered by cartels while they wait in Mexico, unable to seek a truly safe haven from the organized crime that many are fleeing in the first place (Fry 2019; Blitzer 2019b). In June 2019 the administration took their asylum deterrence efforts one step further by announcing that no one would be able to seek asylum in the United States if they had traveled through another safe country on the way. This policy would effectively preemptively block claims by people who do not fly directly to the United States to seek asylum. In September 2019 the US Supreme Court allowed this policy to go forward despite ongoing litigation challenging its departure from both domestic and international law (*Barr v. East Bay Sanctuary Covenant*, 588 U.S. ___ 2019). Meanwhile, the Trump administration signed unprecedented bilateral agreements with Guatemala, El Salvador, and Honduras, declaring them to be safe countries where people should file asylum claims instead of continuing on through Mexico to the southern US border. As a result of these agreements, people from El Salvador and Honduras who arrive at the US/Mexico border are being deported to Guatemala to file their asylum claims there (Human Rights Watch 2020). In June 2020 the Trump administration unveiled yet another set of procedures designed to make every aspect of the asylum process more stringent. If finalized, these rules would make asylum in the United States almost impossible for most applicants (Alvarez and Sands 2020; Schrag 2020).

Taken together, these policies represent a total denial of the notion that people with legitimate humanitarian protection needs may be using the southern border as an access point to the American asylum system. The media focus has been almost exclusively on Central American arrivals, who have been conflated in public discourse with Mexicans, who are assumed not to be refugees. This conflation was most overt during a

Fox News segment when it was reported that people were arriving from "three Mexican countries" (Hernandez 2019). The ironic reality is that, due in part to increased Mediterranean patrols and the European-backed crackdown on foreigners in Libya described in chapter 6, the Trump closure of the US/Mexico border coincided with a spike of arrivals from Africa. An unprecedented number of people from Democratic Republic of the Congo, Angola, Eritrea, Somalia, Sudan, and a handful of other countries have been crossing the Atlantic to destinations in South America, and then walking up through Central America to seek asylum in the United States (Sur 2019). Now, groups of African asylum seekers are being trapped at the Guatemala/Mexico border because Mexico is cracking down and will not let them pass through, for fear they will remain permanently in Mexico.

In the summer of 2019, a major battle arose around the question of whether the detention facilities at the southern border could legitimately be called concentration camps. It began with a Tweet from Democratic congresswoman Alexandria Ocasio-Cortez, and turned into a month-long news flurry. Holocaust survivors weighed in on both sides of the issue. Outlets such as the *New York Times, The Atlantic,* and *The Nation* published articles agreeing with the sentiment, and other news organizations as well as the Trump administration vehemently denied the suggestion, arguing that it was offensive to Jewish people. A columnist in the *Washington Post* declared that it was an irresponsible analogy because "no one is being held for political, ideological or religious reasons" (Cohen 2019).

In many senses, the concentration camp controversy of 2019 was a proxy battle over the question of whether the people at the border were refugees: people in danger and deserving of compassion and protection. Writing for the *New Yorker*, Masha Gessen (2019) observed that the fight was not about facts, but "about imagination . . . about how we perceive history, ourselves, and ourselves in history." If the detention centers were concentration camps holding refugees, the United States was committing an egregious human rights atrocity. If, on the other hand, they were simply migrants in detention, the legitimacy of the state was preserved.

While the concentration camp debate was never fully resolved in American public discourse, the Trump administration's war on asylum at the southern border became so extreme in 2019 that UNHCR finally spoke out in criticism. First, in July, UNHCR issued a statement noting that it was "deeply concerned" about the Trump administration's decision to limit asylum claims from people who had passed through a third country on the way to its territory. "We understand that the U.S. asylum system is under significant strain. And we are ready to play a constructive role if needed in helping alleviate this strain . . . This measure is severe and is not the best way forward" (UNHCR 2019c). Then, in November of 2019, UNHCR issued a similar statement expressing concerns about the Trump administration's asylum practices, noting that they are "at variance with international law that could result in the transfer of highly vulnerable individuals to countries where they may face life-threatening dangers" (UNHCR 2019d). These statements stop just short of declaring that people being deterred are refugees, and only strongly imply that the practices are a violation of the bedrock principle of *non-refoulement*. However, they are by far the most forceful statements that UNHCR has issued toward a major donor in many years, perhaps since it weighed in on the case of Haitian interdiction in the 1990s.

Nonbinary Activism

Asylum-seeking patterns around the world consistently support the theory that people prefer the uncertainty of attempting to reach safe haven and the hope of a better life over the certainty of continuing intolerable circumstances (Hamlin 2015b). The history outlined above of ongoing arrivals in the United States in the face of new deterrence policies further supports this claim. Thus, it is safe to assume that unless circumstances on the ground in the Northern Triangle change dramatically, people will continue to attempt the journey to the United States in large numbers going forward, even if their chances of accessing the American asylum process and ultimately gaining refugee status continue to become more limited. In addition, as safe routes into Europe close down, more and more people from Africa will continue to make the incredibly long journey across the Atlantic to South America, and then continue northward through the Darién Gap (an infamously treacherous sixty-six-mile stretch of terrain where Colombia and Panama meet, and where the Pan-American Highway remains incomplete) into Central America. It will probably also not be too long before Venezuelans begin to come north in larger numbers as regional host states become overwhelmed by the growing burden of hosting.

Perhaps the insistence by many advocates and scholars on the importance of perpetuating distinctions between border crossers based on legal categories stems from fear. Many people who care about vulnerable border crossers are afraid that exposing the dilemmas of classification will erode public support for protecting refugees. However, the recent politics of the United States suggest that binary logic does not prevent refugees from being cast as a tiny fraction of the people whom advocates want to protect. As was so painfully the case during the era of 2 percent acceptance rates for Haitians and Central Americans in the 1980s, a finding that someone is not officially a refugee does not eliminate their humanitarian need or the need for advocacy. Advocates run into trouble when the tropes used to defend refugees automatically make those who are viewed as nonrefugees harder to defend, because their defense focuses on the special needs of refugees. Binary rhetoric by advocates runs the risk of suggesting that arrivals at the US/Mexico border are either all refugees who must be granted protection or all economically motivated migrants (or maybe even terrorists) who must be deterred or removed.

By insisting that "these are refugees" or that "we are in violation of international law," advocates are not acknowledging a fundamental disconnect—many members of the public and many members of Congress do not believe these statements to be true. Public rhetoric has pushed a nuanced reality into a binary driven by concern about people with economic or malevolent motives masquerading in refugees' clothing. Exclusionary policy-makers and their supporters do not care when they are accused of restricting refugees because they believe that genuine refugees are extremely rare, and are waiting somewhere else.

Whereas the Obama administration clearly fell back on binary logic to defend border control measures while pronouncing a commitment to refugees, in many ways, Trump is the hard case. Trump truly does not seem to understand how refugees are defined in law, or care about the binary at all. And much of the public does not seem overly troubled by his self-contradictory rhetoric that simultaneously declares Mexico to be safe enough to house all of Central America's asylum seekers and home to the world's deadliest gangs. By treating all border crossers as equally hostile while paying lip service to the idea of refugee protection in the abstract, the logic of the Trump administration is perfectly compatible with the fundamental assumptions that have governed American refugee politics for decades: refugees are rare, they are particularly vulnerable because they are seeking freedom from ideological persecution, and most importantly, they do not arrive directly into the United States in large numbers.

Ironically, the blanket hostility of the Trump administration to all noncitizens has brought refugee and migrant advocates together with a new sense of urgency, and spawned a powerful nonbinary catchphrase: "No Ban, No Wall." In the spirit of that nonbinary activism, advocates for legal protection both within and outside of government may be better served by reframing their arguments in more practical terms. For instance, efforts to factually dispel the twin myths—that people are drawn by generous welfare policies, and that deterrence policies prevent people from leaving home—might be a good use of public relations resources. Advocacy that works to inform the public about the centrality of US involvement in destabilizing Central America might also pay dividends. Similarly, acknowledgment that the US/Mexico border is a location made up of highly multi-causal border crossers, including people crossing for purely economic reasons, for life and death reasons, for nefarious reasons, and everything in between, could be a refreshing change from the tug-of-war arguments about whether or not the people trying to cross "are refugees."

8

Beyond Binary Thinking

AS THE YEAR 2019 came to a close, a consensus seemed to be forming around the idea that the postwar refugee protection regime was either dead or in critical condition. An article in *Foreign Affairs* declared the "End of Asylum." The piece went on to question whether, since liberal states lack the political will to maintain the long-standing commitment to "this foundational principle," "a pillar of the liberal order is collapsing—but does anybody care?" (Nyabola 2019). A few weeks later, two scholars wrote an article in *The Atlantic* magazine entitled, "The World Is Turning Its Back on Refugees" (Mourad and Norman 2019b). Further evidence of this claim was provided when, in January 2020, Texas governor Greg Abbott announced that his state would not be resettling any refugees that year (Kanno-Youngs 2020). Even before the COVID-19 pandemic swept the globe, it seemed to be the case that many powerful actors, especially in the Global North, were abandoning the notion of refugee protection more overtly and aggressively than in previous decades. Fears about COVID-19 only exacerbated this trend. Conditions for displaced people in the world are arguably much worse today than when Hathaway and Neve declared international refugee law to be in crisis in 1997, almost a quarter century ago. As Agamben observed around that time, all of the apparatus that had been designed ostensibly to help refugees had proved "absolutely incapable not only of solving the problem but also of facing it in an adequate manner" (1993, 17). Today, despite living in "an age of rights," and despite the longevity of the Refugee Convention and many other rights declarations, rightlessness is still rampant (Gündoğdo 2015).

The piece in *The Atlantic* places a lot of blame for the current state of affairs on a lack of commitment to the migrant/refugee binary. For example, Mourad and Norman critique the framing of the 2018 UN Global Compact on Refugees, arguing that the document has failed refugees because it appeals to host countries to help refugees by focusing on the economic benefits they bring. The authors argue that this "framing risks eroding the distinctiveness of the refugee category and the protection it ought to entail." They go on to point out that focusing on the economic potential of refugees has failed before, and "ultimately contributed to the Holocaust." The only way forward, they argue, is to reinvest in the commitment outlined in the 1951 Refugee Convention to the idea "that the term *refugees* has a meaning distinct from the broader category of *migrants*" (emphasis in original).

This book has pushed strenuously against such binary advocacy positions. Instead, I have argued that the migrant/refugee binary is a legal fiction of the type that Fuller contended is dangerous unless it is used "with a complete consciousness of its falsity" (1967, 10). I have argued that the binary is a legal fiction because everything we know about people who decide to move suggests that their motivations and lived experiences are far more complicated than any binary, or even a continuum, can fully encompass. For vulnerable people, the decision to leave home is almost always multi-causal, highly complex, and often involves many stops and hazards along the way. In order to raise consciousness about the fictive nature of this distinction, this book has worked to systematically undermine the three main assumptions that prop up binary logic: that there are two distinct and distinguishable motivations for crossing borders, that refugees are the neediest among the world's border crossers, and that true refugees are rare.

Instead of two distinct groups—vulnerable, needy, yet rare refugees and masses of less vulnerable, less needy migrants—I have worked to show that there are very large numbers of people who deserve compassion and assistance, and that it can be confoundingly difficult to work out which ones should get priority. The legal categories that we use to identify them are not neutral and apolitical. Instead, they often work to help powerful states maintain their sovereignty by justifying deterrence measures, which can harm and even kill border crossers of all types. At the very least, the binary is openly used to justify restrictions on the mobility of people from less powerful states, often in the Global South, to wealthier states, usually in the Global North, with little regard for their level of need. It allows powerful states to sidestep the most difficult political discussions about the ethics of border control by suggesting that border control is just, so long as it makes some rare exceptions for refugees.

This book has shown the ways in which language used to describe border crossers takes on tremendous political importance. People have very strong associations with the terms "migrant" and "refugee," sometimes giving them sociological meanings that do not match their legal definitions. Many people, especially practitioners of immigration law, recognize the migrant/refugee binary as a necessary legal fiction. However, the fiction has been reified and is used in a more essentialist way by people who are outside the field of legal practice, such as politicians and advocates and scholars. So, to move beyond binary thinking, a reframe is needed.

Some readers may be left wondering if I believe people should stop using the words refugee and migrant, and whether I think that people can ever be distinguished as refugees in a way that is not dehumanizing to other border crossers. My goal is not to police the language of other scholars, but rather to inspire us to be more thoughtful about the ways in which we describe people. Ironically, I agree with a key aspect of the UNHCR campaign which declared that "words matter." That is, I believe that when we refer to some people as refugees who have not yet been given any particular legal status, we do so in order to distinguish them as uniquely deserving. Conversely, I believe that when we describe border crossers as migrants, we inevitably suggest that they are less deserving. Ultimately, I believe that it is exceedingly difficult to distinguish refugees as a uniquely deserving group without discrediting the deservingness of other border crossers. That is the work that binaries do. The concept of "mixed flows," which has come into fashion in recent years, is appealing in some ways, but only when used carefully and with clarity. Too often, when scholars, advocates, or policy-makers use this phrase, they use it in the way that UNHCR does: to mean that refugees and migrants are traveling together and need to be sorted, not that the motivations of individual people can be mixed. One way of speaking about mixed flows is binary essentialist, and another way is more nuanced. So, I kindly ask my fellow scholars: If you decide to refer to people without refugee status as refugees in your work, at least add a note explaining that you are doing so for reasons of rhetorical impact, in order to draw attention to a group whom you believe should be recognized as vulnerable and needy. More generally, when speaking and writing about border crossing, ask yourself if your language is falling into binary essentialist traps unnecessarily.

When it is used by states, binary essentialism can become a very dangerous game. It can be manipulated to suggest that few people are truly refugees and the rest are arriving under false pretenses either for economic gain at the expense of a state's citizens or for more devious purposes. Language that suggests most border crossers are migrants posing as refugees allows cruelty to takes place within a framework that pays lip service to protecting refugees. In other words, what makes people "not care" about "the end of asylum" (in the words of the *Foreign Affairs* article) is that they do not actually believe it is ending. Instead, they believe that politicians are simply intent on putting an end to fraud and abuse in order to save room for the imagined "real refugees" coming from somewhere else. It is almost refreshing under those circumstances to hear someone like the Texas governor admit outright that he does not care about refugees, rather than professing a belief in a commitment that he has no intention of fulfilling.

Among all the displacement situations I have examined in the book—Syrians in the Middle East, Venezuelans in Latin America, Africans and others in Europe, and Central Americans and others at the US/Mexico border—one major theme persists: insisting that people are refugees does not seem to make receiving states more open to receiving them. As fervent as the insistence may be, and as compelling the evidence that advocates may have to support the claim, making this claim has not consistently convinced the Lebanese or Jordanian or Colombian or Peruvian or American or European governments to be more willing to host or help people. These types of arguments have worked in the past, but states have turned the tables, and now use the same frames to consistently keep people out.

While this book has not discussed the plight of the persecuted Muslim minority group, the Rohingya, who are being targeted and driven out of their home state of Myanmar by Buddhist nationalists, a similar pattern emerges. Some advocates have critiqued the neighboring states of Southeast Asia that host displaced Rohingya people for not signing onto the UN Refugee Convention and Protocol, and for not referring to them as refugees. For example, Kneebone (2105) wrote that, "ironically, the Rohingya people issue has become a crisis for the very reason that it has not been tackled; namely the labeling of the Rohingya as 'irregular migrants,'

which allows them to be seen solely as victims of smuggling and trafficking rather than of state persecution." This point is a good one: the
label "irregular migrant" seems almost designed to proclaim the "non-
refugeeness" of the arrivals.

Yet, despite the refusal of states such as Thailand, Malaysia, and Indonesia to accede to the Convention and Protocol, and despite their reluctance to refer to the Rohingya as refugees, they host an awful lot of displaced people. Historically, these states have accepted millions of people
into their territories, particularly in the period during and after the Vietnam War. They generally seem to operate under the assumption that the
norm of *non-refoulement* applies to them and that it limits their ability
to restrict entry (Moretti 2018). These days, especially as Australia has
cracked down in draconian ways on maritime arrivals and has stopped resettling refugees directly from Indonesia, Indonesia's position has shifted
from a transit state to a longer-term host, picking up the slack left by Australia's refusal of compassion (McNevin and Missbach 2018; Prabandari
and Dinarto 2016). As Moretti has recently argued, Southeast Asian host
states are de facto protecting people, but do not call them refugees in order to preserve the "fiction" of sovereignty (2018, 5). Meanwhile, Australia's efforts to keep people who might claim refugee status off of their territory, also in the name of sovereignty, have become notorious in some
circles, and a model for deterrence and exclusion for many other powerful
destination states (Pearson 2019).

Uneven sovereignties cause some governments to be chastised, shamed,
or implicitly cast as inhumane or backwards or uncivilized for not em-
bracing people who arrive at their doorstep at any cost. When the EU or
the United States or Australia spend billions to avoid being confronted
with a much smaller number of people, there are no equivalent condem-
nations. This reputational politics too often does not acknowledge that
the current system places heavy burdens on countries that did not partic-
ipate in the actions that created the displacement, and places no obligations on countries that did. The 1951 Convention's silence on this matter
has led to a "troubling deficit of distributive justice" (Coen 2017, 73). Generally speaking, states with the capacity to forcibly keep people out do so.
Funds that could be used to assist vulnerable people, or to help strengthen
the capacity of host states, have been diverted to pay for elaborate exclusion projects and technologies. These tactics of exclusion make vulnerable
people in transit more vulnerable.

On one level then, this exploration of the migrant/refugee binary has exposed the fruitlessness of trying to morally justify harsh border control measures. As Carens famously noted in the opening line of his case for open borders: "Borders have guards and the guards have guns" (1987, 251). Guards and guns and walls and wire and waves cannot tell if a person is a refugee or a migrant. It is not even clear that courts are well suited to the task. But politicians and publics cling to the idea that people are distinct and distinguishable as a shorthand way to avoid making the most difficult decisions. The binary serves to assure us that "real refugees" rise to the top of draconian sorting processes, leaving the undeserving migrants below. In this way, the migrant/refugee binary helps make some lives ungrievable by absolving us of the obligation to grieve them. As Butler put it: "An ungrievable life is one that cannot be mourned because it has never lived, that is, it has never counted as a life at all" (2016, 38). Admitting that the migrant/refugee binary is a legal fiction is akin to admitting that it is all but impossible to distinguish between those whose deaths are grievable and those whose deaths are not. In other words, moving beyond the binary forces us to admit more squarely that borders do violent work and that none of the violence is easily justified.

The current climate is admittedly grim. But I hope this book has helped convince you that insisting on the migrant/refugee binary will not fix the mess we are in. Instead, I believe we must move beyond binary thinking. Ironically, Arendt is an ally in this undertaking because her use of the word refugee was not based in a binary logic. Arendt spoke about refugees because she was reluctantly identified as one. Despite her use of this term, ultimately what she cared about was the link between citizenship and rights, and the ways in which citizenship is deployed to suppress or remove rights. Arendt's experience of displacement made her keenly aware of the sinister side to the connection between people who must ask for protection and the state power that decides whether to grant it. Ultimately, the state is always free to say no. She argued that refugees "represent the vanguard of their peoples" because they expose the ways in which states can show callous disregard for those too vulnerable to fight back (1943, 119). But more than refugees per se, she cared about the rightless. Her arguments can thus be logically extended to other noncitizens whose border crossing experiences lead to rights deprivation, and even to nominal citizens whose rights have been similarly violated by the states of which they are members.

A move beyond binary thinking inevitably begs the question of whether a just border control policy is possible, or whether it is inherently unjust to invoke uneven sovereignties to protect privilege. I believe that a full accounting of the work that the migrant/refugee binary has done over time would call into question the legitimacy of exclusionary border control practices. Binary logic has worked to obscure the degree to which, rather than standing on opposite sides of sovereign borders, "Third and First World peoples are de facto co-sovereigns of neocolonial empire" (Achiume 2019, 1547). I agree with Achiume that Europe's colonial legacy has created "African entitlements to European nation-state admission and inclusion," and also believe that parallel entitlements exist in the Americas (2019, 1521). Song (2009) has argued that in an ideal world, all people who have been subject to the coercive power of a state should have voting rights, regardless of citizenship status. Perhaps more than voting rights, they should also have territorial access.

A reframe beyond binary thinking would also involve having difficult national conversations in which the peoples of popular destination states conduct an honest accounting of responsibility for displacement. There has been surprisingly little scholarly theorizing about the ways in which "capability and culpability" should be considered in conversations about state responses (Coen 2017, 76). Part of the explanation for this lack of attention is that this type of reframe requires us to do what Chimni articulated long ago: consider external causes of displacement, and not just treat it as a function of internal sending-state dysfunction (Souter 2014). Souter further argued that based on externalist logics, asylum should be seen as one form of reparation for past injustice. Drawing on this idea, Coen (2017) has explicitly argued that the United States is culpable for creating displacement crises in the Middle East through military intervention, and should be capable of doing much more to assist with the consequences of these actions. She acknowledges that while culpability arguments can be fraught and complex, they are worth trying, since capability arguments alone have failed. She advocates trying to link culpability arguments to national interests related to security and legitimacy. Similarly, Kritzman-Amir (2009) has pointed out that while it is a complex issue, there are a wide variety of responsibility-sharing formulas that could be implemented fairly easily from a logistical and technical standpoint, if the will to collaborate were there among potential host states.

These works mentioned above begin with the premise that culpability and responsibility should be factors to consider when states are weighing how to protect people who are already considered to be refugees. But the arguments can be broadened. Why should it matter whether a person is a refugee or a migrant when they left home because it was destabilized by a military intervention, or an economic exploitation, or the outside support of a dictator? The links between colonialism, neocolonial interventionism, and instability and poverty in many parts of the world are egregiously underacknowledged in discussions of migration. The migrant/refugee binary has often been enacted to obscure these types of global power dynamics, and reinforce ideas about suffering, deservingness, and protection that perpetuate such dynamics. For example, Coen notes that in the cases of Vietnam and Kosovo, culpability arguments did shape US policy, but that it has been all but impossible to persuade the United States to acknowledge its responsibility in its own backyard, such as its support for the repressive Duvalier regimes in Haiti. Moving past binary rhetoric would only strengthen culpability arguments, by freeing them from the need to classify people as refugees before considering whether an obligation exists.

Discussions of the legitimacy of borders, and assigning culpability for displacement, may feel to some like little more than abstract, ideal theorizing. But more practical moves beyond binary thinking are also possible. Most basically, from an advocacy standpoint, the reframe should involve an active commitment to using nonbinary language to assert "new rights claims" that "inaugurate radically novel understandings of equality and freedom" (Gündoğdu 2015, 180). Talking about border crossers simply as people is one powerful option. Nonbinary slogans such as "No Ban, No Wall" or "All Are Welcome" are significant because they reinforce the notion that what is possible can be expanded. New rights claims, new frames, and new conceptions are animated and made more possible by the practice of repetition, which eventually serves to normalize them.

Finally, and perhaps reassuringly for some, a nonbinary reframe does not have to involve abandoning the concept of refugee protection, or writing a new Convention. Many people legitimately fear opening the Pandora's box of revisiting the 1951 Convention, aware that in the current political moment, there may be nowhere near the widespread support for making an exception to the rule of sovereignty as there was in

1951. As I mentioned in the opening chapter, some people view talk of a new Convention as akin to suggesting a new Constitutional Convention in the United States. While I do not think we have to get rid of the Refugee Convention, even though its definition is a relic of a bygone Cold War era, I do believe such a comparison to the US Constitution is not as apt as some might think. The Refugee Convention is not *the* Constitution. It is one instrument and should not be the only tool for helping people. The assumption that there can be only one definition of a refugee has led to a Eurocentric definition being foisted onto the world, along with its essentialist rhetoric that casts suspicion on the claims of those who do not neatly fit within it. Regional definitions such as the ones that exist in Africa and Latin America have been downplayed and sidelined, but have great potential. There is also great potential in other instruments of protection, and in the concept of *non-refoulement*, which is embedded in customary law and at least theoretically protects a much larger swath of people. As always, someone with power still has to decide if the person is worthy of protection. However, I sincerely believe that a move beyond binary thinking can create new protection possibilities.

Notes

Chapter 1: The Migrant/Refugee Binary

1. The International Organization for Migration's Missing Migrant Project has compiled a record of 33,686 verifiable deaths and disappearances globally in the six-year period between 2014 and 2019. The majority of those deaths occurred as people tried to cross the Mediterranean Sea, although the Sahara and Sonoran deserts are also deadly places. https://missingmigrants.iom.int/ (last accessed June 25, 2020).

2. The list of parties to the 1951 Refugee Convention and 1967 Protocol can be found here: www.unhcr.org/en-us/protection/basic/3b73b0d63/states-parties-1951-convention-its-1967-protocol.html (last accessed June 25, 2020).

3. The Pew Research Center study can be found here: www.pewresearch.org/fact-tank/2019/08/09/people-around-the-world-express-more-support-for-taking-in-refugees-than-immigrants/ (last accessed June 25, 2020).

4. UMass Module, Cooperative Congressional Election Survey, pre-election survey (September–October). N = 1000 for the module, sampling conducted by YouGov's "matched random sample" methodology. For additional details on this survey, see Schaffner, Ansolabehere, and Luks 2019. A special thank you to my colleague Scott Blinder for helping me with question wording and data analysis.

5. The Global North/South binary is another oversimplification that is fraught in its own particular ways, and is equally vulnerable to critiques of "binary essentialism" (Go 2016, 12). While that binary is not the focus of this book, I discuss the choice to use this terminology, and its pitfalls, in much more detail in chapter 5.

6. Donald Trump, Twitter, February 11, 2017, 7:12 a.m., https://twitter.com/realdonaldtrump/status/830389130311921667.

7. International Organization for Migration, "Who Is a Migrant?" www.iom.int/who-is-a-migrant (last accessed June 25, 2020).

8. This line comes from the 1903 poem by Emma Lazarus entitled "The New Colossus."

9. UN Population Division, "International Migrant Stock 2019" (2019), www.un.org /en/development/desa/population/migration/data/estimates2/estimates19.asp (last accessed June 25, 2020).

Chapter 2: Uneven Sovereignties

1. One notable exception is Lucy Mayblin's 2017 book, *Asylum after Empire*.

2. See, for example, *Johnson & Graham's Lessee v. McIntosh*, 21 U.S. 543, 1823.

Chapter 3: Academic Study

1. Oxford University, Refugee Studies Centre, "About Us," www.rsc.ox.ac.uk/about (last accessed June 25, 2020).

Chapter 4: The United Nations High Commissioner for Refugees

1. UNHCR does not keep an archive of every tweet it issues due to the sheer volume of material produced. Rather, UNHCR archivists have been collecting a sample of tweets that are curated to capture a broad range of issues and accounts. The dataset I created by following @Refugees in real time for four years is the only existing full collection of official UNHCR tweets on the topic of the migrant/refugee binary. I elected to present a representative sample of these tweets instead of a more exhaustive presentation of the data, as many of these tweets are highly repetitive, making the same point again and again.

2. UNHCR, "History of UNHCR," www.unhcr.org/en-us/history-of-unhcr.html (last accessed June 26, 2020).

3. UNHCR 2018 Global Funding Overview, http://reporting.unhcr.org/financial #tabs-financial-contributions (last accessed June 26, 2020).

4. Climate change and disaster displacements, www.unhcr.org/en-us/climate-change -and-disasters.html (last accessed June 26, 2020).

5. www.youtube.com/watch?v=SCYmz1fXOiU (last accessed June 26, 2020).

Chapter 5: The Global South

1. UNHCR's Syria fundraising page, www.unhcr.org/ph/campaigns/syria-crisis-8 -years (last accessed June 26, 2020).

2. UNHCR's statistical data on Syrian refugees, https://data2.unhcr.org/en/sit uations/syria#_ga=2.89985176.2072466359.1578506711–1077093284.1570807173 (last accessed June 26, 2020).

3. UNHCR's page on the "Syria Emergency," www.unhcr.org/en-us/syria-emergency .html (last accessed June 26, 2020).

4. The UN's announcement about the campaign to assist people displaced by the Syrian Civil War can be found at https://news.un.org/en/story/2013/06/441682-un-announces -largest-ever-humanitarian-appeal-conflict-torn-syria (last accessed June 26, 2020).

5. The Regional Interagency Coordination Platform for Venezuela, https://r4v.info /en/situations/platform (last accessed June 27, 2020).

6. UNHCR's statement about the Venezuela situation, www.unhcr.org/en-us/news /briefing/2019/5/5ce3bb734/majority-fleeing-venezuela-need-refugee-protection-unhcr .html (last accessed June 27, 2020).

7. Information about this UNHCR/IOM collaboration can be found at https://r4v .info/es/documents/download/73277 (last accessed June 26, 2020).

Chapter 6: Arrivals in Europe

1. UNHCR's statistics on Mediterranean land and sea arrivals, https://data2.unhcr .org/en/situations/mediterranean (last accessed June 29, 2020).

2. The Change.org petition, www.change.org/p/request-bbc-use-the-correct-term -refugee-crisis-instead-of-migrant-crisis (last accessed June 29, 2020).

Chapter 7: American Public Discourse

1. Information about the Presidential Proclamations can be found here: https:// travel.state.gov/content/travel/en/us-visas/visa-information-resources/presidential -proclamation-archive/june_26_supreme_court_decision_on_presidential_proclama tion9645.html (last accessed June 29 2020).

References

Abdelaaty, Lamis. 2021. *Discrimination and Delegation: Explaining State Responses to Refugees*. New York: Oxford University Press.

Abrego, Leisy J. 2018. "Central American Refugees Reveal the Crisis of the State." In *The Oxford Handbook of Migration Crises*, edited by Cecilia Menjívar, Marie Ruiz, and Immanuel Ness, 213–38. Oxford: Oxford University Press.

Achiume, E. Tendayi. 2015. "Syria, Cost-Sharing, and the Responsibility to Protect Refugees." *Minnesota Law Review* 100: 688–89.

Achiume, E. Tendayi. 2019. "Migration as Decolonization." *Stanford Law Review* 71: 1509–74.

Adamson, Fiona B., and Gerasimos Tsourapas. 2019. "The Migration State in the Global South: Nationalizing, Developmental, and Neoliberal Models of Migration Management." *International Migration Review* 20: 1–30.

Adelman, Howard. 2001. "From Refugees to Forced Migration: The UNHCR and Human Security." *International Migration Review* 35(1): 7–32.

Adelman, Howard, and Susan McGrath. 2007. "To Date or To Marry: That Is the Question." *Journal of Refugee Studies* 20(3): 376–80.

Adler-Nissan, Rebecca, Katherine Emilie Andersen, and Lene Hansen. 2020. "Images, Emotion, and International Politics: The Death of Alan Kurdi." *Review of International Studies* 46(1): 75–95.

Agamben, Giorgio. 1993. "Means without End: Notes on Politics." English translation in *Theory Out of Bounds*, vol. 20. Minneapolis: University of Minnesota Press, 2000.

Agamben, Giorgio. 1995. *Homo Sacer: Sovereign Power and Bare Life*. Stanford, CA: Stanford University Press.

Akram, Susan. 2014. "UNRWA and Palestinian Refugees." In *The Oxford Handbook of Refugee and Forced Migration Studies*, edited by Elena Fiddian-Qasmiyeh, Gil Loescher, Katy Long, and Nando Signona, 227–40. Oxford: Oxford University Press.

Allen, William, and Scott Blinder. 2013. "Migration in the News: Portrayals of Immigrants, Migrants, Asylum Seekers and Refugees in National British Newspapers, 2010 to 2012." Migration Observatory, University of Oxford, UK.

Alvarez, Priscilla, and Geneva Sands. 2020. "Trump Administration Proposes Sweeping Changes to US Asylum System in New Rule." *CNN*, June 10. www.cnn .com/2020/06/10/politics/us-asylum-draft-rule/index.html

Amnesty International. 2019. "Syria 2019." www.amnesty.org/en/countries/middle-east -and-north-africa/syria/report-syria/

Anderson, Benedict. 1983. *Imagined Communities: Reflections on the Origins and Spread of Nationalism*. New York: Verso Books.

Andersson, Ruben. 2016. "Europe's Failed 'Fight' against Irregular Migration: Ethnographic Notes on a Counterproductive Industry." *Journal of Ethnic and Migration Studies* 42(7): 1055–75.

Andreas, Peter. 2010. "The Politics of Measuring Illicit Flows and Policy Effectiveness." In *Sex, Drugs, and Body Counts: The Politics of Numbers in Global Crime and Conflict*, edited by Peter Andreas and Kelly M. Greenhill, 23–45. Ithaca, NY: Cornell University Press.

Anghie, Antony. 2004. *Imperialism, Sovereignty, and the Making of International Law*. Cambridge: Cambridge University Press.

Anghie, Antony, and B. S. Chimni. 2003. "Third World Approaches to International Law and Individual Responsibility in Internal Conflicts." *Chinese Journal of International Law* 2(1): 77–103.

Anker, Deborah E., and Michael H. Posner. 1981/1982. "The Forty-Year Crisis: A Legislative History of the Refugee Act of 1980." *San Diego Law Review* 19(9): 9–89.

Anzaldua, Gloria. 1987. *Borderlands / La Frontera*. San Francisco: Aunt Lute Books.

Arar, Rawan. 2017. "The New Grand Compromise: How Syrian Refugees Changed the Stakes in the Global Refugee Assistance Regime." *Middle East Law and Governance* 9: 298–312.

Arboleda, Eduardo. 1991. "Refugee Definition in Africa and Latin America: The Lessons of Pragmatism." *International Journal of Refugee Law* 3(2): 185–207.

Arce, Alberto. 2014. "UN Pushes for Migrants to Be Called Refugees." *Associated Press*, August 7. https://apnews.com/6970d68e6f7942368c00b2290134bofb

Arendt, Hannah. 1943. "We Refugees." *Menorah Journal* 1: 77.

Arendt, Hannah. 1951. *The Origins of Totalitarianism*. New York: Harcourt, Brace.

Baboulias, Yiannis. 2019. "The Next Syrian Refugee Crisis Will Break Europe's Back." *Foreign Policy*, October 24. https://foreignpolicy.com/2019/10/24/syrian-refugee-crisis -europe-greece-turkey-balkans/

Bahar, Dany. 2018. "Latin American Is Facing a Refugee Crisis: Why It Matters That We Call Fleeing Venezuelans Refugees, Not Migrants." *Foreign Affairs*, October 23. www .foreignaffairs.com/articles/venezuela/2018-10-23/latin-america-facing-refugee-crisis

Bahar, Dany, and Meagan Dooley. 2019. "Venezuela Refugee Crisis to Become the Largest and Most Underfunded in Modern History." Brookings Institute Report, December 9. Washington, DC.

Bakewell, Oliver. 2008. "Research beyond the Categories: The Importance of Policy Irrelevant Research into Forced Migration." *Journal of Refugee Studies* 21(4): 432–53.

Banner, Stuart. 2005. "Why Terra Nullius? Anthropology and Property Law in Early Australia." *Law and History Review* 23(1): 95–131.

Bansak, Kirk, Jens Hainmuller, and Dominik Hangartner. 2016. "How Economic, Humanitarian, and Religious Concerns Shape European Attitudes towards Asylum Seekers." *Science* 354: 217–21.

Barnett, Michael. 2001. "Humanitarianism with a Sovereign Face: UNHCR in the Global Undertow." *International Migration Review* 35(1): 244–77.

Barnett, Michael N., and Martha Finnemore. 1999. "The Politics, Power, and Pathologies of International Organizations." *International Organization* 53(4): 699–732.

Barnett, Michael, and Martha Finnemore. 2004. *Rules for the World: International Organizations in Global Politics*. Ithaca, NY: Cornell University Press.

Bauer, Kelly. 2019. "Extending and Restricting the Right to Regularization: Lessons from South America." *Journal of Ethnic and Migration Studies* 20: 1–18.

BenEzer, Gadi, and Roger Zetter. 2015. "Searching for Directions: Conceptual and Methodological Challenges in Researching Refugee Journeys." *Journal of Refugee Studies* 28(3): 297–318.

Benhabib, Seyla. 2004. "The Law of Peoples, Distributive Justice and Migration." *Fordham Law Review* 72(5): 1761–88.

Berry, Mike, Inaki Garcia-Blanco, and Kerry Moore. 2015. "Press Coverage of the Refugee and Migrant Crisis in the EU: A Content Analysis of Five European Countries." Report prepared for the United Nations High Commissioner for Refugees, Cardiff School of Journalism, Media and Cultural Studies.

Betts, Alexander. 2009. *Forced Migration and Global Politics*. Sussex, UK: Wiley-Blackwell.

Betts, Alexander. 2010. "Survival Migration: A New Protection Framework." *Global Governance* 16: 361–82.

Betts, Alexander. 2013. *Survival Migration: Failed Governance and the Crisis of Displacement*. Ithaca, NY: Cornell University Press.

Betts, Alexander. 2019. "Nowhere to Go: How Governments in the Americas Are Bungling the Migration Crisis." *Foreign Affairs* (November/December): 122–33.

Betts, Alexander, and Gil Loescher. 2010. *Refugees in International Relations*. Oxford: Oxford University Press.

Betts, Alexander, and Paul Collier. 2017. *Refuge: Rethinking Refugee Policy in a Changing World*. Oxford: Oxford University Press.

Betts, Alexander, Ali Ali, and Fulda Memisoglu. 2017. "Local Politics and the Syrian Refugee Crisis: Exploring Responses in Turkey, Lebanon, and Jordan." Refugee Policy Centre, Oxford University, Oxford, UK.

Bhambra, Gurminder K. 2017. "The Current Crisis of Europe: Refugees, Colonialism, and the Limits of Cosmopolitanism." *European Law Journal* 23(5): 395–405.

Black, Richard. 2001. "Fifty Years of Refugee Studies: From Theory to Policy." *International Migration Review* 35(1): 57–78.

Bleich, Erik, Hannah Stonebraker, Hasher Nisar, and Rana Abdelhamid. 2015. "Media Portrayals of Minorities: Muslims in British Newspaper Headlines, 2001–2012." *Journal of Ethnic and Migration Studies* 41(6): 942–62.

Blitzer, Jonathan. 2019a. "How Climate Change Is Fueling the U.S. Border Crisis." *New Yorker Magazine,* April 3.

Blitzer, Jonathan. 2019b. "How the U.S. Asylum System Is Keeping Migrants at Risk in Mexico." *New Yorker Magazine,* October 1.

Blouin, Cecile, and Emily Button. 2018. "Addressing Overlapping Migratory Categories within New Patterns of Mobility in Peru." *Anti-Trafficking Review* 11: 69–84.

Bluff, Rachel Ida. 2019. "How President Trump Is Dismantling the World's Refugee Regime." *Washington Post,* February 11. www.washingtonpost.com/outlook/2019/02/11 /why-president-trump-has-won-immigration-standoff-even-if-he-doesnt-get-wall -funding/

Bon Tempo, Carl J. 2008. *Americans at the Gate: The United States and Refugees during the Cold War.* Princeton, NJ: Princeton University Press.

Boomgaarden, Hajo G., and Rens Vliegenthart. 2009. "How News Content Influences Antiimmigration Attitudes: Germany, 1993–2005." *European Journal of Political Research* 48(4): 516–42.

Brigden, Noelle Kateri. 2018. *The Migrant Passage, Clandestine Journeys from Central America.* Ithaca, NY: Cornell University Press.

Broome, André, and Leonard Seabrooke. 2012. "Seeing Like an International Organisation." *New Political Economy* 17(1): 1–16.

Bunce, Mel. 2019. "Humanitarian Communication in a Post-Truth World." *Journal of Humanitarian Affairs* 1(1): 49–55.

Bush, George H. W. 1992. "Executive Order No. 12,807: Interdiction of Illegal Aliens, May 24." 3 C.F.R. 1992 Comp., pp. 303–4.

Butler, Judith. 1990. *Gender Trouble: Feminism and the Subversion of Identity.* London: Routledge.

Butler, Judith. 2009. *Frames of War: When Is Life Grievable?* New York: Verso Books.

Cabot, Heath. 2012. "The Governance of Things: Documenting Limbo in the Greek Asylum Procedure." *Political and Legal Anthropology Review* 35(1): 11–29.

Camilleri, Michael J., and Fen Osler Hampton. 2018. "No Strangers at the Gate: Collective Responsibility and a Region's Response to the Venezuelan Refugee and Migration Crisis." A report for the Centre for International Governance Innovation, Washington, DC.

Cantor, David James. 2018. "Cooperation on Refugees in Latin America and the Caribbean: The 'Cartagena Process' and South-South Approaches." In *The Routledge Handbook of South-South Relations,* edited by Elena Fiddian-Qasmiyeh and Patricia Daley. New York: Routledge.

Carens, Joseph. 1987. "The Case for Open Borders." *Review of Politics* 49(2): 251–73.

Carens, Joseph. 2013. *The Ethics of Immigration.* New York: Oxford University Press.

Carling, Jorgen. 2017. "Refugee Advocacy and the Meaning of 'Migrants.'" *Peace Research Institute Oslo Policy Brief.* Oslo, Norway.

Carpi, Estella, and Pinar H. Senoguz. 2019. "Refugee Hospitality in Lebanon and Turkey: On Making 'The Other.'" *International Migration* 57(2): 126–42.

Carr, Matthew. 2012. *Fortress Europe: Dispatches from a Gated Continent.* London and New York: Hurst and New Press.

Casas-Cortes, Maribel, Sebastian Cobarrubias, and John Pickles. 2015. "Riding Routes and Itinerant Borders: Autonomy of Migration and Border Externalization." *Antipode* 47(4): 894–914.

Castillo, Carlos Maldonado. 2015. "The Cartagena Process: 30 Years of Innovation and Solidarity." *Forced Migration Review* 49: 89–91.

Castles, Steven. 2003. "Towards a Sociology of Forced Migration and Social Transformation." *Sociology* 31(1): 13–34.

Cengel, Katya. 2015. "A Homecoming Racked with Guilt and Shame for Guatemalan Migrant Children." *Al Jazeera America*, October 5. http://america.aljazeera.com/multimedia/2015/10/a-homecoming-racked-with-guilt-and-shame-for-guatemalan-migrant-children.html

Chatty, Dawn. 2016. "The Syrian Humanitarian Disaster: Disparities in Perceptions, Aspirations, and Behavior in Jordan, Lebanon and Turkey." *Institute of Development Studies Bulletin* 47(3). https://bulletin.ids.ac.uk/index.php/idsbo/article/view/2728/HTML

Chavez, Leo R. 2013. *The Latino Threat: Constructing Immigrants, Citizens, and the Nation.* Stanford, CA: Stanford University Press.

Chetail, Vincent. 2014. "Are Refugee Rights Human Rights? An Unorthodox Questioning of the Relations between Refugee Law and Human Rights Law." In *Human Rights and Immigration*, edited by Ruth Rubio-Marin, 19–72. Oxford: Oxford University Press.

Chimni, B. S. 1998. "The Geopolitics of Refugee Studies: A View from the South." *Journal of Refugee Studies* 11(4): 350–74.

Chimni, B. S. 2009. "The Birth of a 'Discipline': From Refugee to Forced Migration Studies." *Journal of Refugee Studies* 22(1): 11–29.

Coen, Alise. 2017. "Capable and Culpable? The United States, RtoP, and Refugee Responsibility Sharing." *Ethics & International Affairs* 31(2): 71–92.

Cohen, Dara Kay, and Amelia Hoover Green. 2012. "Dueling Incentives: Sexual Violence in Liberia and the Politics of Human Rights Advocacy." *Journal of Peace Research* 49: 445–58.

Cohen, Richard. 2019. "There Are No Concentration Camps on the Border." *Washington Post*, June 24. www.washingtonpost.com/opinions/there-are-no-concentration-camps-on-the-border/2019/06/24/0229e886–96bb-11e9–830a-21b9bs36b64ad_story.html

Collyer, Michael, and Hein de Haas, 2012. "Developing Dynamic Categorizations of Transit Migration." *Population, Space and Place* 18(4): 468–81.

Connell, Raewyn. 2007. *Southern Theory: The Global Dynamics of Knowledge in Social Science.* Cambridge: Polity Press.

Cooper, Holly, and Jayashri Srikantiah. 2015. "Op-Ed: The Refugee Tragedy in Our Own Backyard." *Los Angeles Times*, October 8. www.latimes.com/opinion/op-ed/la-oe-cooper-and-srikantiah-refugees-without-rights-in-us-20151007-story.html

Cornelius, Wayne, and Marc Rosenblum. 2005. "Immigration and Politics." *Annual Review of Political Science* 8: 99–119.

Cottle, Simon, and David Nolan. 2007. "Global Humanitarianism and the Changing Aid-Media Field: 'Everyone Was Dying for Footage.'" *Journalism Studies* 8(6): 862–78.

Coutin, Susan B. 2006. "Cause Lawyering and Political Advocacy: Moving Law on Behalf of Central American Refugees." In *Cause Lawyers and Social Movements*, edited by Austin Sarat and Stuart Scheingold, 101–19. Stanford, CA: Stanford University Press.

Crawley, Heaven, and Dimitris Skleparis. 2018. "Refugees, Migrants, Neither, Both: Categorical Fetishism and the Politics of Bounding in Europe's 'Migration Crisis'." *Journal of Ethnic and Migration Studies* 44(1): 1–16.

Crisp, Jeff. 1999. "Who Has Counted the Refugees? UNHCR and the Politics of Numbers." *New Issues in Refugee Research*, Working Paper no. 12. Geneva: Centre for Documentation and Research.

Crisp, Jeff. 2010. "Forced Displacement in Africa: Dimensions, Difficulties, and Policy Directions." *Refugee Survey Quarterly* 29(1): 1–27.

Cuellar, Mariano-Florentino. 2006. "Refugee Security and the Organizational Logic of Legal Mandates." *Georgetown Journal of International Law* 37: 583–723.

Dahl, Adam. 2018. *Empire of the People: Settler Colonialism and the Foundations of Modern Democratic Thought*. Lawrence: University Press of Kansas.

Dauvergne, Catherine. 2008. *Making People Illegal: What Globalization Means for Migration and Law*. Cambridge: Cambridge University Press.

Dauvergne, Catherine. 2016. *The New Politics of Immigration and the End of Settler Societies*. Cambridge: Cambridge University Press.

Davies, Sara E. 2006. "'The Asian Rejection?': International Refugee Law in Asia." *Australian Journal of Politics and History* 52(4): 562–75.

Davies, Sara E. 2007. "Redundant or Essential? How Politics Shaped the Outcome of the 1967 Protocol." *International Journal of Refugee Law* 19(4): 703–28.

De Genova, Nicholas. 2004 "The Legal Production of Mexican/Migrant 'Illegality'." *Latino Studies* 2(2): 160–85.

De Genova, Nicholas. 2016. "The European Question: Migration, Race, and Postcoloniality in Europe." *Social Text* 34(3): 75–102.

De Haas, Hein. 2007. "The Myth of Invasion: Irregular Migration from West Africa to the Maghreb and the European Union." International Migration Institute Report. Oxford University, Oxford, UK.

De Leon, Jason. 2015. *The Land of Open Graves: Living and Dying on the Migrant Trail*. Berkeley: University of California Press.

De Menezes, Fabiano L. 2016. "Utopia or Reality: Regional Cooperation in Latin America to Enhance the Protection of Refugees." *Refugee Survey Quarterly* 35(4): 122–41.

Denti, Antonio, and Wladamiro Pantaleone. 2019. "German Migrant Rescue Ship Captain Goes before Italian Court." *Reuters*, July 1. www.reuters.com/article/us-europe-migrants-italy-captain/german-migrant-rescue-ship-captain-goes-before-italian-court-idUSKCN1TW2OR

Department of State. 2015. "Cumulative Summary of Refugee Admissions 1975–2015." Bureau of Population, Refugees, and Migration, December 31. Washington, DC. https://2009–2017.state.gov/j/prm/releases/statistics/251288.htm

Department of State. 2019. "Report to Congress on Proposed Refugee Admissions for FY 2020." Office of the Spokesperson, September 26. Washington, DC. www.state.gov /report-to-congress-on-proposed-refugee-admissions-for-fy-2020/

Derrida, Jacques. [1972] 1981. *Positions.* Translated by Alan Bass. Chicago: University of Chicago Press.

Diamond, Jeremy. 2017. "Trump Orders Construction of Border Wall, Boosts Deportation Force." *CNN,* January 25. www.cnn.com/2017/01/25/politics/donald-trump -build-wall-immigration-executive-orders/index.html

Dinnerstein, Leonard. 1986. *America and the Survivors of the Holocaust.* New York: Columbia University Press.

Dionigi, Filippo. 2017. "Rethinking Borders: The Case of the Syrian Refugee Crisis in Lebanon." *Refugees and Migration Movements in the Middle East* 25: 22–29.

Druckman, James N. 2011. "What's It All About? Framing in Political Science." In *Perspectives on Framing,* edited by Gideon Keren, 279–302. New York: Psychology Press.

Eilperin, Juliet. 2016. "White House Raises Refugee Target to 110,000." *Washington Post,* September 14. www.washingtonpost.com/news/post-politics/wp/2016/09/14/white -house-plans-to-accept-at-least-110000-refugees-in-2017/

Elie, Jérôme. 2014. "Histories of Refugee and Forced Migration Studies." In *The Oxford Handbook of Refugee and Forced Migration Studies,* edited by Elena Fiddian-Qasmiyeh, Gil Loescher, Katy Long, and Nando Signoa, 23–35. Oxford: Oxford University Press.

Entman, Robert M. 1993. "Framing: Toward Clarification of a Fractured Paradigm." *Journal of Communication* 43(4): 50–58.

Erdal, Marta Bivand, and Ceri Oeppen. 2018. "Forced to Leave? The Discursive and Analytical Significance of Describing Migration as Forced and Voluntary." *Journal of Ethnic and Migration Studies* 44(6): 981–98.

Espiritu, Yen Le. 2006. "Toward a Critical Refugee Study: The Vietnamese Refugee Subject in US Scholarship." *Journal of Vietnamese Studies* 1(1–2): 410–33.

Espiritu, Yen Le. 2014. *Body Counts: The Vietnam War and Militarized Refuge(es).* Berkeley: University of California Press.

European Council. 2016. "EU-Turkey Statement." *Council of the European Union,* March 18. www.consilium.europa.eu/en/press/press-releases/2016/03/18/eu-turkey-statement/

European Union. 2003. "Council Regulation (EC) no. 343/2003 of 18 February 2003 Establishing the Criteria and Mechanisms for Determining the Member State Responsible for Examining an Asylum Application Lodged in One of the Member States by a Third-Country National." *Official Journal of the European Union,* February 18. https:// eur-lex.europa.eu/legal-content/EN/TXT/PDF/?uri=CELEX:32003R0343&from=EN

European Union. 2010. "Charter of Fundamental Rights of the European Union." *Official Journal of the European Union C83,* vol. 53. Brussels: European Union. www .europarl.europa.eu/charter/pdf/text_en.pdf

Executive Committee of the High Commissioner's Programme. 2015. "UNHCR's Communications Strategy," June 3. EC/66/SC/CRP.14. Geneva: UNHCR.

Fassin, Didier. 2016. "From Right to Favor: The Refugee Question as Moral Crisis." *The Nation*, April 5.

Fekete, Liz. 2018. "Migrants, Borders and the Criminalization of Solidarity in the EU." *Race and Class* 59(4): 65–83.

Feller, Ericka. 2005. "Refugees Are Not Migrants." *Refugee Survey Quarterly* 24(4): 27–35.

Fessy, Thomas. 2013. "Niger Migrants' Bodies Found near Algerian Border." *BBC News*, October 31. www.bbc.com/news/av/world-africa-24754492/niger-migrants-bodies-found-near-algerian-border

Fiddian-Qasmiyeh, Elena, Gil Loescher, Katy Long, and Nando Signoa, eds. 2014. *The Oxford Handbook of Refugee and Forced Migration Studies*. Oxford: Oxford University Press.

Fineman, Martha A. 2008. "The Vulnerable Subject: Anchoring Equality in the Human Condition." *Yale Journal of Law and Feminism* 20(1). https://digitalcommons.law.yale.edu/yjlf/vol20/iss1/2

Fischel de Andrade, Jose H. 2019. "The 1984 Cartagena Declaration: A Critical Review of Some Aspects of Its Emergence and Relevance." *Refugee Survey Quarterly* 38(4): 341–62.

FitzGerald, David. 2014. "The Sociology of International Migration." In *Migration Theory: Talking across Disciplines*, edited by James F. Hollifield and Caroline B. Brettell, 115–47. New York: Routledge.

FitzGerald, David. 2019. *Refuge beyond Reach: How Rich Democracies Repel Asylum Seekers*. New York: Oxford University Press.

FitzGerald, David, and Rawan Arar. 2016. "What Drives Refugee Migration." *American Political Science Association, Migration and Citizenship Newsletter* 4(2): 7–12.

FitzGerald, David, and Rawan Arar. 2018. "The Sociology of Refugee Migration." *Annual Review of Sociology* 44: 387–406.

FitzGerald, David, and David Cook-Martin. 2014. *Culling the Masses: The Democratic Origins of Racist Immigration Policy in the Americas*. Cambridge, MA: Harvard University Press.

Forero, Juan. 2019. "Colombia Grants Citizenship to Babies Born to Venezuelan Refugees." *Wall Street Journal*, August 5. www.wsj.com/articles/colombia-grants-citizenship-to-babies-born-to-venezuelan-refugees-11565040915

Foret, François, and Oriane Calligaro. 2018. *European Values: Challenges and Opportunities for EU Governance*. London: Routledge.

Forsythe, David. 2001. "UNHCR's Mandate: The Politics of Being Non-Political." *New Issues in Refugee Research*, Working Paper no. 33. Geneva: UNHCR.

Franco, Leonardo. 1994. "Forward." *Refugee Survey Quarterly* 1(13): 2–3.

Freier, Luisa Feline, and Nicolas Parent. 2019. "The Regional Response to the Venezuelan Exodus." *Current History* 118(805): 56–61.

Frelick, Bill, Ian M. Kysel, and Jennifer Podkul. 2016. "The Impact of Externalization of Migration Controls on the Rights of Asylum Seekers and Other Migrants." *Journal on Migration and Human Security* 4(4): 190–220.

Frontex. 2020. "Invitation to Frontex Industry Days." Frontex European Border and Coast Guard Agency, January 15. https://frontex.europa.eu/research/invitations/invitation-to-frontex-industry-days-si8nYe

Fry, Wendy. 2019. "Central American Migrant Who Sought U.S. Asylum Slain in Tijuana." *Los Angeles Times*, December 12. www.latimes.com/california/story/2019-12-12/attorney-central-american-in-mpp-program-murdered-in-tijuana

Fuller, Lon. 1967. *Legal Fictions*. Stanford, CA: Stanford University Press.

Gallagher, Dennis. 1989. "The Evolution of the International Refugee System." *International Migration Review* 23(3): 579–98.

Gammeltoft-Hansen, Thomas, and James C. Hathaway. 2015. *"Non-Refoulement* in a World of Cooperative Deterrence." *Columbia Journal of Transnational Law* 53: 235–84.

Garcia, Maria Cristina. 2006. *Seeking Refuge: Central American Migration to Mexico, the United States, and Canada*. Berkeley: University of California Press.

Gatrell, Peter. 2013. *The Making of the Modern Refugee*. Oxford: Oxford University Press.

Georgiou, Myria, and Rafal Zaborowski. 2017. "Media Coverage of the 'Refugee Crisis': A Cross-European Perspective." A report for the Council of Europe, London School of Economics.

Gessen, Masha. 2019. "The Unimaginable Reality of American Concentration Camps." *New Yorker Magazine*, June 21.

Ghezelbash, David. 2018. *Refuge Lost: Asylum in an Interdependent World*. Cambridge: Cambridge University Press.

Gibney, Matthew J. 2004. *The Ethics and Politics of Asylum: Liberal Democracy and the Responses to Refugees*. Cambridge: Cambridge University Press.

Gibney, Matthew J. 2013. "Is Deportation a Form of Forced Migration?" *Refugee Survey Quarterly* 32(2): 116–29.

Gill, Nick, and Anthony Good. 2019. *Asylum Determination in Europe: Ethnographic Perspectives*. Cham, Switz.: Palgrave Macmillan.

Go, Julian. 2016. "Globalizing Sociology, Turning South: Perspectival Realism and the Southern Standpoint." *Sociologica* 2: 1–42.

Goodman, Simon, and Susan A. Speer. 2007. "Category Use in the Construction of Asylum Seekers." *Critical Discourse Studies* 4: 165–86.

Goodman, Simon, Ala Sirreyeh, and Simon McMahon. 2017. "The Evolving (Re)Categorisations of Refugees throughout the Refugee Crisis." *Journal of Community and Applied Social Psychology* 27(2): 105–14.

Gorman, Cynthia S. 2017. "Redefining Refugees: Interpretive Control and the Bordering Work of Legal Categorization in U.S. Asylum Law." *Political Geography* 58: 1–10.

Gould, Jon, Colleen Sheppard, and Johannes Wheeldon. 2010. "A Refugee from Justice? Disparate Treatment in the Federal Court of Canada." *Law and Policy* 32(4): 454–86.

Grahl-Madsen, Atle. 1972. *The Status of Refugees in International Law*, vol. 2, *Asylum, Entry, and Sojourn*. Leiden, Neth.: A. W. Sijthoff.

Gray, Benjamin. 2011. "From Exile of Citizens to Deportation of Non-Citizens: Ancient Greece as a Mirror to Illuminate a Modern Transition." *Citizenship Studies* 15(5): 565–82.

Grillo, Ioan. 2018. "'There Is No Way We Can Turn Back': Why Thousands of Refugees Will Keep Coming to America Despite Trump's Crackdown." *Time Magazine*, June 21. https://time.com/5318718/central-american-refugees-crisis/

Grovogui, Siba. 2011. "A Revolution Nonetheless: The Global South in International Relations." *Global South* 5(1): 175–90.

Gündoğdu, Ayten. 2015. *Rightlessness in an Age of Rights: Hannah Arendt and the Contemporary Struggles of Migrants*. New York: Oxford University Press.

Haddad, Emma. 2003. "The Refugee: The Individual between Sovereigns." *Global Society* 17(3): 297–322.

Hamlin, Rebecca. 2012a. "International Law and Administrative Insulation: A Comparison of Refugee Status Determination Regimes in the United States, Canada, and Australia." *Law and Social Inquiry* 37(4): 933–68.

Hamlin, Rebecca. 2012b. "Illegal Refugees: Competing Policy Ideas and the Rise of the Regime of Deterrence in American Asylum Politics." *Refugee Survey Quarterly* 31(2): 33–53.

Hamlin, Rebecca. 2014. *Let Me Be a Refugee: Administrative Justice and the Politics of Asylum in the United States, Canada, and Australia*. New York: Oxford University Press.

Hamlin, Rebecca. 2015a. "Ideology, International Law, and the INS: The Development of American Asylum Politics 1948–Present." *Polity* 47(3): 320–36.

Hamlin, Rebecca. 2015b. "Why the Rohingya Will Continue to Flee Myanmar, Even if We Deter Them." *Washington Post*, May 28. www.washingtonpost.com/blogs/monkey-cage/wp/2015/05/28/why-the-rohingyas-will-continue-to-flee-myanmar-even-if-we-try-to-deter-them/

Hamlin, Rebecca, and Philip E. Wolgin. 2012. "Symbolic Politics and Policy Feedback: The United Nations Protocol Relating to the Status of Refugees and American Refugee Policy in the Cold War." *International Migration Review* 46(3): 586–623.

Hathaway, James C. 1984. "The Evolution of Refugee Status in International Law: 1920–1950." *International and Comparative Law Quarterly* 33(2): 348–80.

Hathaway, James C. 1991. "Reconceiving Refugee Law as Human Rights Protection." *Journal of Refugee Studies* 4(2): 113–31.

Hathaway, James C. 2007a. "Forced Migration Studies: Could We Agree Just to 'Date'?" *Journal of Refugee Studies* 20(3): 349–69.

Hathaway, James C. 2007b. "Rejoinder." *Journal of Refugee Studies* 20(3): 385–90.

Hathaway, James C., and R. Alexander Neve. 1997. "Making International Refugee Law Relevant Again: A Proposal for Collectivized and Solution-Oriented Protection." *Harvard Human Rights Journal* 10: 115–43.

Hein, Jeremy. 1993. "Refugees, Immigrants, and the State." *Annual Review of Sociology* 19: 43–59.

Helton, Arthur C. 2002. *The Price of Indifference: Refugees and Humanitarian Action in the New Century*. Oxford: Oxford University Press.

Hernandez, David. 2019. "'3 Mexican Countries': When All Latin American Migrants Become Mexicans." *Radical History Review*, Forum 3.4, September 10. www.radicalhistoryreview.org/abusablepast/forum-3-4-3-mexican-countries-when-all-latin-american-migrants-become-mexicans-by-david-hernandez/

Hiskey, Jonathan T., Abby Cordova, Diana Orces, and Mary Fran Malone. 2016. "Understanding the Central American Refugee Crisis: Why They Are Fleeing and How U.S. Policies Are Failing to Deter Them." Special report for the American Immigration Council, Washington, DC.

Hiskey, Jonathan T., Abby Cordova, Mary Fran Malone, and Diana Orces. 2018. "Leaving the Devil You Know: Crime Victimization, US Deterrence Policy, and the Emigration Decision in Central America." *Latin American Research Review* 53(3): 429–547.

Holborn, Louise Wilhelmine. 1975. *Refugees: A Problem of Our Time—The Work of the United Nations High Commissioner for Refugees, 1951–1972*. Metuchen, NJ: Scarecrow Press.

Hollifield, James F. 2004. "The Emerging Migration State." *International Migration Review* 38(3): 885–912.

Human Rights Watch. 2019. "No Escape from Hell: EU Policies Contribute to Abuse of Migrants in Libya." January 21. www.hrw.org/report/2019/01/21/no-escape-hell/eu-policies-contribute-abuse-migrants-libya#

Human Rights Watch. 2020. "Deportation with a Layover: Failure of Protection under the U.S.–Guatemala Asylum Cooperative Agreement." May 19. Washington, DC. www.hrw.org/report/2020/05/19/deportation-layover/failure-protection-under-us-guatemala-asylum-cooperative

Hunter, Ian. 2013. "Kant and Vattel in Context: Cosmopolitan Philosophy and Diplomatic Casuistry." *History of European Ideas* 39(4): 477–502.

Immigration and Naturalization Services. 1996. Table 27: "Asylum Cases Filed with INS District Directors and Asylum Officers, Fiscal Years 1973–96." *Statistical Yearbook*, Washington, DC.

Inter-American Commission on Human Rights. 2019. *Principles on the Rights of All Migrants, Refugees, Stateless Persons, and Victims of Trafficking*. www.oas.org/es/cidh/informes/pdfs/Principios%20DDHH%20migrantes%20-%20ES.pdf

Isayev, Elena. 2017. *Migration, Mobility and Place in Ancient Italy*. Cambridge: Cambridge University Press.

Iyengar, Shanto. 1987. "Television News and Citizens' Explanations of National Affairs." *American Political Science Review* 81: 815–31.

Jacobson, David. 1996. *Rights across Borders: Immigration and the Decline of Citizenship*. Baltimore, MD: Johns Hopkins University Press.

Janmyr, Maja. 2017. "No Country of Asylum: 'Legitimizing' Lebanon's Rejection of the 1951 Refugee Convention." *International Journal of Refugee Law* 29(3): 438–65.

Janmyr, Maja. 2018. "UNHCR and the Syrian Refugee Response: Negotiating Status and Registration in Lebanon." *International Journal of Human Rights* 22(3): 393–419.

Janmyr, Maya, and Lama Mourad. 2018. "Modes of Ordering: Labelling, Classification and Categorization in Lebanon's Refugee Response." *Journal of Refugee Studies* 31(4): 544–65.

Jensen, Elizabeth. 2015. "'Refugee' or 'Migrant': How to Refer to Those Fleeing Home." *NPR*, August 21. www.npr.org/sections/publiceditor/2015/08/21/433493813/refugee-or-migrant-how-to-refer-to-those-fleeing-home

Kahn, Jeffrey S. 2019. *Islands of Sovereignty: Haitian Migration and the Borders of Empire.* Chicago: University of Chicago Press.

Kang, S. Deborah. 2017. *The INS on the Line: Making Immigration Law on the US/Mexico Border, 1917–1954.* Oxford: Oxford University Press.

Kanno-Youngs, Zolan. 2020. "Texas Governor Shuts State to Refugees, Using New Power Granted by Trump." *New York Times,* January 10. www.nytimes.com/2020/01/10/us /politics/texas-governor-refugees.html

Kant, Immanuel. 1996. "Toward Perpetual Peace: A Philosophical Project." In *Immanuel Kant: Practical Philosophy,* edited and translated by Mary J. Gregor. Cambridge: Cambridge University Press.

Karatani, Rieko. 2003. *Defining British Citizenship: Empire, Commonwealth, and Modern Britain.* London: Frank Cass.

Karatani, Rieko. 2005. "How History Separated Refugee and Migrant Regimes: In Search of Their Institutional Origins." *International Journal of Refugee Law* 17: 517–41.

Kasimis, Demetra. 2018. *The Perpetual Immigrant and the Limits of Athenian Democracy.* Cambridge: Cambridge University Press.

Katwala, Sunder, and Will Somerville. 2016. "Engaging the Anxious Middle on Immigration Reform: Evidence from the UK Debate." Washington, DC: Migration Policy Institute.

Kaushal, Asha, and Catherine Dauvergne. 2011. "The Growing Culture of Exclusion: Trends in Canadian Refugee Exclusions." *International Journal of Refugee Law* 23(1): 54–92.

Kennedy, David. 1986. "International Refugee Protection." *Human Rights Quarterly* 8(1): 1–69.

Kent, Tom. 2015. "Migrants, Refugees, or Both?" *Associated Press,* September 14. https:// blog.ap.org/behind-the-news/migrants-refugees-or-both

Keohane, Robert O., and David G. Victor. 2011. "The Regime Complex for Climate Change." *Perspectives on Politics* 9(1): 7–23.

Kihato, Caroline Wanjiku, and Loren B. Landau. 2017. "Stealth Humanitarianism: Negotiating Politics, Precarity and Performance Management in Protecting the Urban Displaced." *Journal of Refugee Studies* 30(3): 407–25.

King, Wayne. 1985. "Hispanic Alien Surge Fuels Asylum Debate." *New York Times,* August 19.

Kington, Tom. 2015. "Italy Pledges to Return Migrants to Africa." *The Times,* June 26. www.thetimes.co.uk/article/italy-pledges-to-return-migrants-to-africa-lrd3907gk7w

Kneebone, Susan. 2015. "The Labeling Problem in Southeast Asia's Refugee Crisis." *The Diplomat,* August 12. https://thediplomat.com/2015/08/the-labeling-problem-in -southeast-asias-refugee-crisis/

Kritzman-Amir, Tally. 2009. "Not in My Backyard: On the Morality of Responsibility Sharing in Refugee Law." *Brooklyn Journal of International Law* 34(2): 355–93.

Kukathas, Chandran. 2016. "Are Refugees Special?" In *Migration in Political Theory: The Ethics of Movement and Membership,* edited by Sarah Fine and Leah Ypi, 249–68. Oxford: Oxford University Press.

Kumin, Judith. 2008. "Orderly Departure from Vietnam? Cold War Anomaly or Humanitarian Innovation?" *Refugee Survey Quarterly* 27(1): 104–17.

Kunz, E. F. 1973. "The Refugee in Flight: Kinetic Models and Forms of Displacement." *International Migration Review* 7(2): 125–46.

Kuschminder, Katie, and Khalid Koser. 2016. "Why Don't Refugees Just Stay in Turkey or Greece? We Asked Them." *The Conversation,* December 13. https://theconversation.com/why-dont-refugees-just-stay-in-turkey-or-greece-we-asked-them-70257

Landau, Loren B. 2019. "A Chronotope of Containment Development: Europe's Migrant Crisis and Africa's Reterritorialisation." *Antipode* 51(1): 169–86.

Landau, Loren B., and Roni Amit. 2014. "Wither Policy? Southern African Perspectives on Understanding Law, 'Refugee' Policy and Protection." *Journal of Refugee Studies* 27(4): 534–52.

Landau, Loren B., and E. Tendayi Achiume. 2017. "Misreading Mobility?: Bureaucratic Politics and Blindness in the United Nations' Migration Reports." *Development and Change* 48(5): 1182–95.

Latour, Bruno. 2004. "Why Has Critique Run Out of Steam? From Matters of Fact to Matters of Concern." *Critical Inquiry* 30: 225–48.

Lee, Ju-Sung, and Adina Nerghes. 2018. "Refugee or Migrant Crisis? Labels, Perceived Agency, and Sentiment Polarity in Online Discussions." *Social Media + Society* (July–September 2018): 1–22.

Lee, Sang. 2011. "Between Displacement and Migration: Neoliberal Reform and the Residues of War in Rural Nicaragua." In *The Migration-Displacement Nexus: Patterns, Processes, and Policies,* edited by Khalid Koser and Susan Martin, 119–30. Oxford: Berghahn Books.

Levenson, Eric, and Ralph Ellis. 2017. "'We Love Refugees, but . . .': Listen to the Voicemails of Trump's Travel Ban Supporters." *CNN,* January 31. https://edition.cnn.com/2017/01/30/politics/travel-ban-supporters-trump/index.html

Levine, Philippa. 2010. "Anthropology, Colonialism, and Eugenics." In *The Oxford Handbook of the History of Eugenics,* edited by Philippa Levine and Alison Bashford, 43–61. Oxford: Oxford University Press.

Lindskoog, Carl. 2018. *Detain and Punish: Haitian Refugees and the Rise of the World's Largest Immigration Detention System.* Gainesville: University of Florida Press.

Lister, Matthew. 2014. "Climate Change Refugees." *Critical Review of International Social and Political Philosophy* 17(5): 618–34.

Loescher, Gil. 1993. *Beyond Charity: International Cooperation and the Global Refugee Crisis.* New York: Oxford University Press.

Loescher, Gil. 2001. *The UNHCR and World Politics: A Perilous Path.* Oxford: Oxford University Press.

Loescher, Gil, and John A. Scanlan. 1986. *Calculated Kindness: Refugees and America's Half-Open Door, 1945–Present.* New York: Free Press.

Long, Katy. 2013. "When Refugees Stopped Being Migrants: Movement, Labour, and Humanitarian Protection." *Migration Studies* 1(1): 4–26.

Ludwig, Bernadette. 2013. "'Wiping the Dust from My Feet': Advantages and Burdens of Refugee Status and the Refugee Label." *International Migration* 54(1): 5–18.

Lyman, Rick, and Alison Smale. 2015. "Paris Attacks Shift Europe's Migrant Focus to Security." *New York Times,* November 15. www.nytimes.com/2015/11/16/world/europe /paris-attacks-shift-europes-migrant-focus-to-security.html

Mackey, Robert. 2015. "Hungarian Leader Rebuked for Saying Muslim Migrants Must Be Blocked 'to Keep Europe Christian'." *New York Times,* September 3. www.nytimes .com/2015/09/04/world/europe/hungarian-leader-rebuked-for-saying-muslim-mi grants-must-be-blocked-to-keep-europe-christian.html

Macklin, Audrey. 2009. "Refugee Roulette in the Canadian Casino." In *Refugee Roulette: Disparities in Asylum Adjudication and Proposals for Reform,* edited by Jaya Ramji-Nogales, Andrew I. Schoenholtz, and Philip G. Schrag, 135–63. New York: New York University Press.

Maddaloni, Domenico, and Garzia Moffa. 2019. "Migration Flows and Migration Crisis in Southern Europe." In *The Oxford Handbook of Migration Crises,* edited by Cecilia Menjivar, Marie Ruiz, and Immanuel Ness, 603–18. Oxford: Oxford University Press.

Madianou, Mirca. 2013. "Humanitarian Campaigns in Social Media: Network Architectures and Polymedia Events." *Journalism Studies* 14(2): 249–66.

Malkki, Liisa H. 1995. "Refugees and Exile: From 'Refugee Studies' to the National Order of Things." *Annual Review of Anthropology* 24: 495–523.

Malone, Barry. 2015. "Why Al Jazeera Will Not Say Mediterranean 'Migrant'." *Al Jazeera,* August 20. www.aljazeera.com/blogs/editors-blog/2015/08/al-jazeera-mediterranean -migrants-150820082226309.html

Marfleet, Philip. 2007. "Refugees and History: Why We Must Address the Past." *Refugee Survey Quarterly* 26(3): 136–48.

Martin, David, ed. 1988. *The New Asylum Seekers: Refugee Law in the 1980s.* Dordrecht, Neth.: Martinus Nijhoff.

Martinez, Michael, and Miguel Marquez. 2015. "What's the Difference between Immigrant and Refugee?" *CNN,* July 16. www.cnn.com/2014/07/15/us/immigrant-refugee -definition/

Martinez, Sofia. 2018. "Today's Migrant Flow Is Different." *The Atlantic,* June 26. www .theatlantic.com/international/archive/2018/06/central-america-border-immigra tion/563744/

Massey, Douglas S. 1999. "Why Does Immigration Occur? A Theoretical Synthesis." In *The Handbook of International Migration: The American Experience,* edited by Charles Hirschman, Phillip Kasinitz and Josh DeWind, 34–52. New York: Russell Sage Foundation.

Matar, Dina. 2017. "Media Coverage of the Migration Crisis in Europe: A Confused and Polarized Narrative." In *Mediterranean Yearbook 2017: Strategic Sectors—Culture & Society,* 292–95. Barcelona: European Institute of the Mediterranean (IEMed).

Mathema, Silva. 2016. "They Are Refugees: An Increasing Number of People Are Fleeing Violence in the Northern Triangle." Center for American Progress, February 24. Washington, DC.

Mayblin, Lucy. 2017. *Asylum after Empire: Colonial Legacies in the Politics of Asylum Seeking.* London: Roman & Littlefield.

McAdam, Jane. 2012. *Climate Change, Forced Migration, and International Law*. Oxford: Oxford University Press.

McMahon, Simon, and Nando Sigona. 2018. "Navigating the Central Mediterranean in a Time of 'Crisis': Disentangling Migration Governance and Migrant Journeys." *Sociology* 52: 497–514.

McNevin, Anne, and Antje Missbach. 2018. "Hospitality as a Horizon of Aspiration (or, What the International Refugee Regime Can Learn from Acehnese Fishermen)." *Journal of Refugee Studies* 31(3): 292–313.

Medrano, Celia. 2017. "Securing Protection for De Facto Refugees: The Case of Central America's Northern Triangle." *Ethics & International Affairs* 31(2): 129–42.

Meissner, Doris, Faye Hipsman, and T. Alexander Aleinikoff. 2018. "The U.S. Asylum System in Crisis: Charting a Way Forward." Washington, DC: Migration Policy Institute.

Menjívar, Cecilia. 1993. "History, Economy, and Politics: Macro and Micro Level Factors in Recent Salvadoran Migration to the US." *Journal of Refugee Studies* 6: 350–71.

Menjívar, Cecilia. 2006. "Liminal Legality: Salvadoran and Guatemalan Immigrants' Lives in the United States." *American Journal of Sociology* 111(4): 999–1037.

Miglierini, Julian. 2016. "Migrant Tragedy: Anatomy of a Shipwreck." *BBC News*, May 24. www.bbc.com/news/world-europe-36278529

Miller, David. 2016. *Strangers in Our Midst: The Political Philosophy of Immigration*. Cambridge, MA: Harvard University Press.

Moeller, Susan. 1999. *Compassion Fatigue: How the Media Sell Disease, Famine, War and Death*. London: Routledge.

Moncrieffe, Joy. 2007. "Introduction: Labelling, Power and Accountability: How and Why 'Our' Categories Matter." In *The Power of Labelling: How People Are Categorized and Why It Matters,* edited by Joy Moncrieffe and Rosalind Eyben, 1–16. London: Earthscan.

Mongia, Radhika Viyas. 1999. "Race, Nationality, Mobility: A History of the Passport." *Public Culture* 11(3): 527–56.

Moretti, Sebastien. 2018. "Keeping Up Appearances: State Sovereignty and the Protection of Refugees in Southeast Asia." *European Journal of East Asian Studies* 17: 3–30.

Motomura, Hiroshi. 2020. "The New Migration Law: Migrants, Refugees, and Citizens in an Anxious Age." *Cornell Law Review* 105(2): 457–548.

Mountz, Alison. 2010. *Seeking Asylum: Human Smuggling and Bureaucracy at the Border*. Minneapolis: University of Minnesota Press.

Mourad, Lama, and Kelsey P. Norman. 2019a. "Transforming Refugees into Migrants: Institutional Change and the Politics of International Protection." *European Journal of International Relations* 26(3): 1–27.

Mourad, Lama, and Kelsey P. Norman. 2019b. "The World Is Turning Its Back on Refugees." *The Atlantic*, December 24. www.theatlantic.com/ideas/archive/2019/12/world -turning-its-back-refugees/604042/

National Journal. 2015. "Why Won't Obama Call These Kids Refugees?" www.national journal.com/s/72691/why-wont-obama-call-these-kids-refugees?

Natter, Katerina. 2018. "Rethinking Immigration Policy Theory beyond 'Western Liberal Democracies'." *Comparative Migration Studies* 6(4): 1–21.

Nawyn, Stephanie J. 2019. "Refugees in the United States and the Politics of Crisis." In *The Oxford Handbook of Migration Crises,* edited by Cecilia Menjívar, Marie Ruiz, and Immanuel Ness, 163–79. Oxford: Oxford University Press.

Nazario, Sonia. 2014. "A Refugee Crisis, Not an Immigration Crisis." *New York Times,* July 11. www.nytimes.com/2014/07/13/opinion/sunday/a-refugee-crisis-not-an-immigration-crisis.html

Ngai, Mae. 2003. "The Strange Career of the Illegal Alien: Immigration Restriction and Deportation Policy in the United States, 1921–1965." *Law and History Review* 21(1): 69–107.

Nguyen, Viet Thanh. 2016. "The Hidden Scars All Refugees Carry." *New York Times,* September 2. www.nytimes.com/2016/09/03/opinion/the-hidden-scars-all-refugees-carry.html

Noack, Rick. 2019. "The E.U.'s Ominous New Name for a Top Migration Job? Vice President for 'Protecting Our European Way of Life'." *Washington Post,* September 10. www.washingtonpost.com/world/2019/09/10/eus-ominous-new-name-top-migration-job-vice-president-protecting-our-european-way-life/

Nyabola, Nanjala. 2019. "End of Asylum: A Pillar of the Liberal Order Is Collapsing—But Does Anybody Care?" *Foreign Affairs,* October 10, 1–11.

Nyers, Peter. 2006. *Rethinking Refugees: Beyond States of Emergency.* London: Routledge.

Obama, Barack. 2014. "Letter from the President—Efforts to Address the Humanitarian Situation in the Rio Grande Valley Areas of Our Nation's Southwest Border." June 30. Washington, DC: White House, Office of the Press Secretary. www.whitehouse.gov/the-press-office/2014/06/30/letter-president-efforts-address-humanitarian-situation-rio-grande-valle

Oberoi, Pia. 2001. "South Asia and the Creation of the International Refugee Regime." *Refuge: Canada's Journal on Refugees* 19(5): 36–45.

Oberoi, Pia. 2018. "Words Matter; But Rights Matter More." *Anti-Trafficking Review* 11: 129–32.

O'Keefe, Ed, and Robert Costa. 2014. "House Passes Two Republican Measures in Response to Surge of Child Migrants." *Washington Post,* August 14. www.washingtonpost.com/politics/house-gop-moves-closer-on-immigration-bill-ahead-of-recess/2014/08/01/11084a2e-1983-11e4-9e3b-7f2f110c6265_story.html

Okoth-Obbo, George. 2001. "Thirty Years On: A Legal Review of the 1969 OAU Refugee Convention Governing the Specific Aspects of Refugee Problems in Africa." *Refugee Survey Quarterly* 20(1): 79–138.

Orchard, Phillip. 2014. *A Right to Flee: Refugees, States, and the Construction of International Cooperation.* Cambridge: Cambridge University Press.

Ordóñez, Juan Thomas, and Hugo Eduardo Ramírez Arcos. 2019. "At the Crossroads of Uncertainty: Venezuelan Migration to Colombia." *Journal of Latin American Geography* 18(2): 158–64.

Ottonelli, Valeria, and Tiziana Torresi. 2013. "When Is Migration Voluntary?" *International Migration Review* 47(4): 783–813.

Patel, Sujata. 2018. "Sociology through the 'South' Prism." In *The Routledge Handbook of South-South Relations*, edited by Elena Fiddian-Qasmiyeh and Patricia Daley, 31–47. Oxford: Routledge.

Paz, Moria. 2016. "Between the Kingdom and the Desert Sun: Human Rights, Immigration, and Border Walls." *Berkeley Journal of International Law* 34: 1–43.

Pearson, Elaine. 2019. "Trump's Attack on Asylum Seekers Was Made In Australia." *Foreign Policy*, July 24.

Peterson, William. 1958. "A General Typology of Migration." *American Sociological Review* 23(3): 256–66.

Pisarevskaya, Asya, Nathan Levy, Peter Scholten, and Joost Jansen. 2019. "Mapping Migration Studies: An Empirical Analysis of the Coming of Age of a Research Field." *Migration Studies* 20(10): 1–27.

Planas, Rocque. 2013. "Goodlatte Demands Investigation into Mexico Asylum Claims, Calling Them 'Fake'." *Huffington Post*, August 22. www.huffingtonpost.com/2013/08 /22/goodlatte-mexico-asylum_n_3797209.html

Pompeo, Michael R. 2018. "We Remain the World's Most Generous Nation." *USA Today*, September 20. www.state.gov/we-remain-the-worlds-most-generous-nation/

Prabandari, Atin, and Dedi Dinarto. 2016. "The Connecting Issue of Asylum Seekers and Irregular Migrants in Southeast Asia." *E-International Relations*. www.e-ir.info /2016/08/11/the-connecting-issue-of-asylum-seekers-and-irregular-migrants-in-south east-asia/

Price, Matthew E. 2009. *Rethinking Asylum: History, Purpose, and Limits*. Cambridge: Cambridge University Press.

Radford, Jynnah, and Phillip Connor. 2019. "Canada Now Leads the World in Refugee Resettlement, Surpassing the U.S." June 19. Washington, DC: Pew Research Center. www.pewresearch.org/fact-tank/2019/06/19/canada-now-leads-the-world-in-refugee -resettlement-surpassing-the-u-s/

Ram, Melanie H. 2017. "International Organization Autonomy and Issues Emergence: The World Bank's Roma Inclusion Agenda." *Global Governance* 23(4): 565–82.

Ramji-Nogales, Jaya. 2017a. "Migration Emergencies." *Hastings Law Journal* 68: 609–55.

Ramji-Nogales, Jaya. 2017b. "Moving beyond the Refugee Law Paradigm." *American Journal of International Law* 111: 8–12.

Ramji-Nogales, Jaya, Andrew I. Schoenholtz, and Philip G. Schrag, eds. 2009. *Refugee Roulette: Disparities in Asylum Adjudication and Proposals for Reform*. New York: New York University Press.

Reed-Hurtado, Michael. 2013. "The Cartagena Declaration on Refugees and the Protection of People Fleeing Armed Conflict and Other Situations of Violence in Latin America." *UNHCR Legal and Protection Policy Research Series*. Geneva: UNHCR.

Rehaag, Sean. 2009. "Troubling Patterns in Canadian Refugee Adjudication." *Ottawa Law Review* 39: 335–66.

Richmond, Anthony H. 1988. "Sociological Theories of International Migration: The Case of Refugees." *Current Sociology* 20(1): 7–25.

Robertson, Shanthi. 2018. "Status-Making: Rethinking Migrant Categorization." *Journal of Sociology* 55(2): 219–33.

Robinson, Vaughn. 1990. "Into the Next Millennium: An Agenda for Refugee Studies." A report of the First Annual Meeting of the International Advisory Panel, January. *Journal of Refugee Studies* 3(1): 3–15.

Robson, Laura. 2017. "Refugees and the Case for International Authority in the Middle East: The League of Nations and the United Nations Relief Works Agency for Palestinian Refugees in the Near East Compared." *International Journal of Middle East Studies* 49: 625–44.

Romo, Vanessa, Martina Stewart, and Brian Naylor. 2017. "Trump Ends DACA, Calls on Congress to Act." *NPR*, September 5. www.npr.org/2017/09/05/546423550/trump -signals-end-to-daca-calls-on-congress-to-act

Rubinstein, Lene. 2018. "Immigration and Refugee Crises in Fourth-Century Greece: An Athenian Perspective." *European Legacy* 23(1–2): 5–24.

Ruhs, Martin. 2012. "The Human Rights of Migrant Workers: Why Do So Few Countries Care?" *American Behavioral Scientist* 56(9): 1277–93.

Rutinwa, Bonaventure. 2017. "Relationship between the 1951 Refugee Convention and the 1969 OAU Convention on Refugees." In *Flight from Conflict and Violence: UNHCR's Consultations on Refugee Status and Other Forms of International Protection*, edited by Volker Turk, Alice Edwards, and Cornelius Wouters, 94–115. Cambridge: Cambridge University Press.

Ruz, Camila. 2015. "The Battle over the Words Used to Describe Migrants." *BBC News Magazine*, August 28. www.bbc.com/news/magazine-34061097

Sajjad, Tazreena. 2018. "What's in a Name? 'Refugees', 'Migrants' and the Politics of Labelling." *Race and Class* 60(2): 40–62.

Sassen, Saskia. 2002. "The Repositioning of Citizenship: Emergent Subjects and Spaces for Politics." *Berkeley Journal of Sociology* 46: 4–25.

Scalettaris, Giulia. 2007. "Refugee Studies and the International Refugee Regime: A Reflection on a Desirable Separation." *Refugee Survey Quarterly* 26(3): 36–50.

Schaffner, Brian, Stephen Ansolabehere, and Sam Luks. 2019. *Guide to the 2018 Cooperative Congressional Election Survey, 2018.* Harvard Dataverse: CCES Common Content. https://doi.org/10.7910/DVN/ZSBZ7K/WZWCZ1

Schrag, Phillip G. 2020. "The End of Asylum for Now." *The Hill*, June 16. https://thehill .com/opinion/immigration/502881-the-end-of-asylum-for-now

Seipel, Arnie. 2015. "30 Governors Call for Halt to U.S. Resettlement of Syrian Refugees." *NPR*, November 17. www.npr.org/2015/11/17/456336432/more-governors-oppose -u-s-resettlement-of-syrian-refugees

Sengupta, Somini. 2015. "Migrant or Refugee? There Is a Difference, with Legal Implications." *New York Times*, August 27. www.nytimes.com/2015/08/28/world/migrants -refugees-europe-syria.html

Shachar, Ayelet. 2009. *The Birthright Lottery: Citizenship and Global Inequality.* Cambridge, MA: Harvard University Press.

Shacknove, Andrew E. 1985. "Who Is a Refugee?" *Ethics* 95: 274–84.

Sharpe, Marina. 2018. *The Regional Law of Refugee Protection in Africa.* Oxford: Oxford University Press.

Sharpe, Marina. 2019. "The Supervision (or Not) of the 1969 OAU Refugee Convention." *International Journal of Refugee Law* 31(2/3): 261–89.

Shields, Michael. 2015. "Hungary Won't Shoot at Migrants Crossing Fence: Orban." *Reuters,* September 7. www.reuters.com/article/us-europe-migrants-hungary-orban /hungary-wont-shoot-at-migrants-crossing-fence-orban-idUSKCN0R70GC20150907

Sigona, Nando. 2018. "The Contested Politics of Naming in Europe's 'Refugee Crisis'." *Ethnic and Racial Studies* 41(3): 456–60.

Simpson, Sir John Hope. 1938. *The Refugee Problem: Report of a Survey.* London: Oxford University Press.

Skran, Claudena, and Carla N. Daughtry. 2007. "The Study of Refugees before 'Refugee Studies'." *Refugee Survey Quarterly* 26(3): 15–35.

Soguk, Nevzat. 1999. *States and Strangers, Refugees and the Displacements of Statecraft.* Minneapolis: University of Minnesota Press.

Song, Sarah. 2009. "Democracy and Non-Citizen Voting Rights." *Citizenship Studies* 13(6): 607–20.

Song, Sarah. 2019. *Immigration and Democracy.* New York: Oxford University Press.

Souter, James. 2014. "Towards a Theory of Asylum as Reparation for Past Injustice." *Political Studies* 62: 326–42.

Soysal, Yasemin. 1994. *Limits of Citizenship: Migrants and Postnational Membership in Europe.* Chicago: University of Chicago Press.

Specia, Megan. 2019. "What Is Happening in Venezuela and Why It Matters." *New York Times,* April 30. www.nytimes.com/2019/04/30/world/americas/venezuela-crisis.html

Squire, Vicki, Angeliki Dimitriadi, Nina Perkowski, Maria Pisani, Dallal Stevens, and Nick Vaughan-Williams. 2017. *Crossing the Mediterranean Sea by Boat: Mapping and Documenting Migratory Journeys and Experiences.* Final Project Report, University of Warwick.

Stallings, A. E. 2018. *Like.* New York: Farrar, Straus Giroux.

Stein, Barry N. 1981. "The Refugee Experience: Defining the Parameters of a Field of Study." *International Migration Review* 15(1): 320–30.

Stein, Barry N., and Silvano M. Tomasi. 1981. "Forward." *International Migration Review* 15(1): 5–7.

Steinhilper, Elias, and Rob J. Gruijters. 2018. "A Contested Crisis: Policy Narratives and Empirical Evidence on Border Deaths in the Mediterranean." *Sociology* 52: 515–33.

Stevens, Dallal. 2013. "Legal Status, Labelling, and Protection: The Case of Iraqi 'Refugees' in Jordan." *International Journal of Refugee Law* 25(1): 1–38.

Sur, Priyali. 2019. "Why Record Numbers of African Migrants Are Showing Up at the U.S./Mexico Border." *Foreign Policy,* June 26. https://foreignpolicy.com/2019/06 /26/why-record-numbers-of-african-migrants-are-showing-up-at-the-u-s-mexican -border/

Tacoma, Laurens E. 2016. *Moving Romans: Migration to Rome in the Principate.* Oxford: Oxford University Press.

Taparata, Evan. 2019. "'Refugees as You Call Them': The Politics of Refugee Recognition in the Nineteenth-Century United States." *Journal of American Ethnic History* 38(2): 9–35.

Taylor, Adam. 2015a. "Italy Ran an Operation That Saved Thousands of Migrants from Drowning in the Mediterranean. Why Did It Stop?" *Washington Post*, April 20. www.washingtonpost.com/news/worldviews/wp/2015/04/20/italy-ran-an-operation-that-save-thousands-of-migrants-from-drowning-in-the-mediterranean-why-did-it-stop/

Taylor, Adam. 2015b. "Is It Time to Ditch the Word 'Migrant'?" *Washington Post*, August 24. www.washingtonpost.com/news/worldviews/wp/2015/08/24/is-it-time-to-ditch-the-word-migrant/

Taylor, Alan. 2002. *American Colonies: The Settling of North America, Volume 1*. New York: Penguin Books.

The Economist. 2015. "How Many Migrants to Europe Are Refugees?" September 8. www.economist.com/the-economist-explains/2015/09/07/how-many-migrants-to-europe-are-refugees

The Guardian. 2015. "*The Guardian* View on Europe's Refugee Crisis: A Little Leadership, at Last." *The Guardian Editorial*, September 1. www.theguardian.com/commentisfree/2015/sep/01/guardian-view-on-europe-refugee-crisis-leadership-at-last-angela-merkel

Thomaz, Diana. 2018. "What's in a Category? The Politics of Not Being a Refugee." *Social & Legal Studies* 27(2): 200–218.

Thompson, Andrea. 2018. "Wave of Climate Migration Looms, but It Doesn't Have to Be a Crisis." *Scientific American*, March 23.

Tichenor, Daniel J. 2002. *Dividing Lines: The Politics of Immigration Control in America*. Princeton, NJ: Princeton University Press.

Ticktin, Miriam. 2016. "Thinking beyond Humanitarian Borders." *Social Research: An International Quarterly* 83(2): 255–71.

Toksabay, Ece. 2017. "Turkey May Cancel Migrant Readmission Deal with EU, Says Foreign Minister." *Reuters*, March 15. www.reuters.com/article/us-turkey-eu-refugees/turkey-may-cancel-migrant-readmission-deal-with-eu-says-foreign-minister-idUSKBN16M2YA

Tondo, Lorenzo. 2019. "I Have Seen the Tragedy of Mediterranean Migrants: This 'Art' Makes Me Uneasy." *The Guardian*. May 12. www.theguardian.com/world/2019/may/12/venice-biennale-migrant-tragedy-art-makes-me-uneasy

Torpey, John. 2000. *The Invention of the Passport: Surveillance, Citizenship and the State*. New York: Cambridge University Press.

Trump, Donald. 2015. (@realDonaldTrump). "13 Syrian Refugees Were Caught Trying to Get into the U.S. through the Southern Border. How Many Made It? WE NEED THE WALL!" Twitter, November 22, 7:53 a.m.

Trump, Donald. 2018. "President Donald J. Trump's State of the Union Address." January 30. www.whitehouse.gov/briefings-statements/president-donald-j-trumps-state-union-address/

Trump, Donald. 2019a. "President Donald Trump Full Speech at the Republican Jewish Convention in Las Vegas, Nevada." *C-SPAN*, April 6. www.c-span.org/video/?459585-1/president-trump-asylum-program-scam.

Trump, Donald. 2019b. "Statement from the President Regarding Emergency Measures to Address the Border Crisis." Statements and Releases, May 30. www.whitehouse .gov/briefings-statements/statement-president-regarding-emergency-measures -address-border-crisis/

Trump, Donald. 2019c. "Presidential Determination on Refugee Admissions for Fiscal Year 2020." Presidential Memoranda, November 1. www.whitehouse.gov/presidential -actions/presidential-determination-refugee-admissions-fiscal-year-2020/

Tuitt, Patricia. 1996. *False Images: Law's Construction of the Refugee.* London: Pluto Press.

Türk, Volker. 2017. "Statement to the 68th Session of the Executive Committee of the High Commissioner's Programme." Assistant High Commissioner for Protection, October 5. www.unhcr.org/en-us/admin/dipstatements/59d4b99d10/statement-68th -session-executive-committee-high-commissioners-programme.html

United Nations General Assembly. 1951. *Convention Relating to the Status of Refugees,* July 28. UN Treaty Series, vol. 189, p. 137.

United Nations General Assembly. 2016. "New York Declaration for Refugees and Migrants." A/Res/7/1 (October 3), Seventy-First Session, Agenda items 13 and 117.

United Nations General Assembly. 2018a. "Intergovernmental Conference to Adopt the Global Compact for Safe, Orderly, and Regular Migration: Draft Outcome Document of the Conference." A/CONF.231/3, July 30. https://undocs.org/A/CONF.231/3

United Nations General Assembly. 2018b. *Report of the United Nations High Commissioner for Refugees: Part II—Global Compact on Refugees.* Supplement no. 12 (A/73/12), August 2. www.unhcr.org/gcr/GCR_English.pdf

UNHCR (United Nations High Commissioner for Refugees). 1992. Amicus Curiae brief, October. www.refworld.org/docid/3f336bbc4.html

UNHCR. 2007a. "Refugee Protection and Mixed Migration: A 10-Point Plan of Action." January. Geneva: UNHCR. www.unhcr.org/en-us/protection/migration/4742a30b4 /refugee-protection-mixed-migration-10-point-plan-action.html

UNHCR. 2007b. "Refugee or Migrant? Why It Matters." *Refugees Magazine,* no. 148, December 12. Geneva: UNHCR.

UNHCR. 2009. "Africa—40th Anniversary of the OAU 1969 Refugee Convention." Geneva: UNHCR. www.unhcr.org/news/briefing/2009/9/4aa641da6/africa-40th-an niversary-oau-1969-refugee-convention.html

UNHCR. 2015a. "UNHCR's Communications Strategy." Executive Committee of the High Commissioner's Programme, June 3. EC/66/SC/CRP.14. Geneva: UNHCR.

UNHCR. 2015b. "Women on the Run: Firsthand Accounts of Refugees Fleeing El Salvador, Guatemala, Honduras and Mexico." Geneva: UNHCR.

UNHCR. 2016a. *The 10-Point Plan in Action, 2016 Update.* Geneva: UNHCR.

UNHCR. 2016b. "Refugees and Migrants: Frequently Asked Questions." March 16. Geneva: UNHCR. www.unhcr.org/584689257

UNHCR. 2016c. "UNHCR Viewpoint: 'Refugee' or 'Migrant,' Which Is Right?" July 11. Geneva: UNHCR. www.unhcr.org/news/latest/2016/7/55df0e556/unhcr-view point-refugee-migrant-right.html

UNHCR. 2017. "'Migrants in Vulnerable Situations': UNHCR's Perspective." June. Geneva: UNHCR.

UNHCR. 2019a. *Handbook on Procedures and Criteria for Determining Refugee States under the 1951 Convention and the 1967 Protocol Relating to the Status of Refugees.* Updated February 2019. Geneva: UNHCR.

UNHCR. 2019b. *Global Trends 2018.* Geneva: UNHCR.

UNHCR. 2019c. "UNHCR Deeply Concerned about New U.S. Asylum Restrictions." Press release, July 15. www.unhcr.org/en-us/news/press/2019/7/5d2cdf114/unhcr-deeply -concerned-new-asylum-restrictions.html

UNHCR. 2019d. "Statement on New U.S. Asylum Policy." Press release, November 19. www.unhcr.org/5dd426824

UNHCR. n.d. "UNHCR, Refugee Protection, and International Migration." Geneva: UNHCR. www.unhcr.org/en-us/protection/migration/4a24efoca2/unhcr-refugee-pro tection-international-migration.html

United Nations High Commissioner for Refugees USA. 2014. "Children on the Run." Washington, DC.

Van Hear, Nicholas. 2014. "Reconsidering Migration and Class." *International Migration Review* 48: 100–121.

Vaughan-Williams, Nick. 2015. *Europe's Border Crisis: Biopolitical Security and Beyond.* Oxford: Oxford University Press.

Venzke, Ingo. 2012. *How Interpretation Makes International Law: On Semantic Change and Normative Twists.* Oxford: Oxford University Press.

Vernant, Jacques. 1953. *The Refugee in the Post-War World.* New Haven, CT: Yale University Press.

Walzer, Michael. 1983. *Spheres of Justice: A Defense of Pluralism and Equality.* Oxford: Blackwell.

Weiss, Brennan. 2018. "The Trump Administration Has Ended Protections for Immigrants from Four Countries: Here's When They Will Have to Leave the US." *Business Insider,* January 11. www.businessinsider.com/trump-has-ended-temporary-pro tection-status-for-4-countries-2018–1

White, Gregory. 2011. *Climate Change and Migration: Security and Borders in a Warming World.* Oxford: Oxford University Press.

Wimmer, Andreas, and Nina Glick Schiller. 2003. "Methodological Nationalism, the Social Sciences, and the Study of Migration: An Essay in Historical Epistemology." *International Migration Review* 37(3): 576–610.

Witt, Charlotte. 1995. "Anti-Essentialism in Feminist Theory." *Philosophical Topics* 23(2): 321–44.

Wolgin, Phillip E. 2011. *Beyond National Origins: The Development of Modern Immigration Policymaking, 1948–1968.* PhD diss., University of California, Berkeley.

Wolgin, Philip E. 2016. "A Short-Term Plan to Address the Central American Refugee Situation." May. Washington, DC: Center for American Progress.

Wong, Tom K., Sebastian Bonilla, and Anna Colemana. 2019. *Seeking Asylum: Part 1.* La Jolla: U.S. Immigration Policy Center (USIPC) at UC San Diego.

Wood, Tamara. 2019. "Who Is a Refugee in Africa? A Principled Framework for Interpreting and Applying Africa's Expanded Refugee Definition." *International Journal of Refugee Law* 31(2/3): 290–320.

Worrall, Patrick. 2017. "Are Most Asylum Seekers Really Economic Migrants?" *Channel 4 News*, March 2. www.channel4.com/news/factcheck/factcheck-are-most-asylum-seekers-really-economic-migrants

Xenos, Nicholas. 1993. "Refugees: The Modern Political Condition." *Alternatives* 18: 419–30.

Zahra, Tara. 2016. *The Great Departure: Mass Migration from Eastern Europe and the Making of the Free World*. New York: W. W. Norton.

Zetter Roger. 1988. "Refugees and Refugee Studies: A Label and an Agenda." *Journal of Refugee Studies* 1(1): 1–6.

Zetter, Roger. 1991. "Labeling Refugees: Forming and Transforming a Bureaucratic Identity." *Journal of Refugee Studies* 4(1): 39–62.

Zetter, Roger. 2007. "More Labels, Fewer Refugees: Remaking the Refugee Label in an Era of Globalization." *Journal of Refugee Studies* 20(2): 172–92.

Zezima, Katie. 2016. "Mike Pence Wants to Keep Syrian Refugees Out of Indiana: They're Coming Anyway." *Washington Post*, August 28. www.washingtonpost.com/politics/mike-pence-wants-to-keep-syrian-refugees-out-of-indiana-theyre-coming-anyway/2016/08/28/2847f4dc-6576-11e6-8b27-bb8ba39497a2_story.html

Zolberg, Aristide R., Astri Suhrke, and Sergio Aguayo. 1989. *Escape from Violence: Conflict and the Refugee Crisis in the Developing World*. New York: Oxford University Press.

Zucker, Norman, and Naomi Flink Zucker. 1991. "The 1980 Refugee Act: A 1990 Perspective." In *Refugee Policy: Canada and the United States*, edited by Howard Adelman, 224–52. Toronto: York Lanes Press.

Index

CPSIA information can be obtained
at www.ICGtesting.com
Printed in the USA
JSHW021426200421
13749JS00001B/49

9 781503 627871